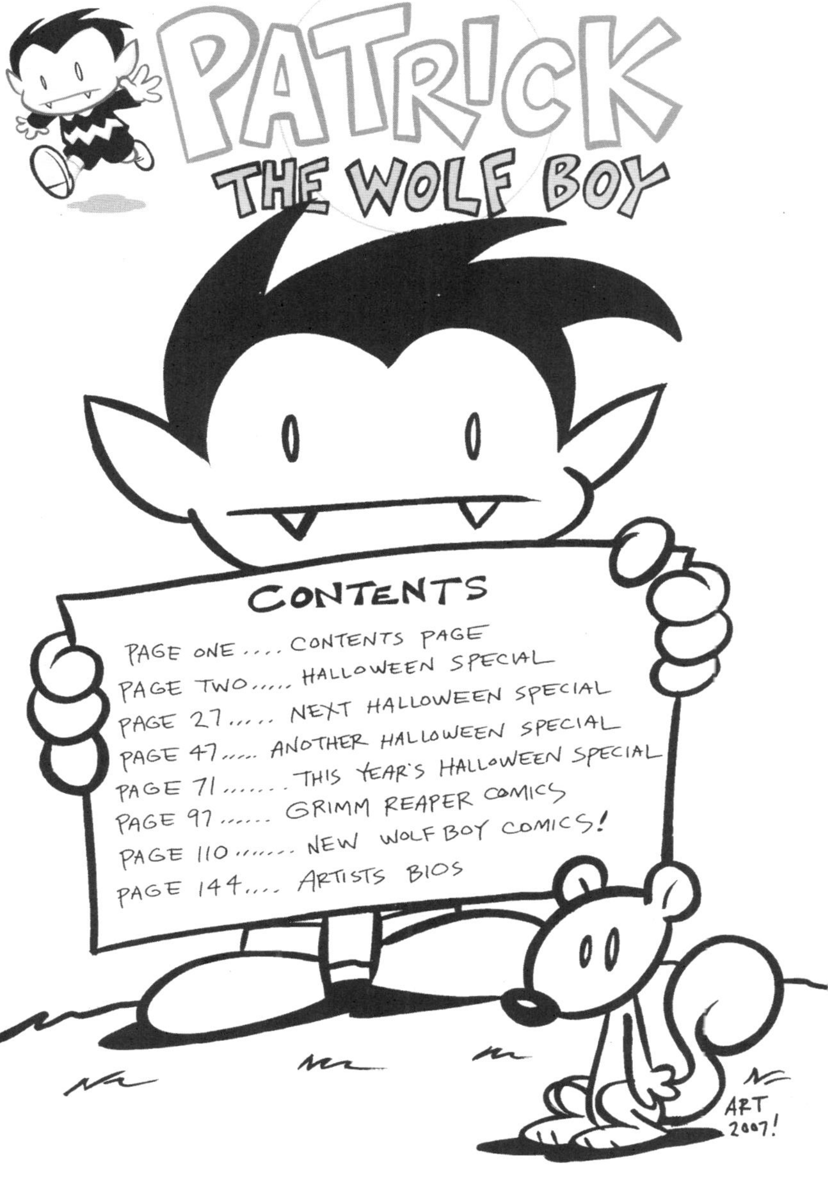
PATRICK
THE WOLF BOY
CONTENTS
PAGE ONE.... CONTENTS PAGE
PAGE TWO..... HALLOWEEN SPECIAL
PAGE 27..... NEXT HALLOWEEN SPECIAL
PAGE 47..... ANOTHER HALLOWEEN SPECIAL
PAGE 71....... THIS YEAR'S HALLOWEEN SPECIAL
PAGE 97...... GRIMM REAPER COMICS
PAGE 110....... NEW WOLF BOY COMICS!
PAGE 144.... ARTISTS BIOS
ART 2007!

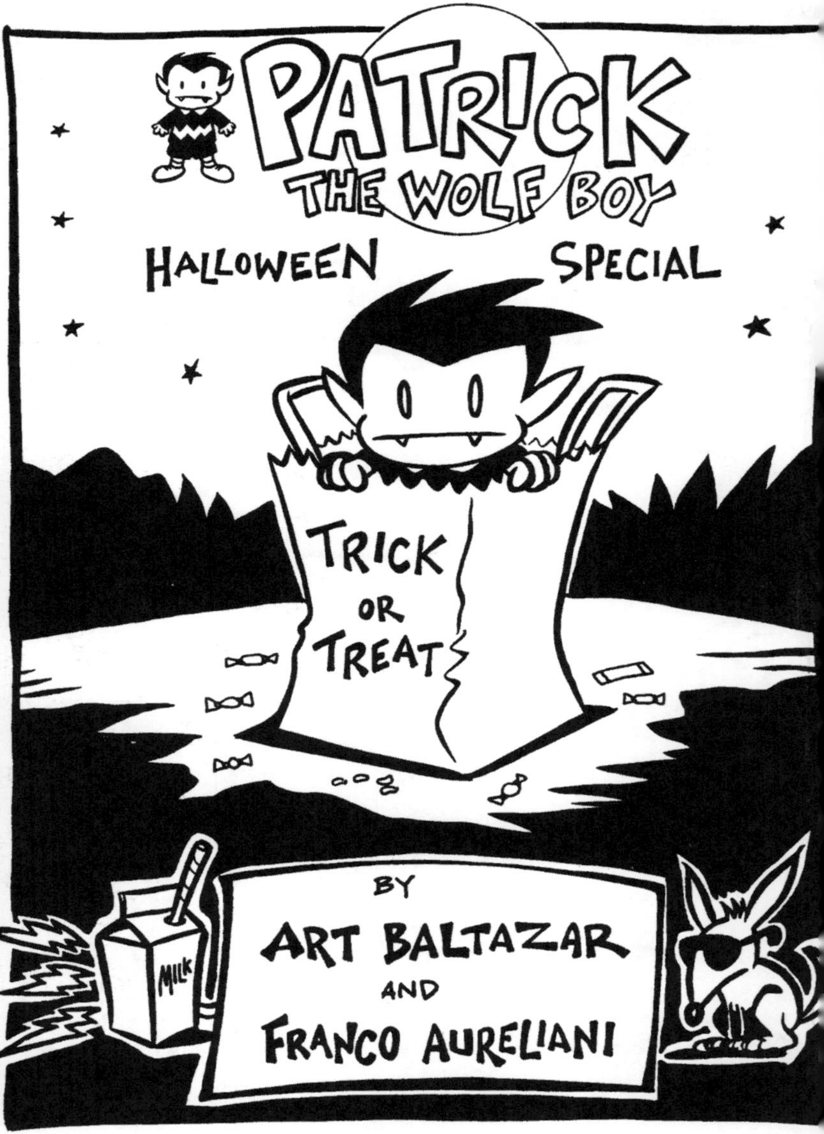
PATRICK THE WOLF BOY
HALLOWEEN SPECIAL
TRICK OR TREAT
MILK
BY
ART BALTAZAR
AND
FRANCO AURELIANI

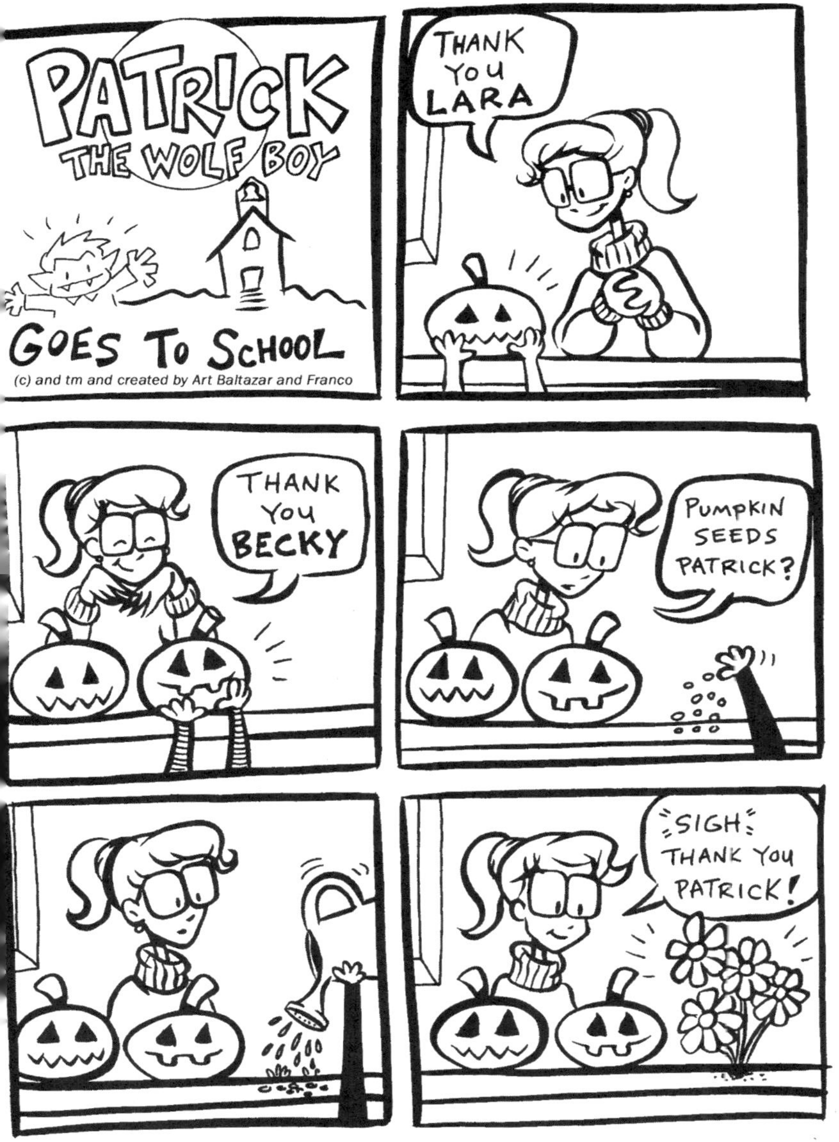
PATRICK THE WOLF BOY
GOES TO SCHOOL
(c) and tm and created by Art Baltazar and Franco
THANK YOU LARA
THANK YOU BECKY
PUMPKIN SEEDS PATRICK?
SIGH
THANK YOU PATRICK!

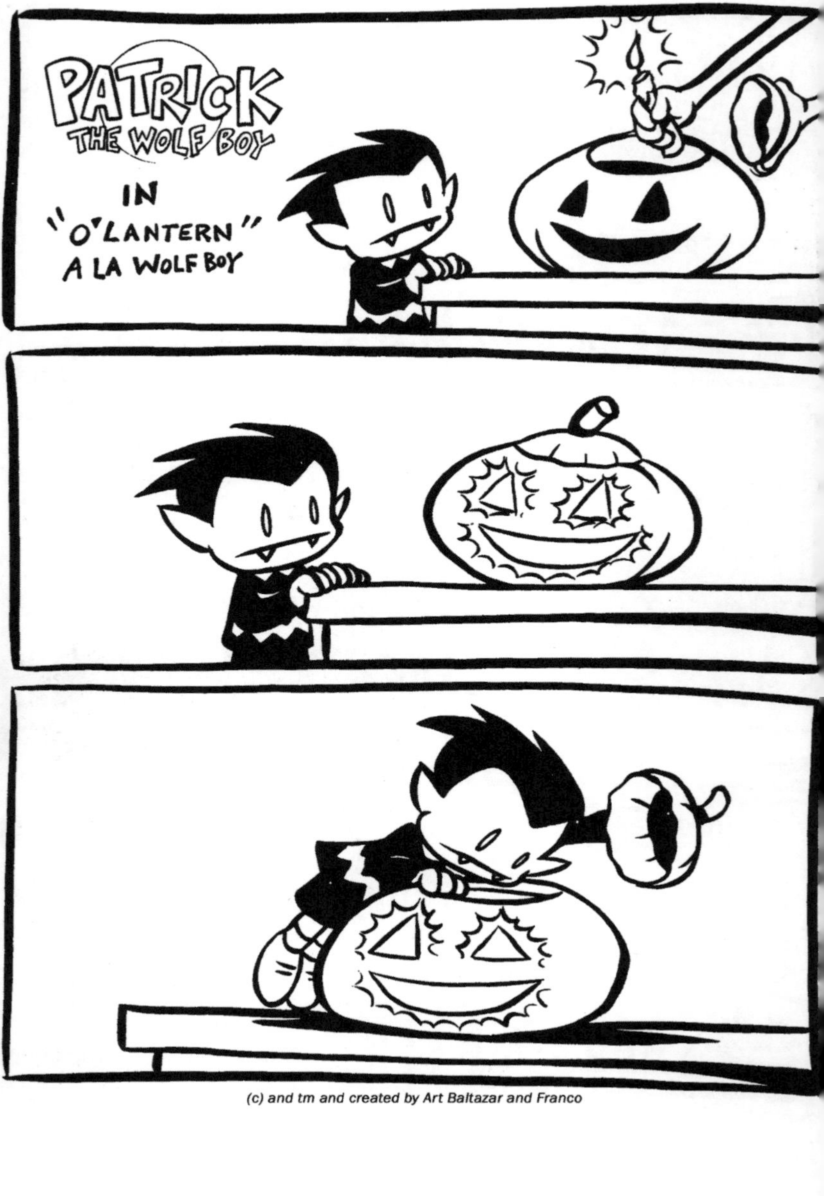
PATRICK THE WOLF BOY
IN "O'LANTERN" A LA WOLF BOY

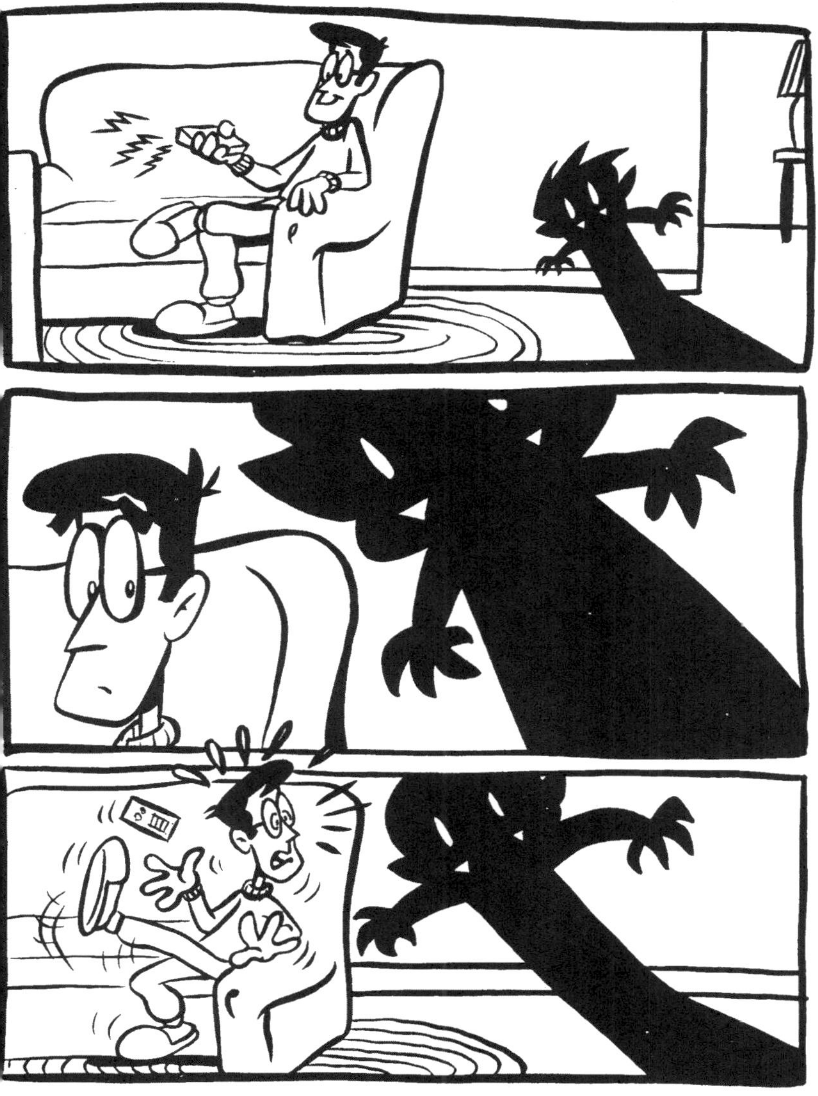

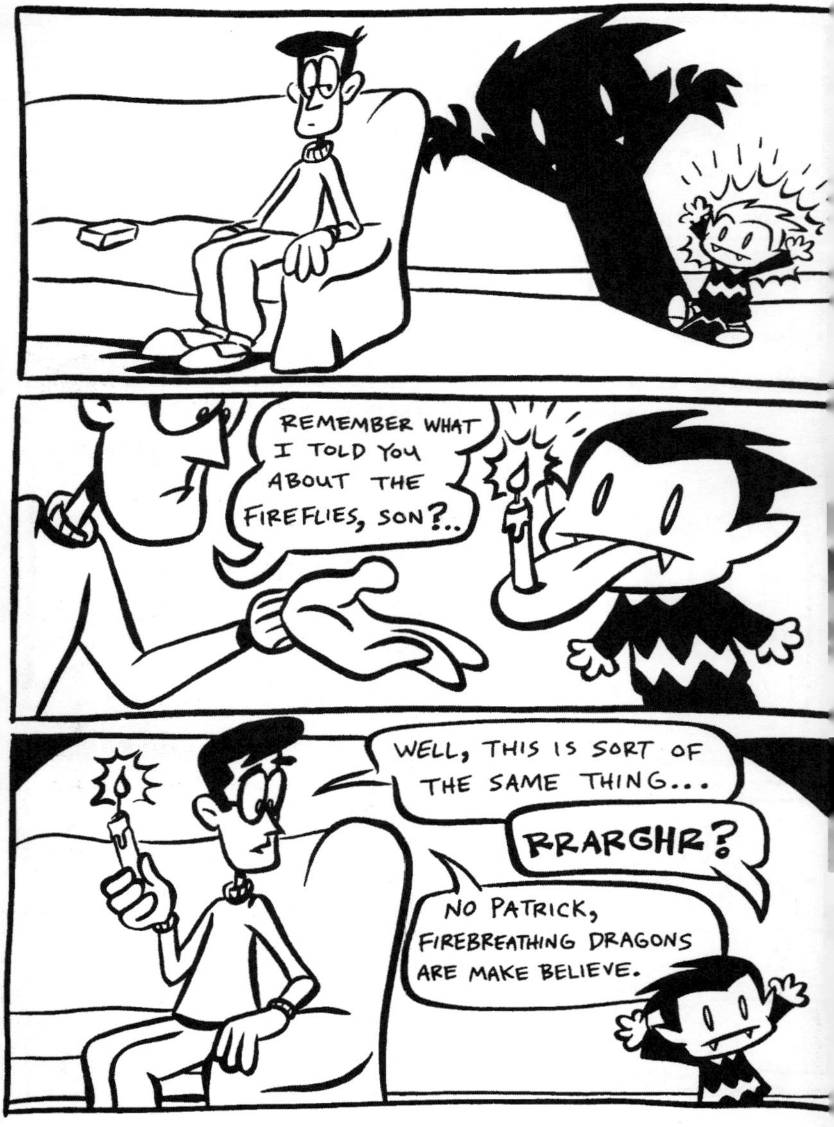
REMEMBER WHAT I TOLD YOU ABOUT THE FIREFLIES, SON?..
WELL, THIS IS SORT OF THE SAME THING...
RRARGHR?
NO PATRICK, FIREBREATHING DRAGONS ARE MAKE BELIEVE.

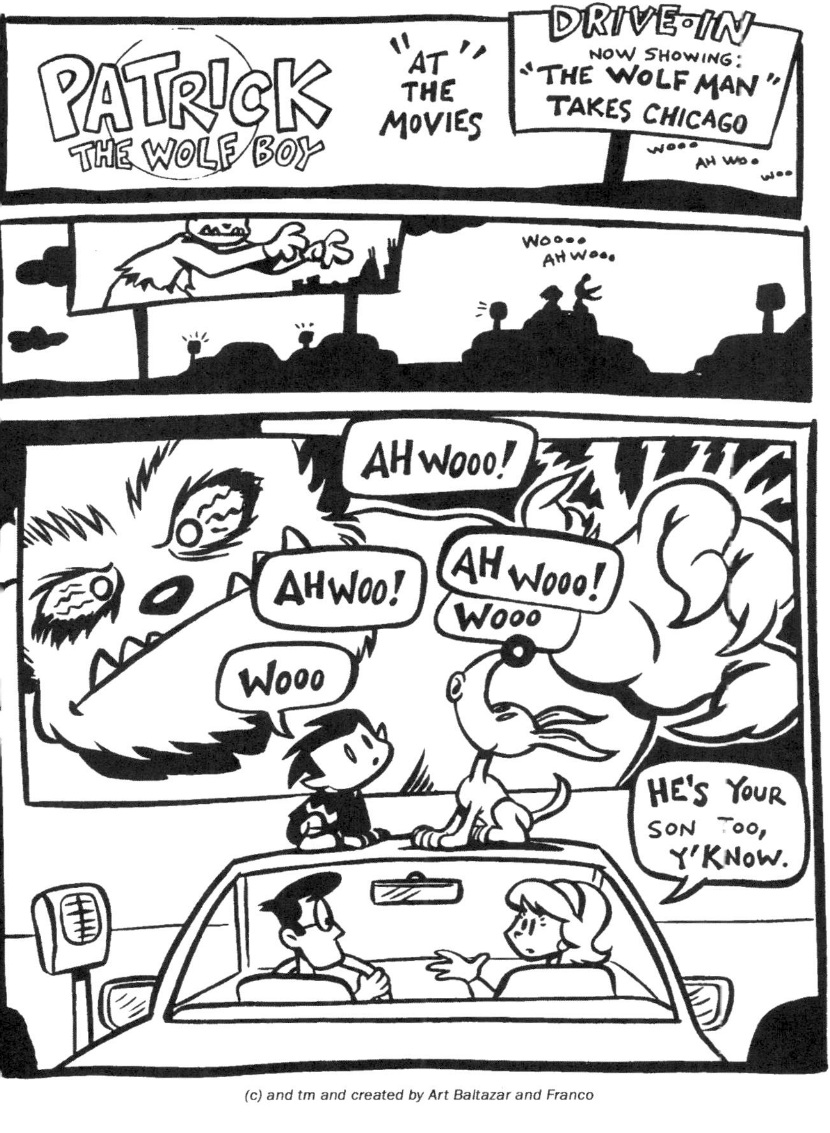
PATRICK THE WOLF BOY
"AT THE MOVIES"
DRIVE-IN
NOW SHOWING:
"THE WOLF MAN" TAKES CHICAGO
WOOO
AH WOO
WOO
WOOOO
AH WOOO
AH WOOO!
AH WOO!
AH WOOO!
WOOO
WOOO
HE'S YOUR SON TOO, Y'KNOW.

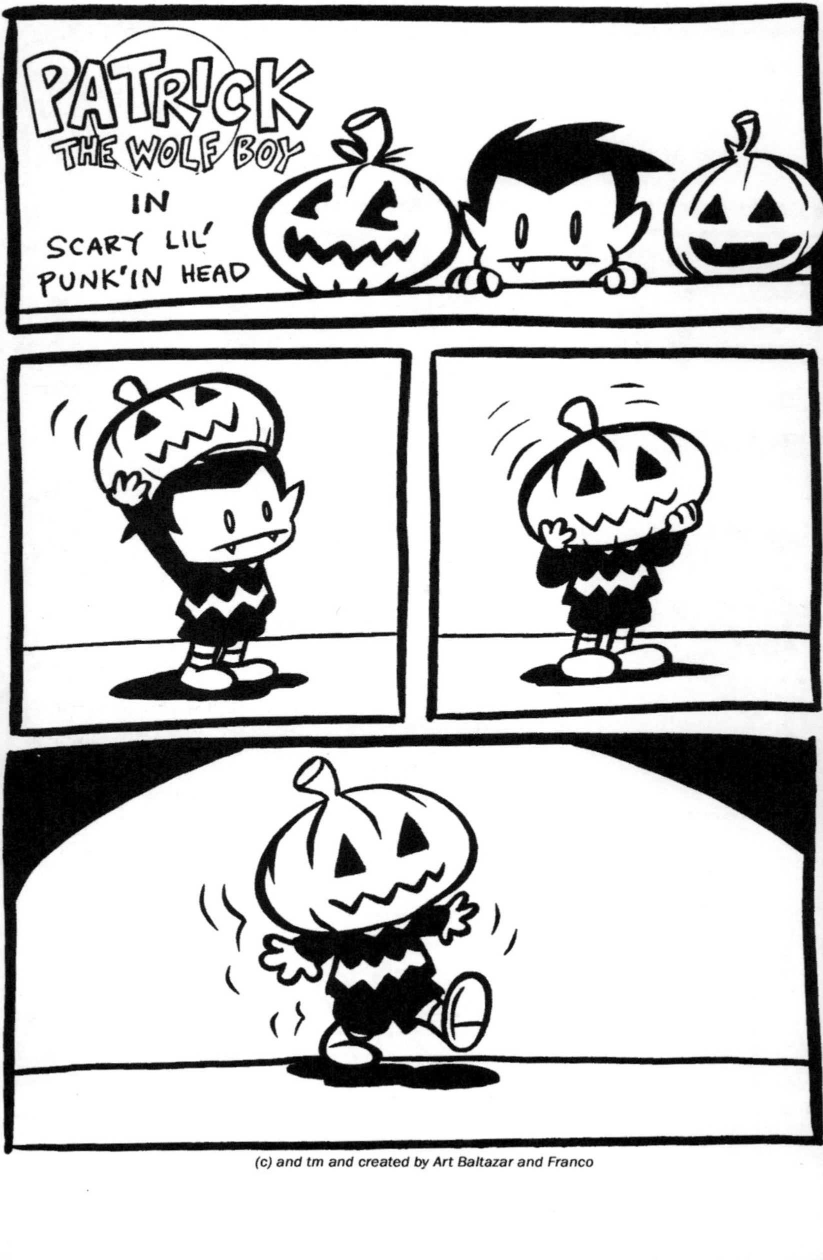
PATRICK THE WOLF BOY
IN
SCARY LIL' PUNK'IN HEAD

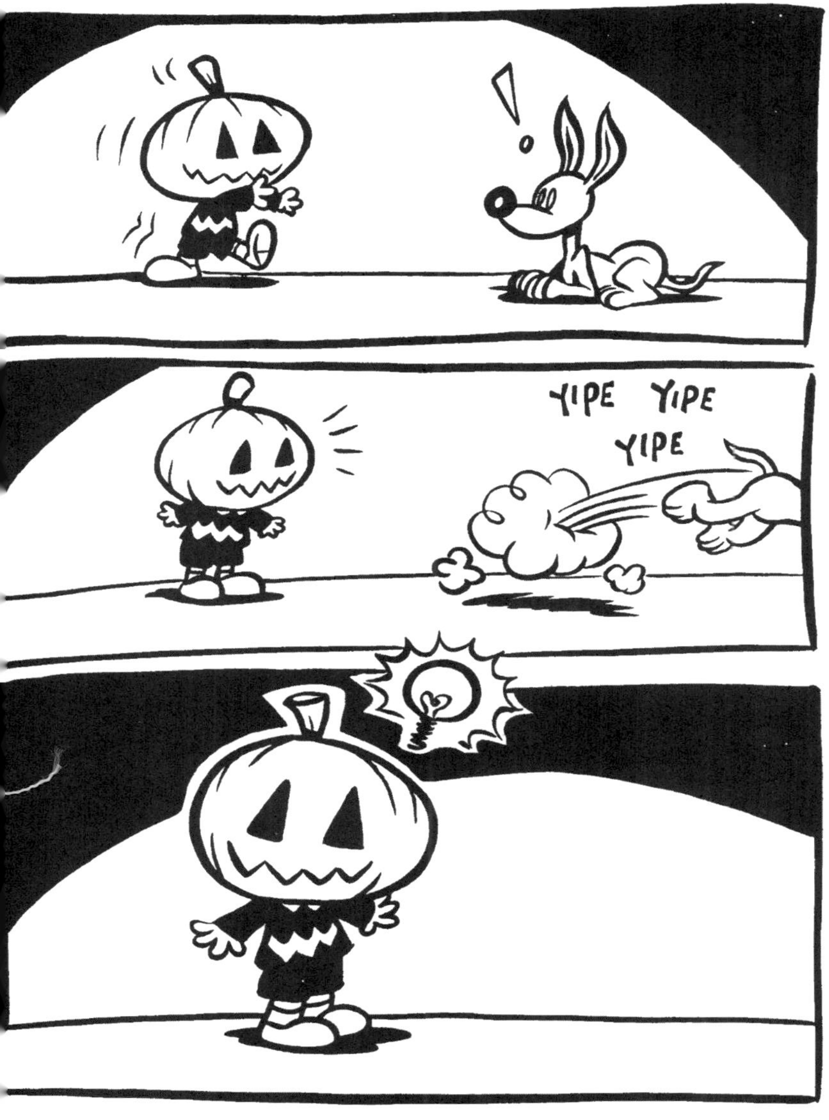
!
YIPE YIPE
YIPE

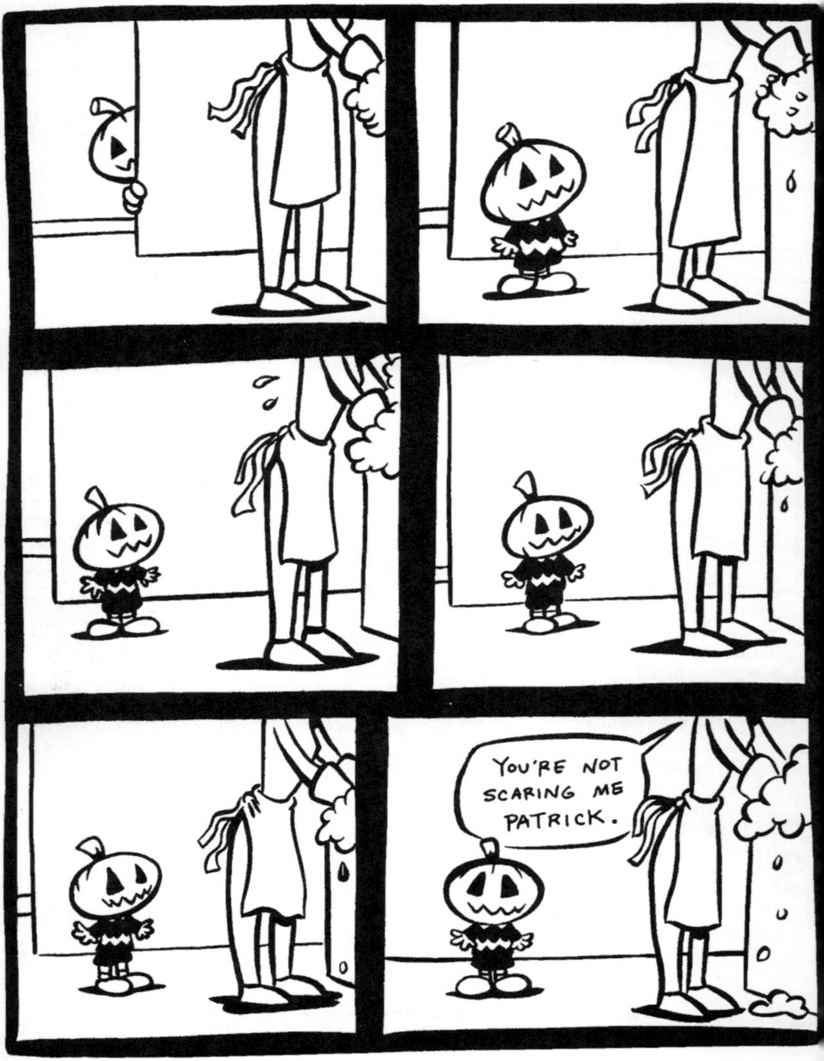
YOU'RE NOT SCARING ME PATRICK.

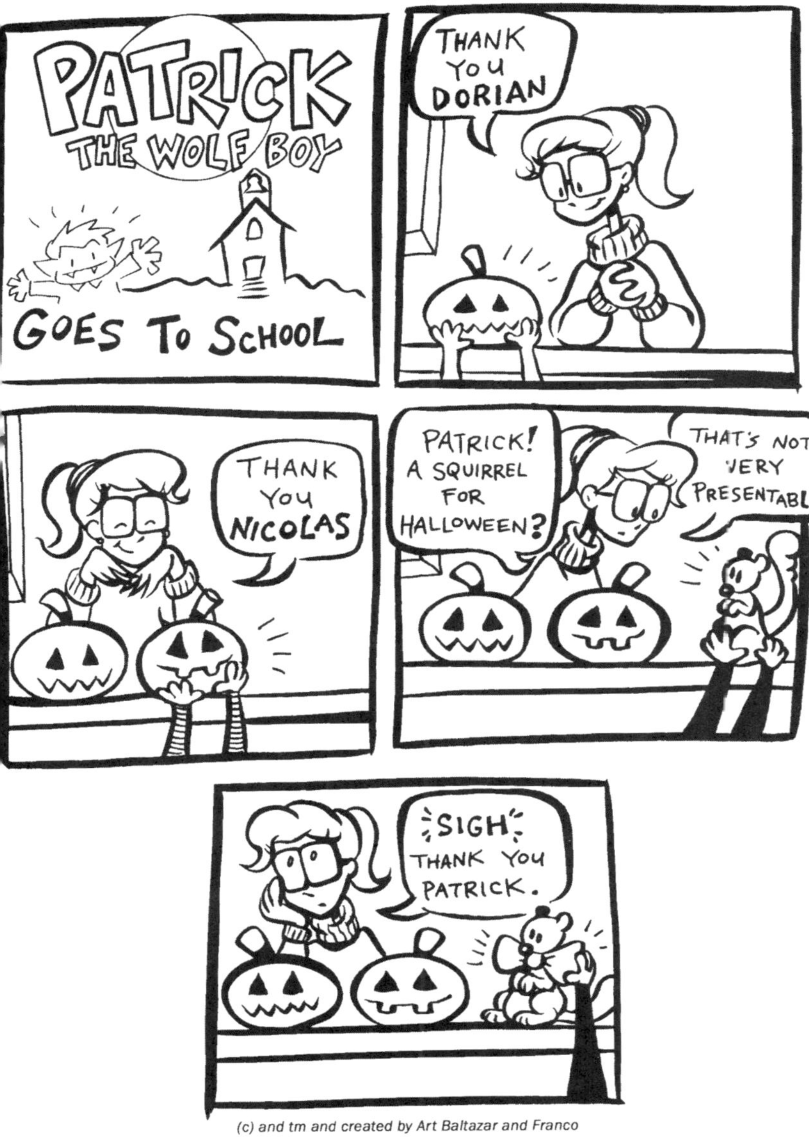
PATRICK THE WOLF BOY
GOES TO SCHOOL
THANK YOU DORIAN
THANK YOU NICOLAS
PATRICK! A SQUIRREL FOR HALLOWEEN?
THAT'S NOT VERY PRESENTABLE
SIGH THANK YOU PATRICK.

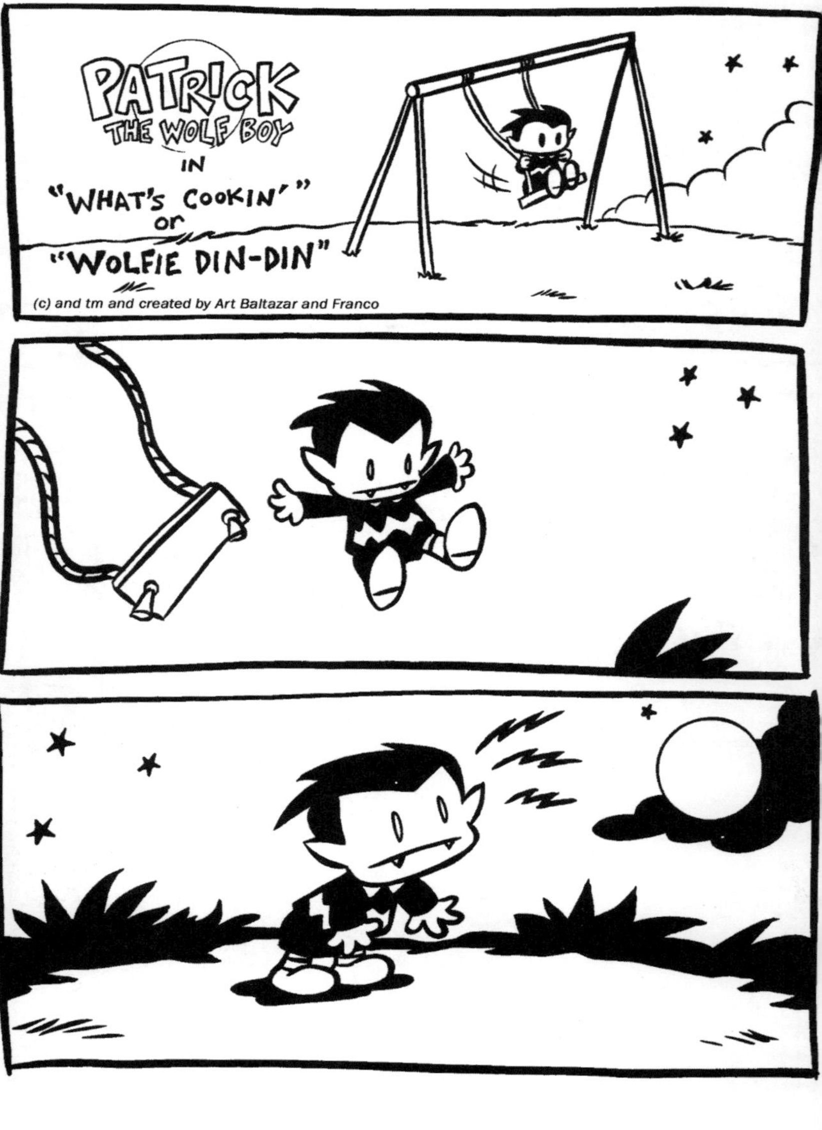
PATRICK THE WOLF BOY
IN
"WHAT'S COOKIN'"
or
"WOLFIE DIN-DIN"
(c) and tm and created by Art Baltazar and Franco

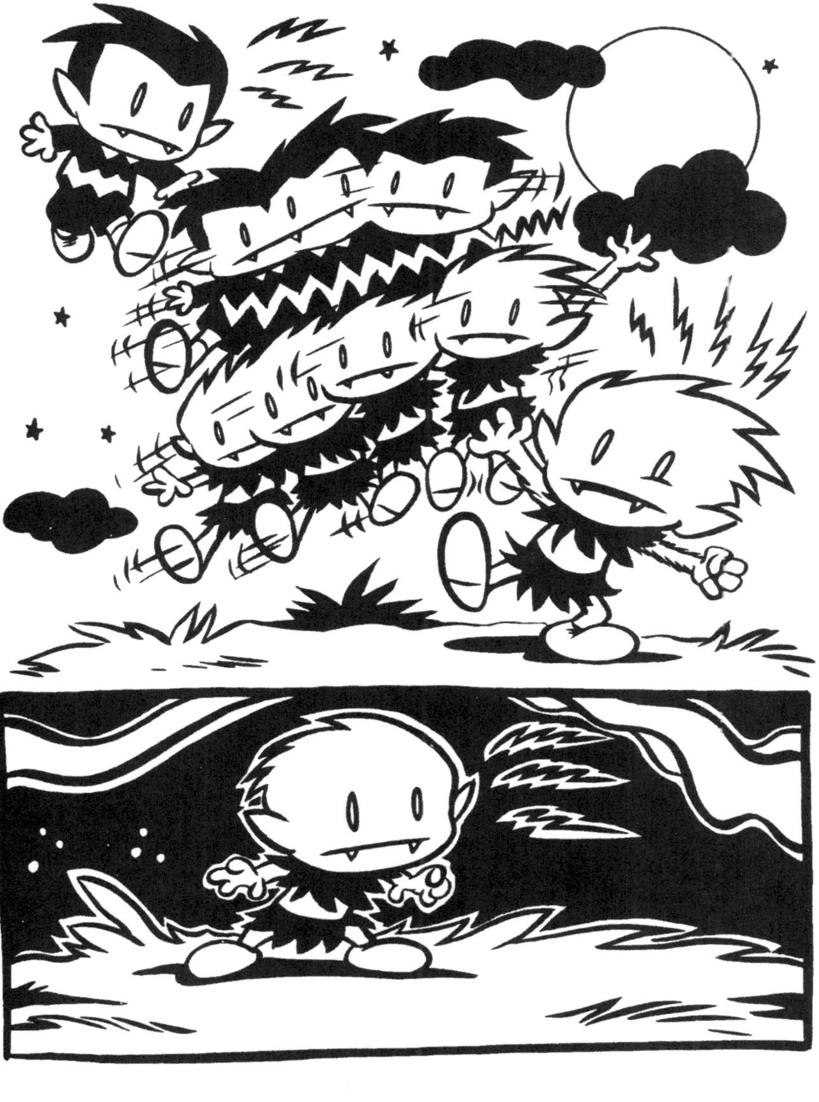

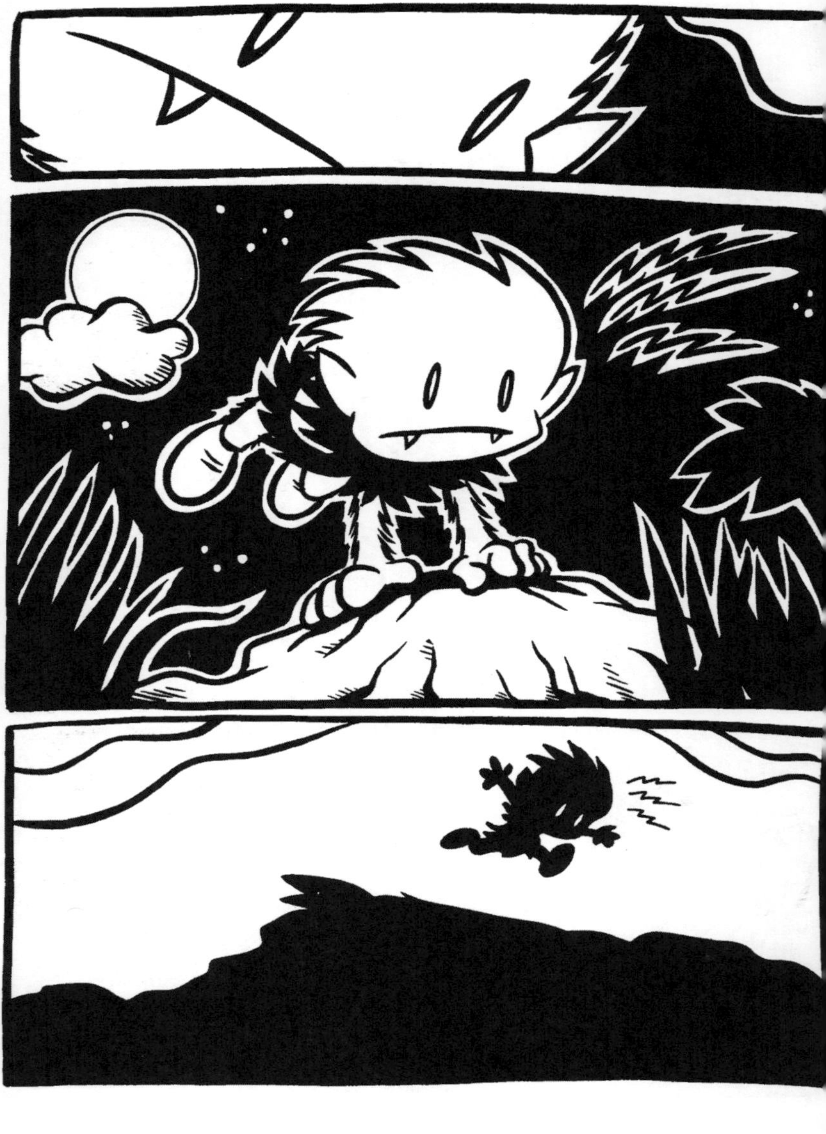

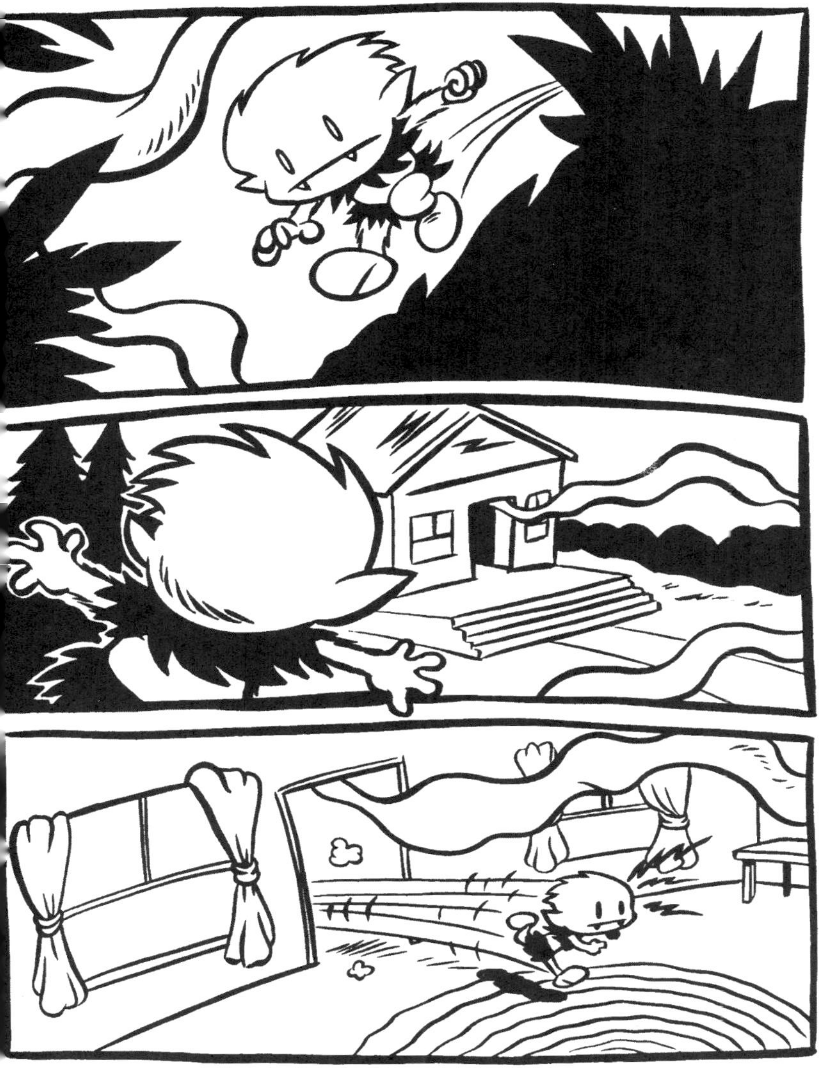

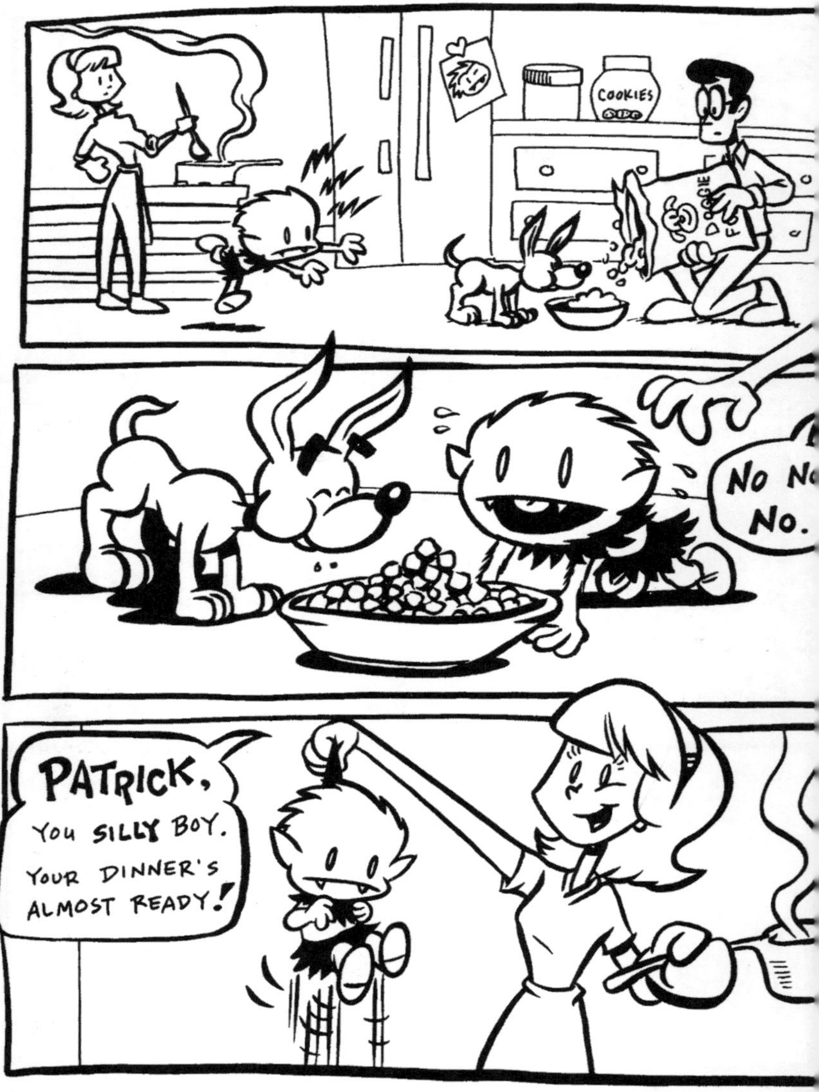
COOKIES
No
No.
PATRICK,
YOU SILLY BOY.
YOUR DINNER'S
ALMOST READY!

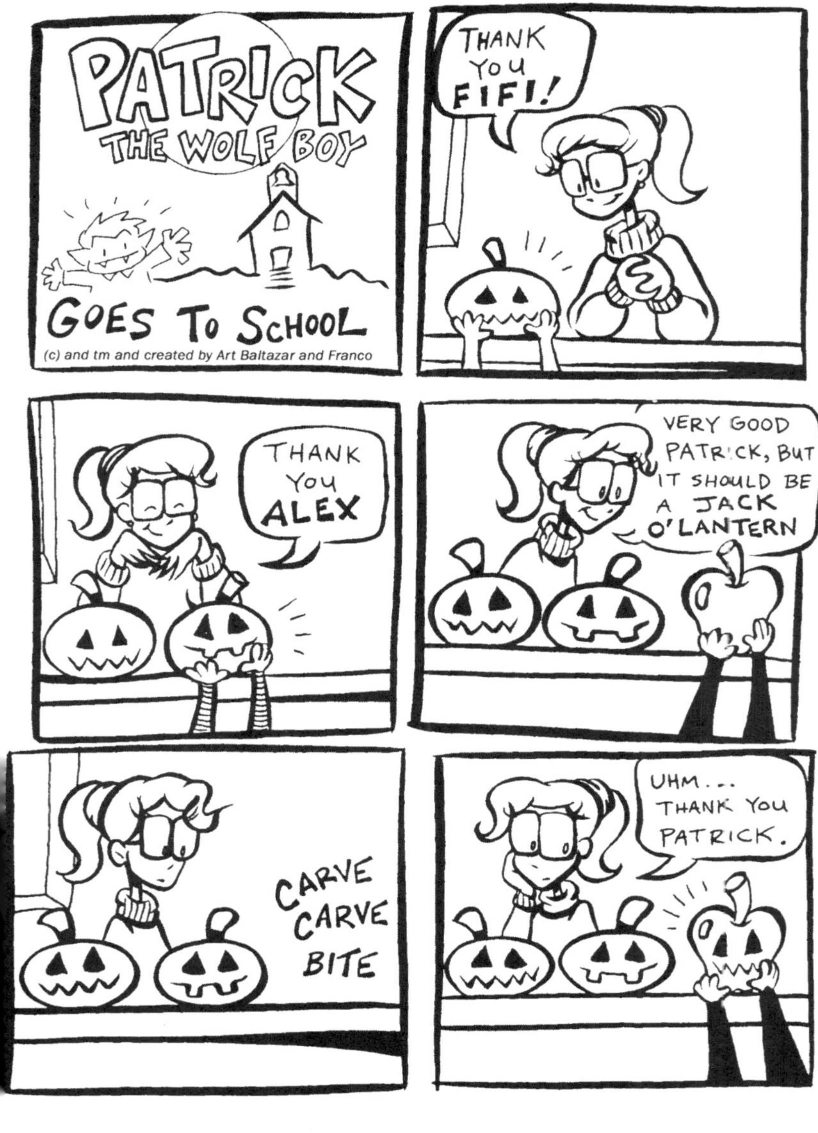
PATRICK THE WOLF BOY
GOES TO SCHOOL
(c) and tm and created by Art Baltazar and Franco
THANK YOU FIFI!
THANK YOU ALEX
VERY GOOD PATRICK, BUT IT SHOULD BE A JACK O'LANTERN
CARVE CARVE BITE
UHM... THANK YOU PATRICK.

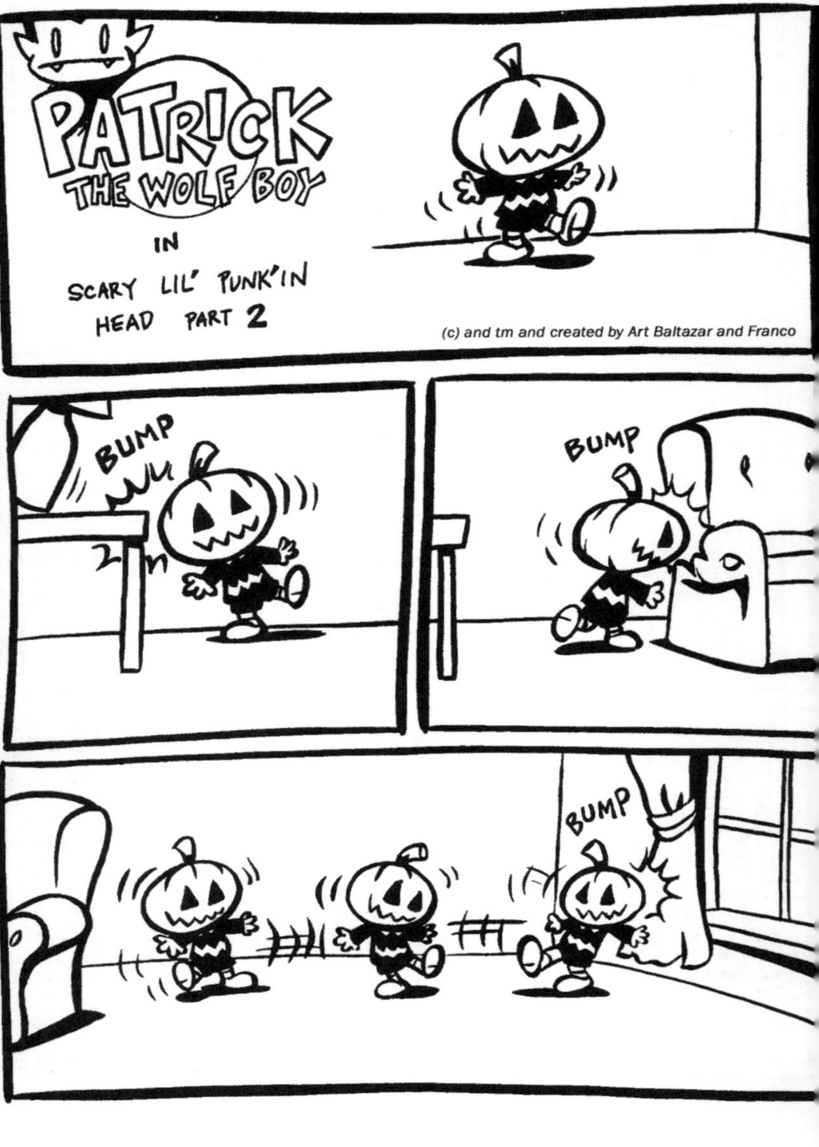
PATRICK THE WOLF BOY
IN
SCARY LIL' PUNK'IN HEAD PART 2
(c) and tm and created by Art Baltazar and Franco
BUMP
BUMP
BUMP

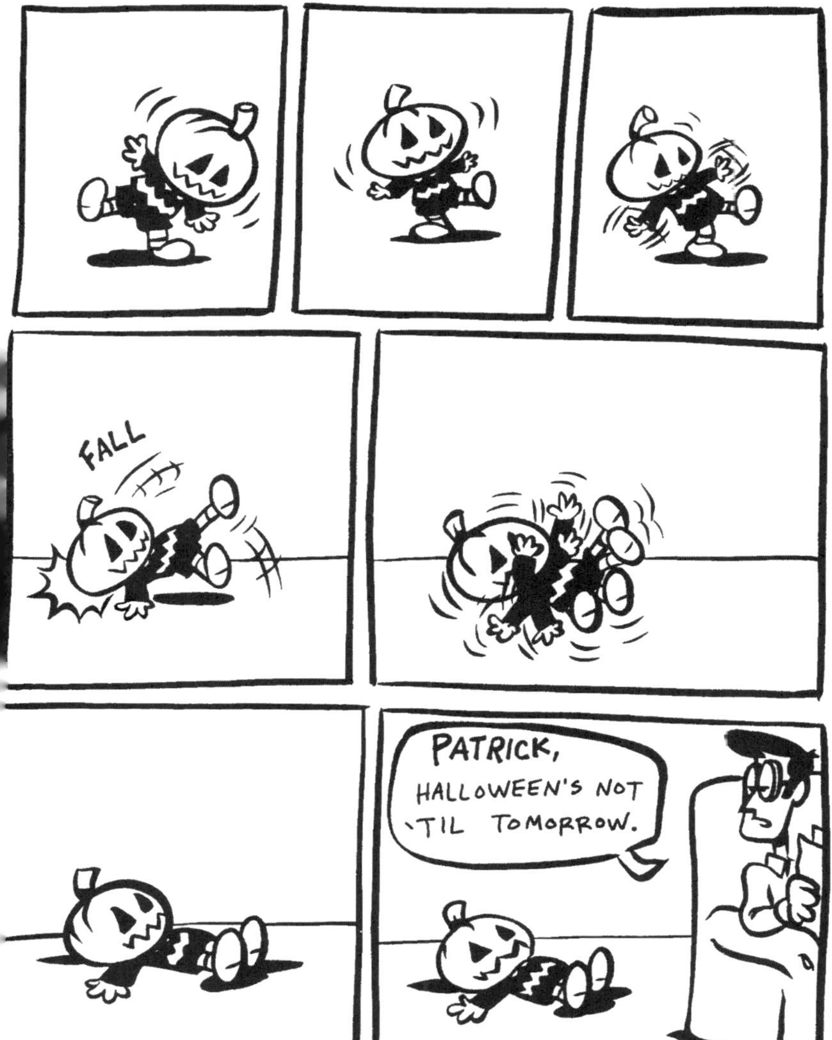
FALL
PATRICK, HALLOWEEN'S NOT 'TIL TOMORROW.

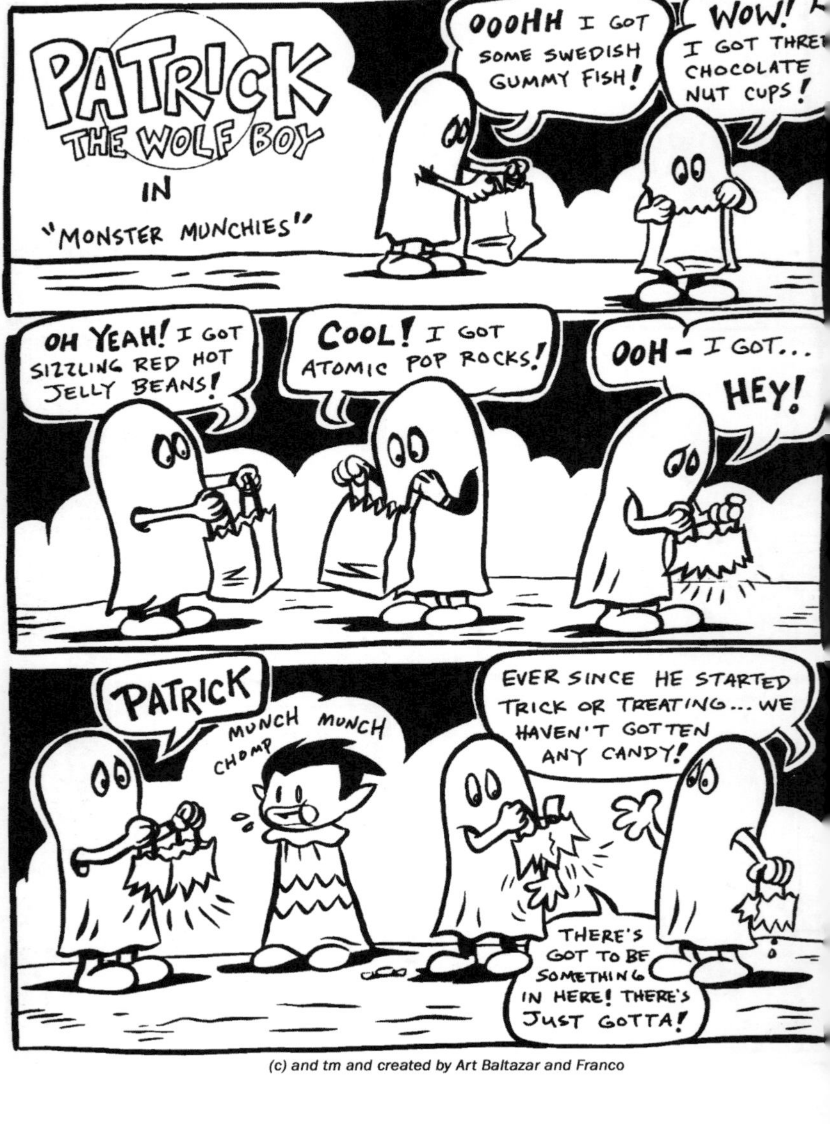

(c) and tm and created by Art Baltazar and Franco

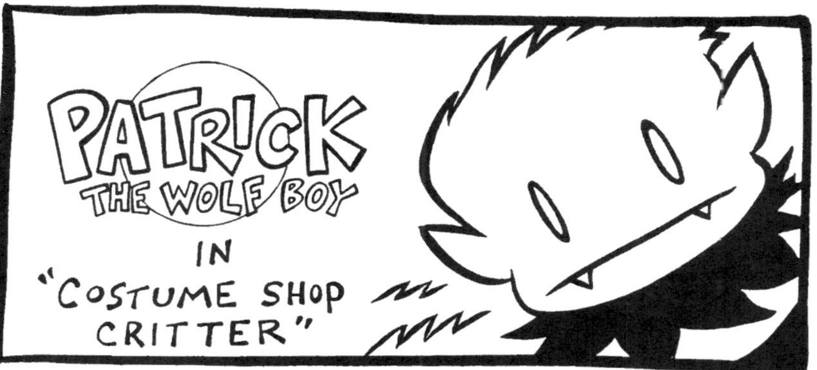
PATRICK THE WOLF BOY
IN
"COSTUME SHOP CRITTER"

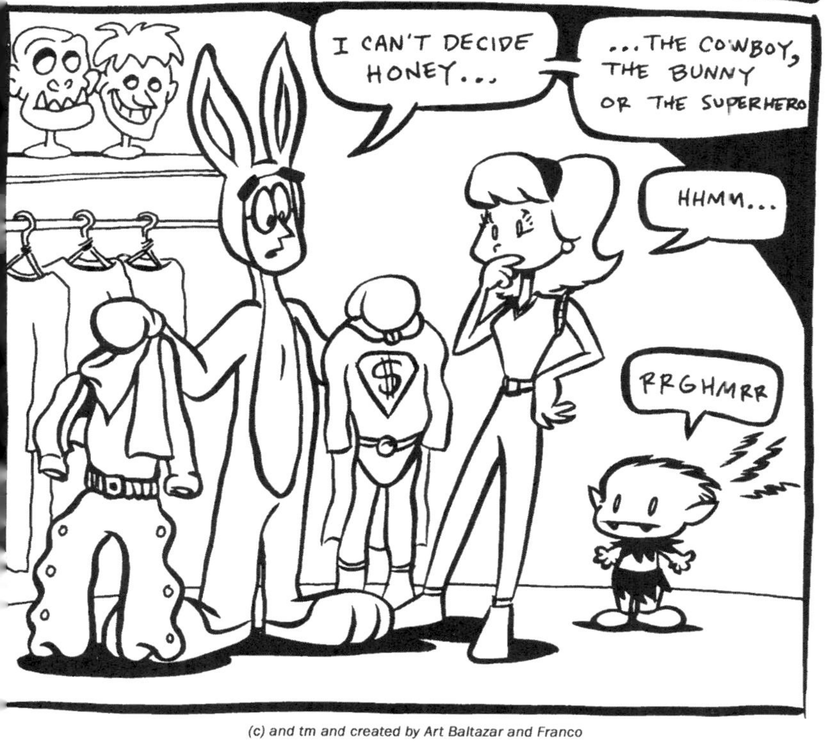
I CAN'T DECIDE HONEY...
...THE COWBOY, THE BUNNY OR THE SUPERHERO
HHMM...
RRGHMRR

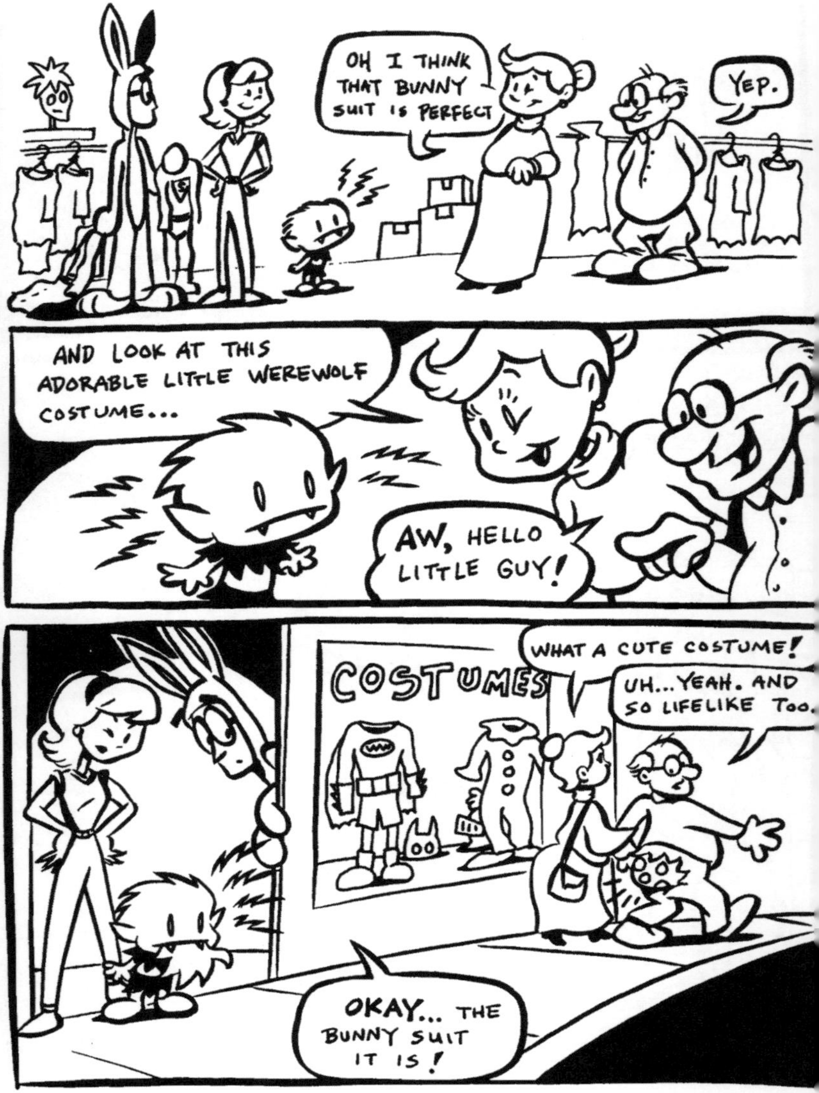

OH I THINK THAT BUNNY SUIT IS PERFECT
YEP.
AND LOOK AT THIS ADORABLE LITTLE WEREWOLF COSTUME...
AW, HELLO LITTLE GUY!
COSTUMES
WHAT A CUTE COSTUME!
UH... YEAH. AND SO LIFELIKE TOO.
OKAY... THE BUNNY SUIT IT IS!

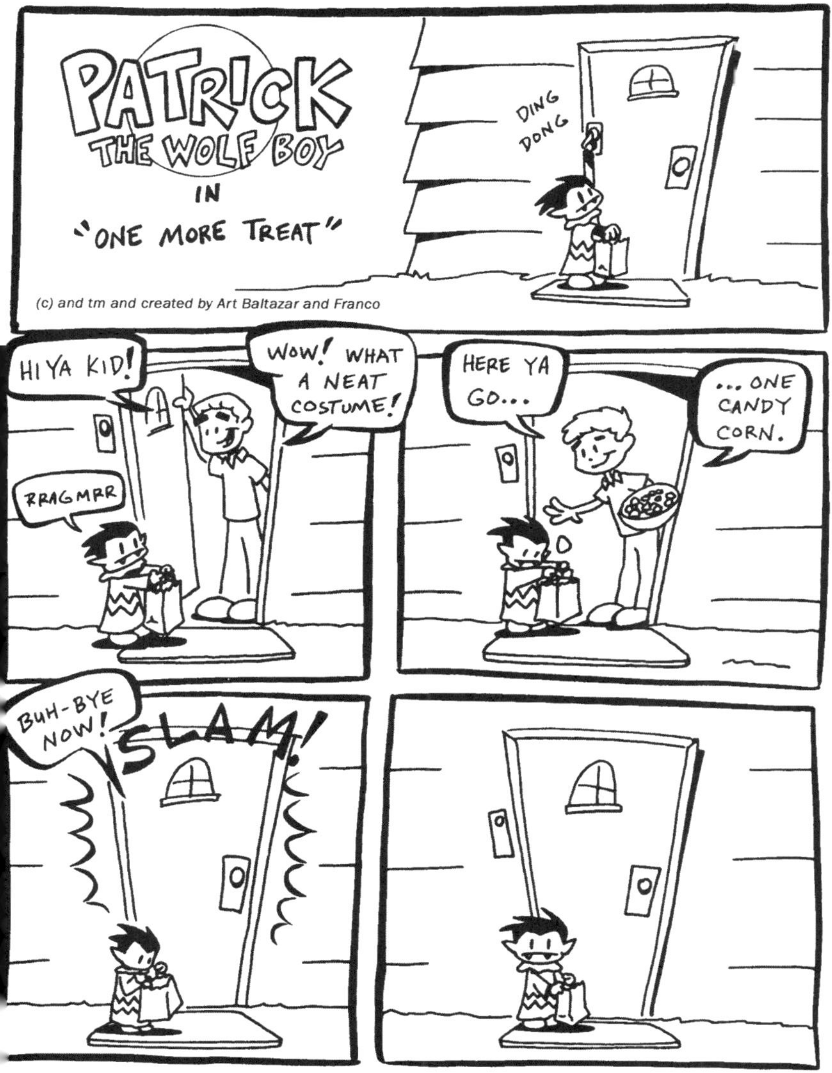
PATRICK THE WOLF BOY
IN
"ONE MORE TREAT"
DING DONG
(c) and tm and created by Art Baltazar and Franco
HI YA KID!
WOW! WHAT A NEAT COSTUME!
RRAGMRR
HERE YA GO...
...ONE CANDY CORN.
BUH-BYE NOW!
SLAM!

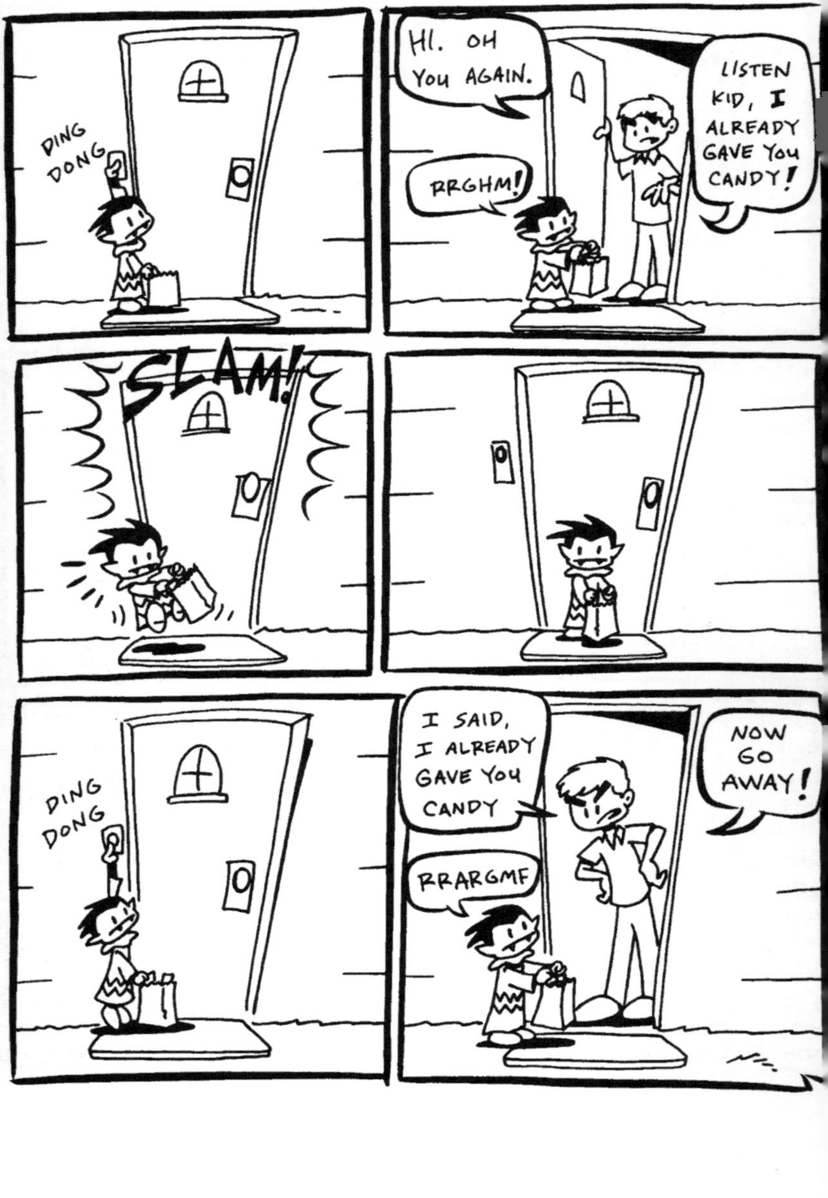

DING DONG
HI. OH YOU AGAIN.
RRGHM!
LISTEN KID, I ALREADY GAVE YOU CANDY!
SLAM!
DING DONG
I SAID, I ALREADY GAVE YOU CANDY
RRARGMF
NOW GO AWAY!

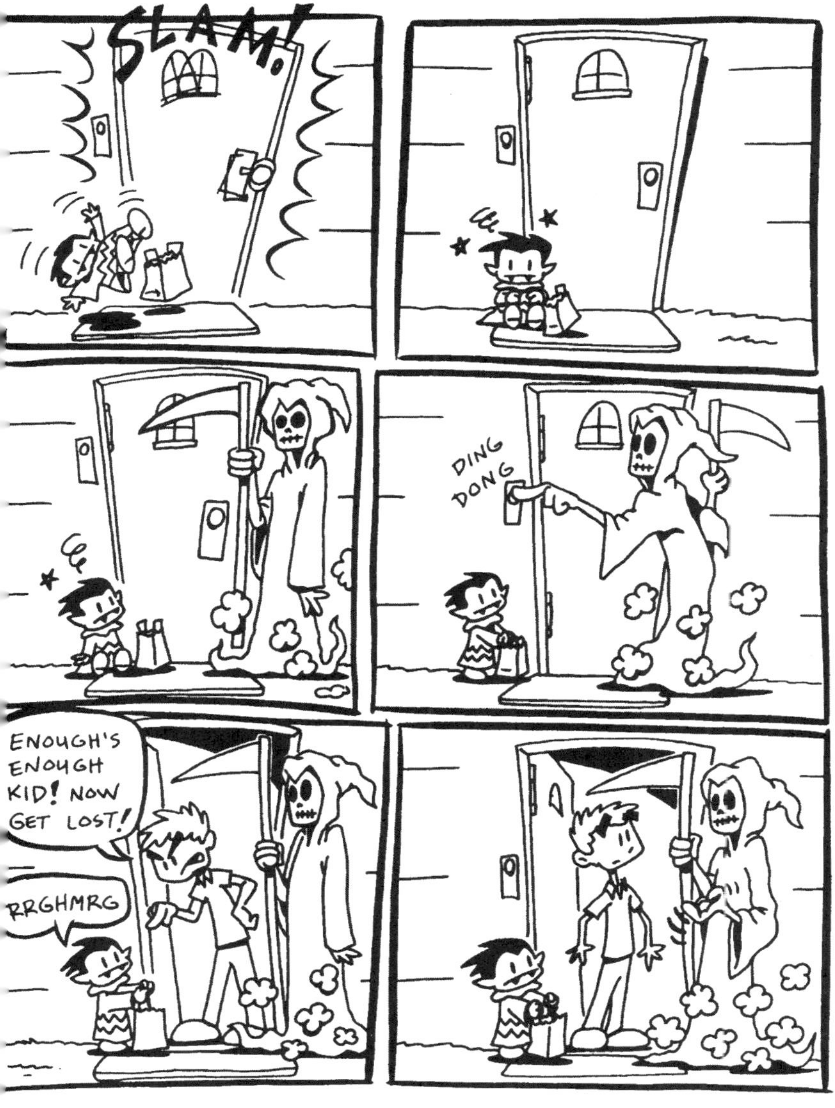
SLAM!
DING DONG
ENOUGH'S ENOUGH KID! NOW GET LOST!
RRGHMRG

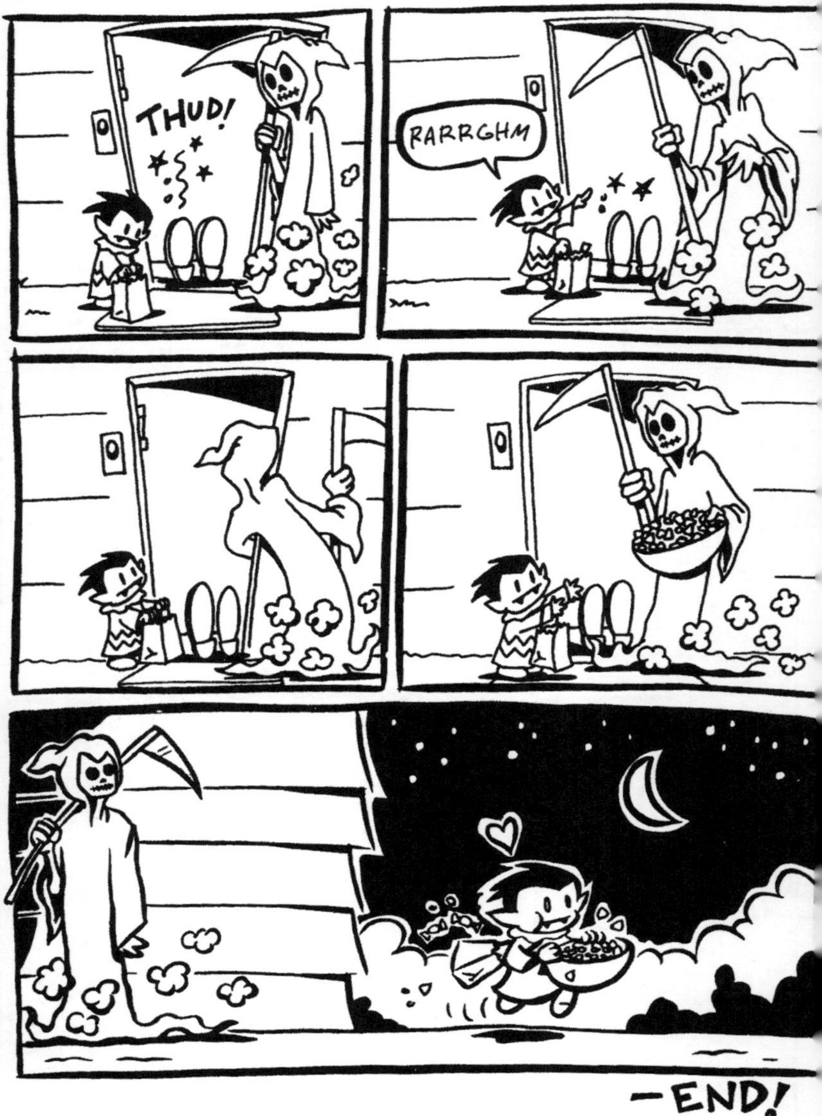
THUD!
RARRGHM

—END!

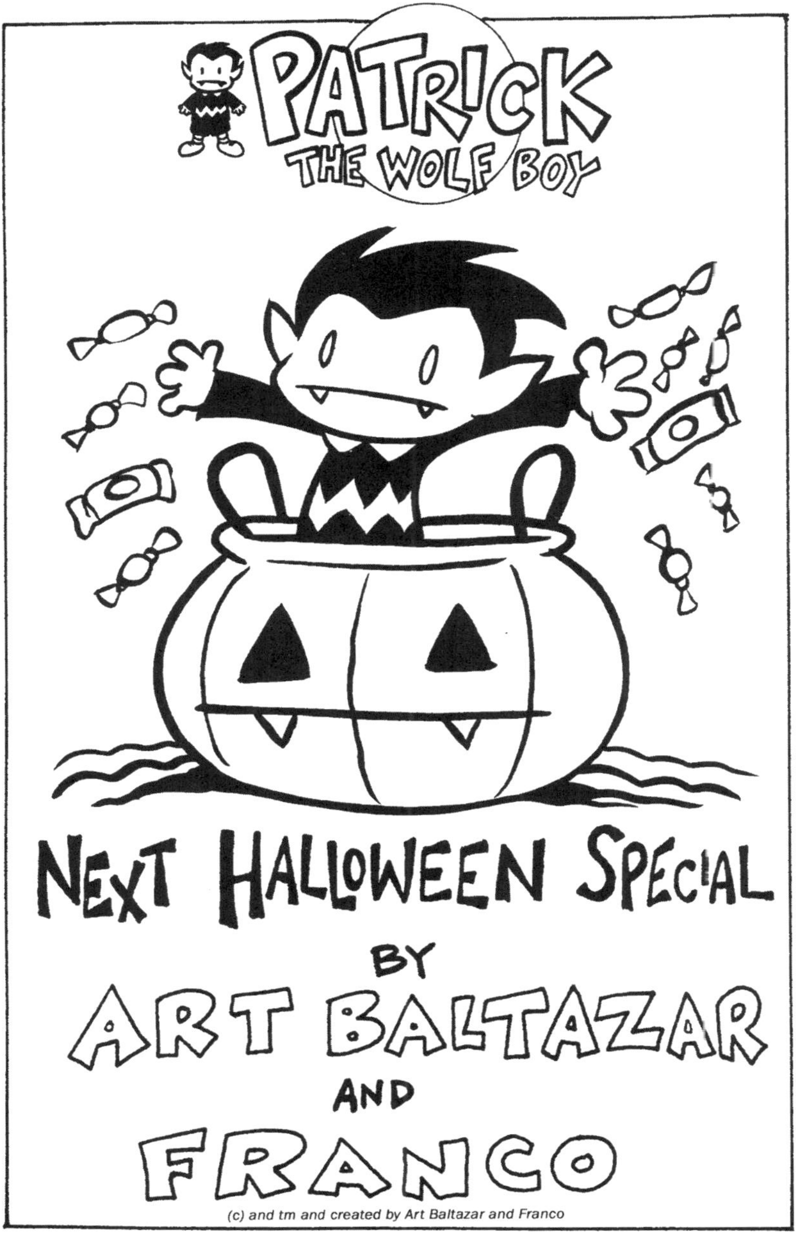
PATRICK THE WOLF BOY
NEXT HALLOWEEN SPECIAL
BY
ART BALTAZAR
AND
FRANCO

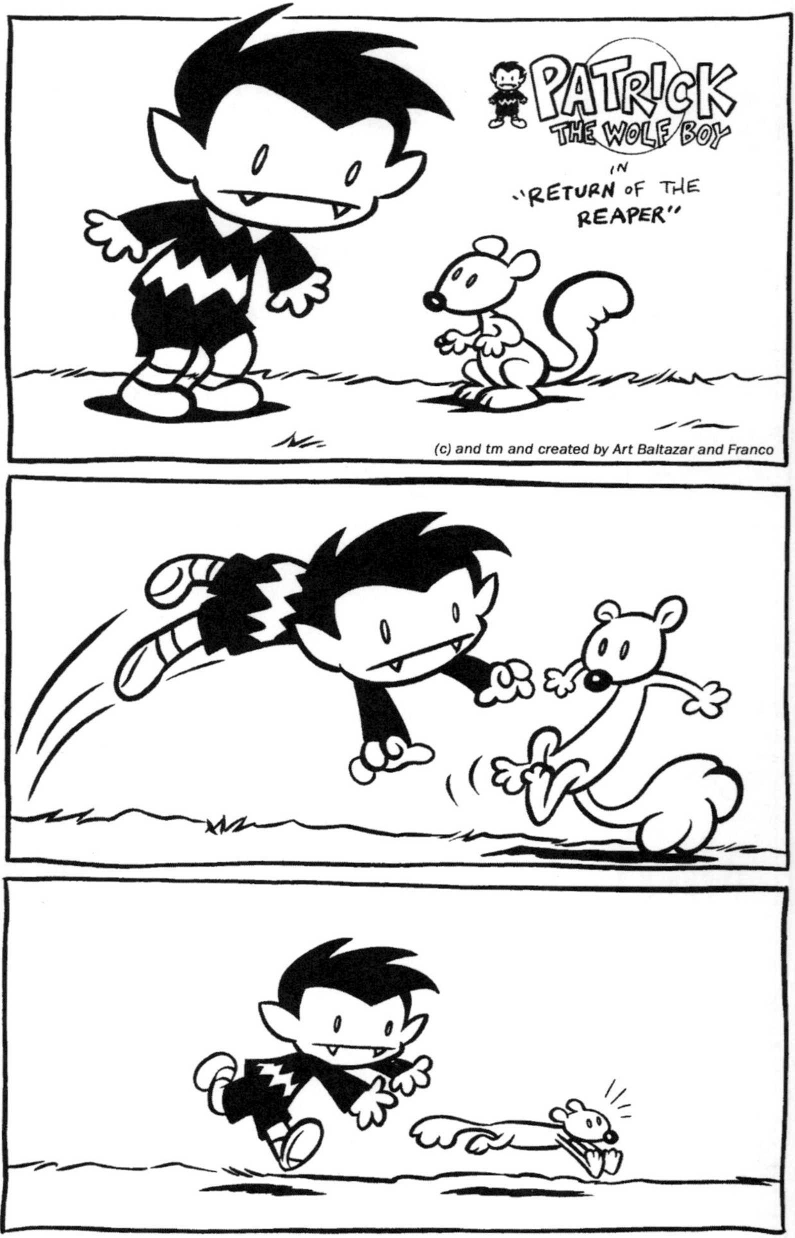
PATRICK THE WOLF BOY
IN
"RETURN OF THE REAPER"
(c) and tm and created by Art Baltazar and Franco

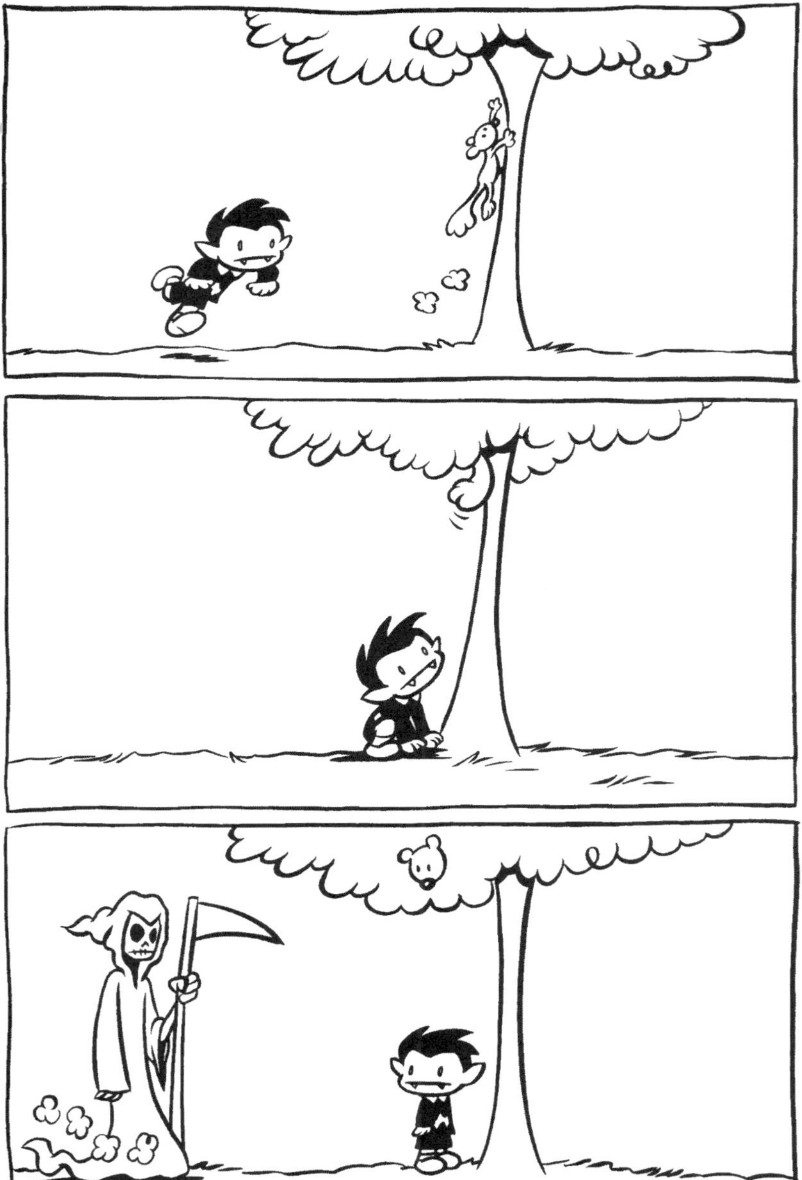

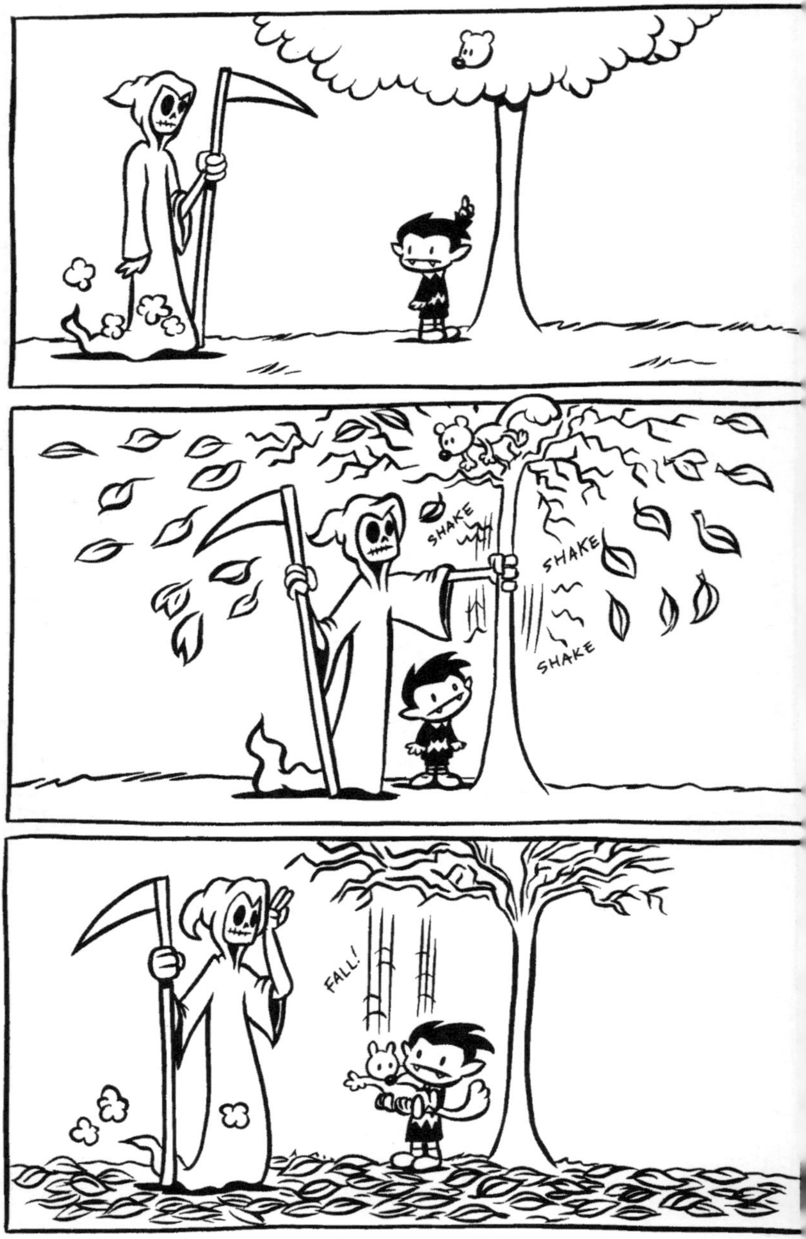
SHAKE
SHAKE
SHAKE
FALL!

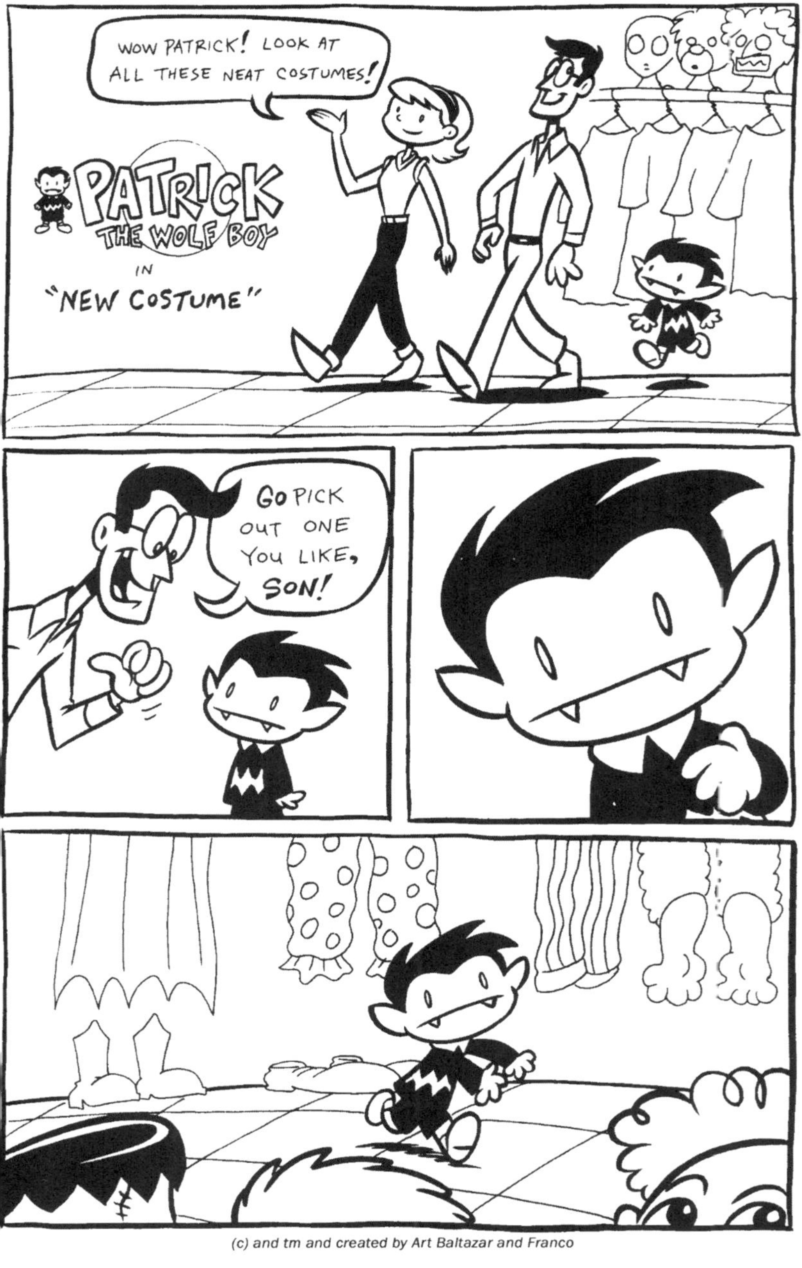
WOW PATRICK! LOOK AT ALL THESE NEAT COSTUMES!
PATRICK THE WOLF BOY
IN
"NEW COSTUME"
GO PICK OUT ONE YOU LIKE, SON!

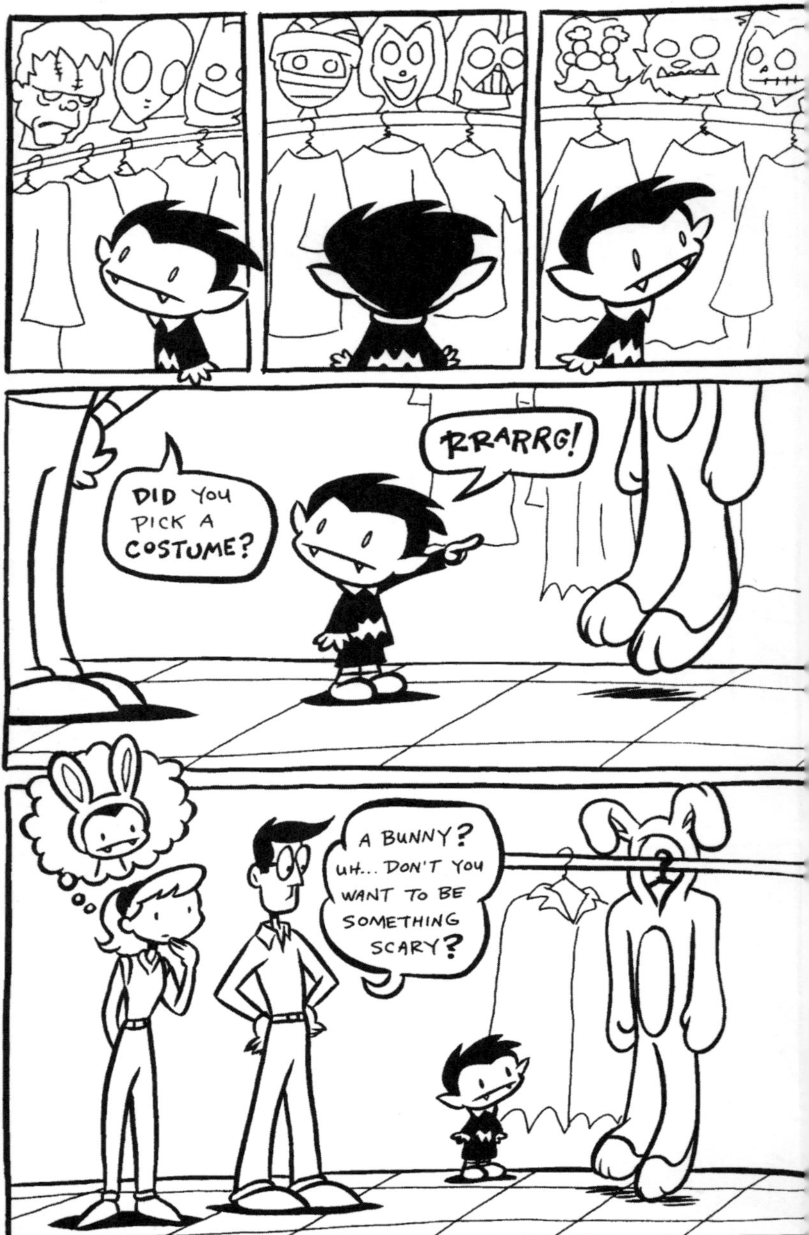

DID YOU PICK A COSTUME?
RRARRG!
A BUNNY? UH... DON'T YOU WANT TO BE SOMETHING SCARY?

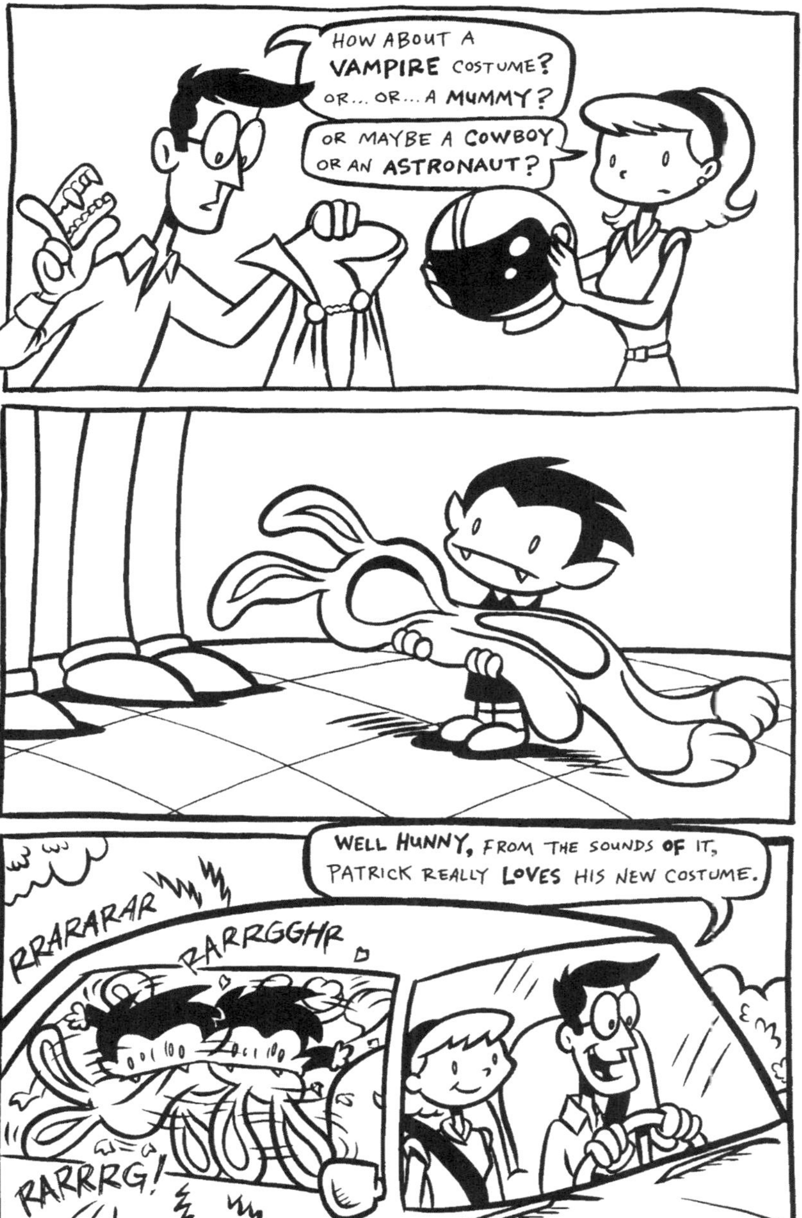
HOW ABOUT A VAMPIRE COSTUME? OR... OR... A MUMMY?
OR MAYBE A COWBOY OR AN ASTRONAUT?
WELL HUNNY, FROM THE SOUNDS OF IT, PATRICK REALLY LOVES HIS NEW COSTUME.
RRARARAR
RARRGGHR
RARRRG!

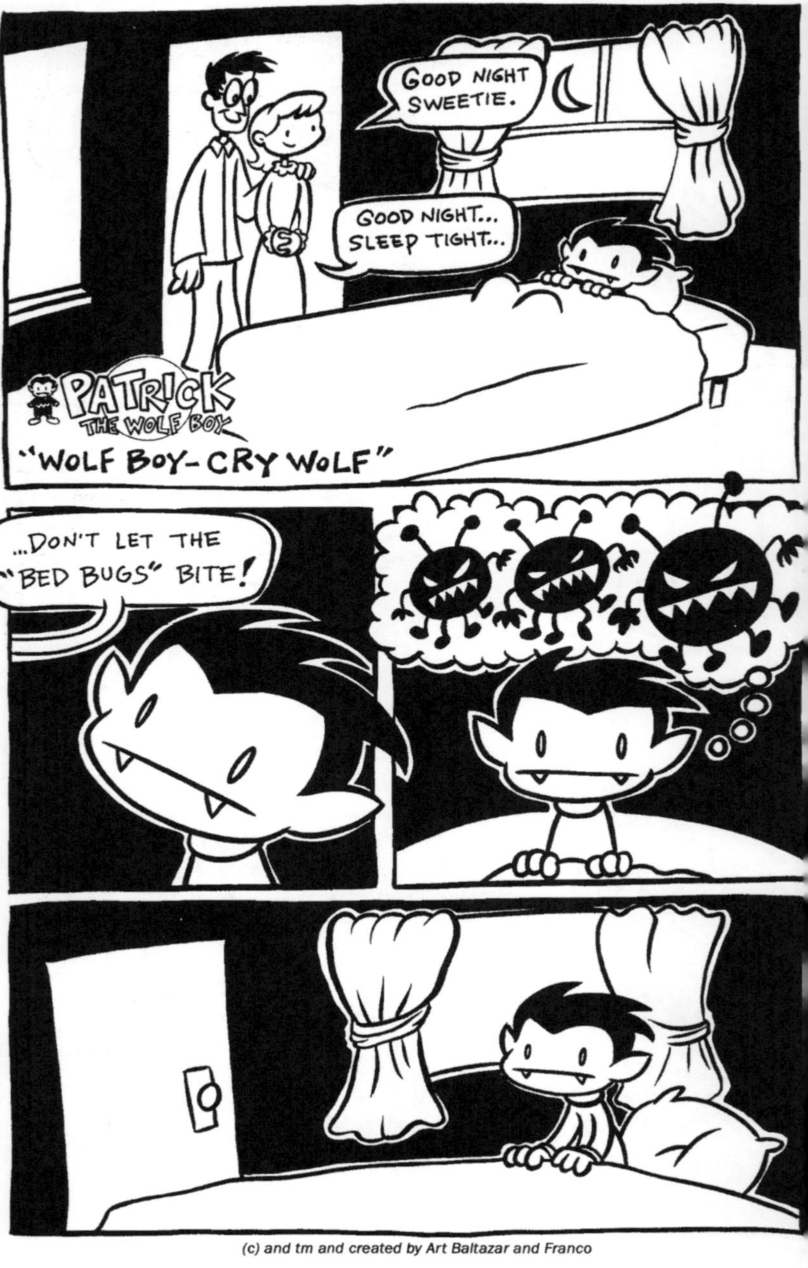
GOOD NIGHT SWEETIE.
GOOD NIGHT... SLEEP TIGHT...
PATRICK THE WOLF BOY
"WOLF BOY- CRY WOLF"
...DON'T LET THE "BED BUGS" BITE!

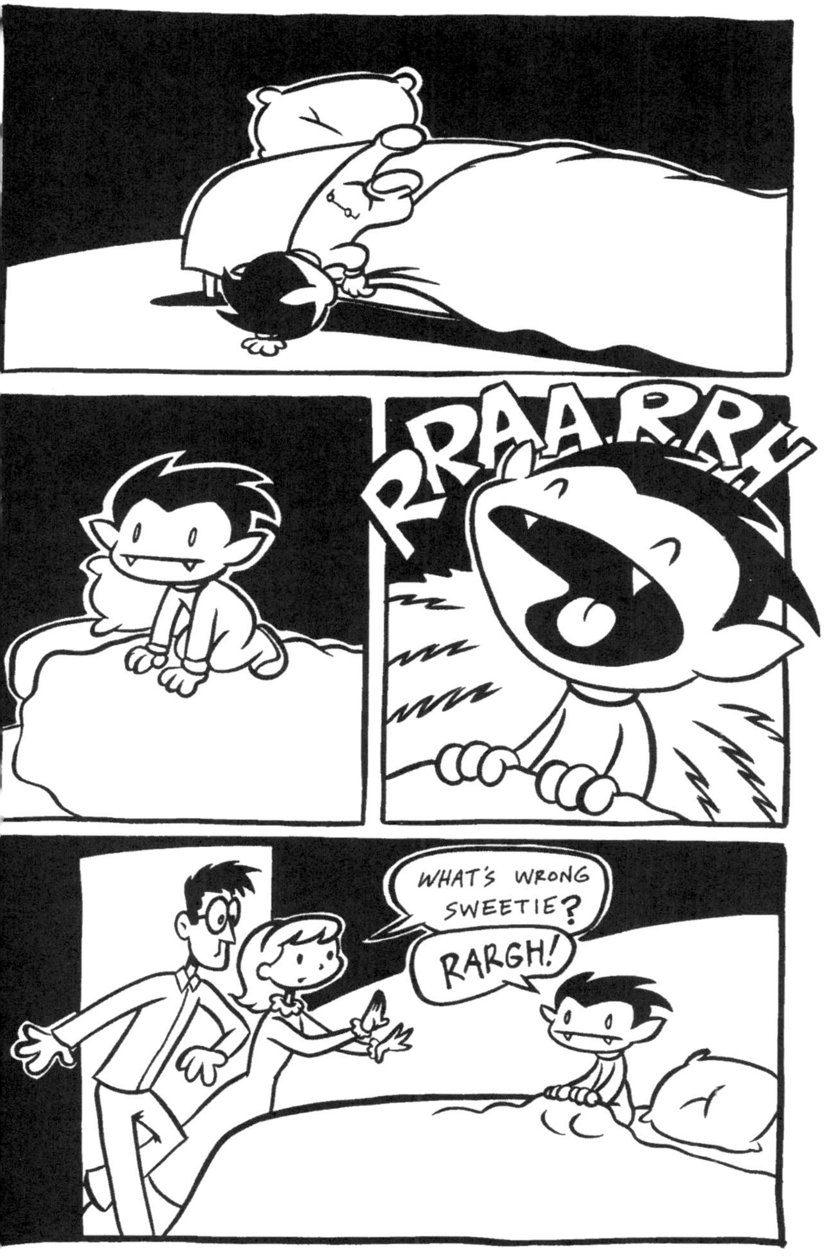
RRAARRH
WHAT'S WRONG SWEETIE?
RARGH!

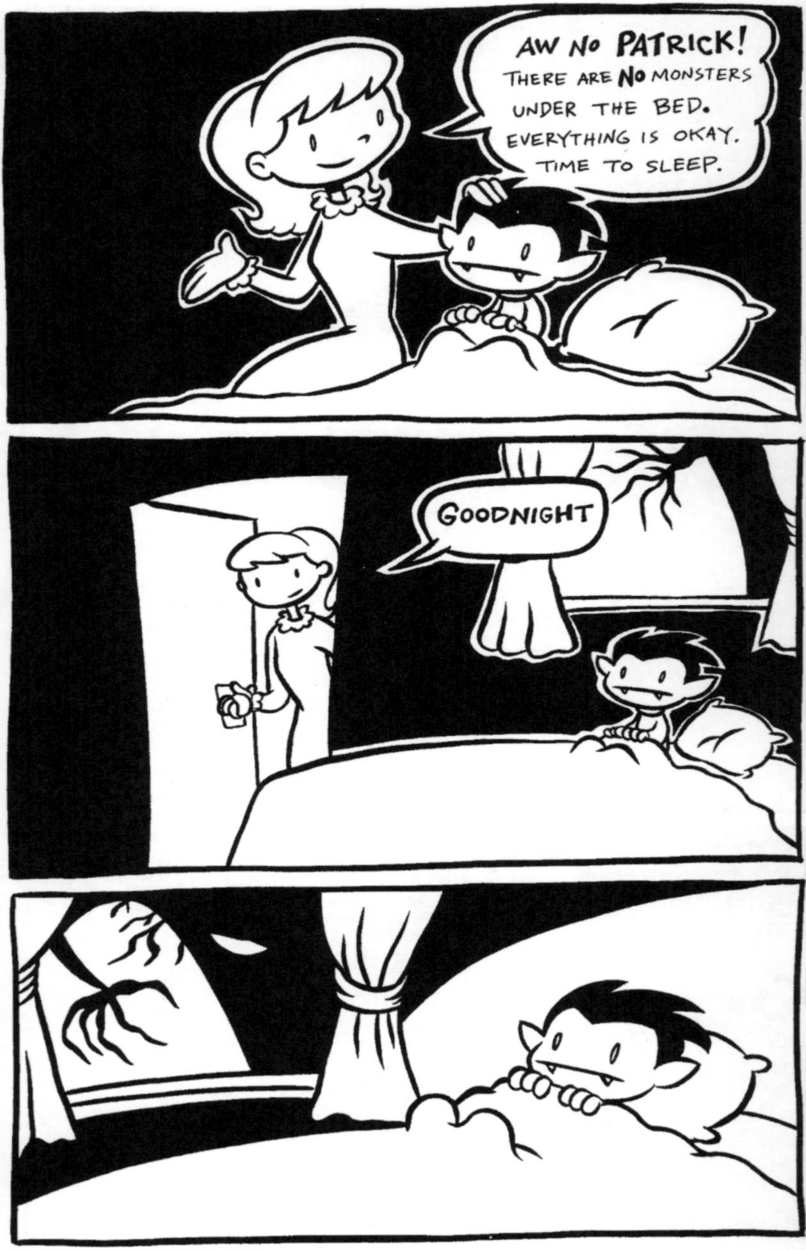
AW NO PATRICK! THERE ARE NO MONSTERS UNDER THE BED. EVERYTHING IS OKAY. TIME TO SLEEP.
GOODNIGHT

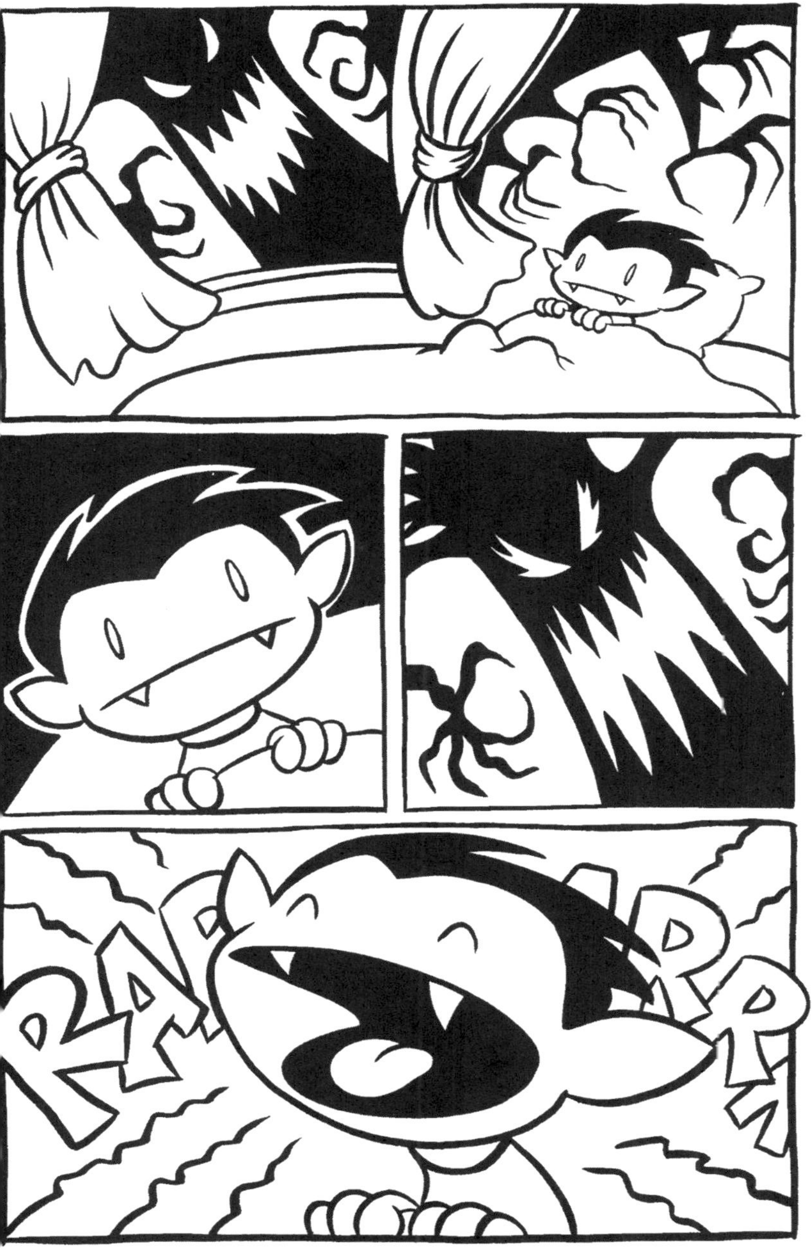

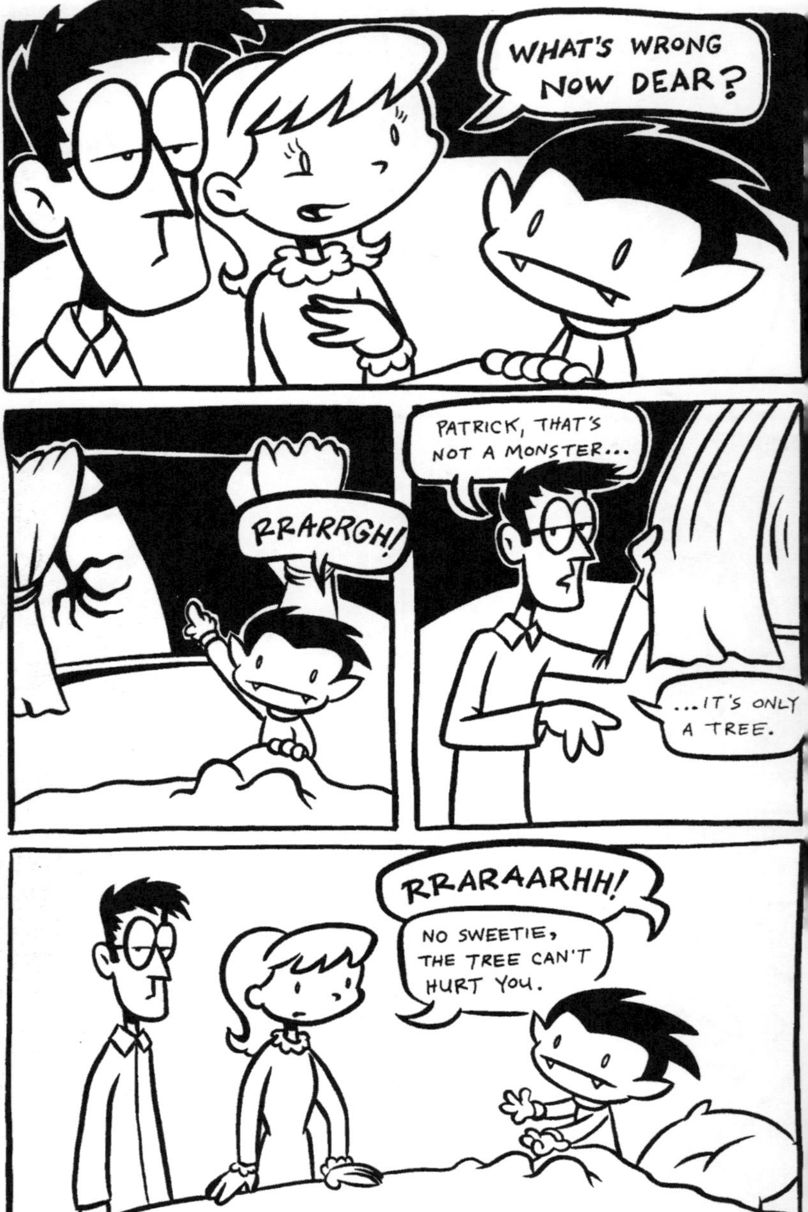
WHAT'S WRONG NOW DEAR?
RRARRGH!
PATRICK, THAT'S NOT A MONSTER...
...IT'S ONLY A TREE.
RRARAARHH!
NO SWEETIE, THE TREE CAN'T HURT YOU.

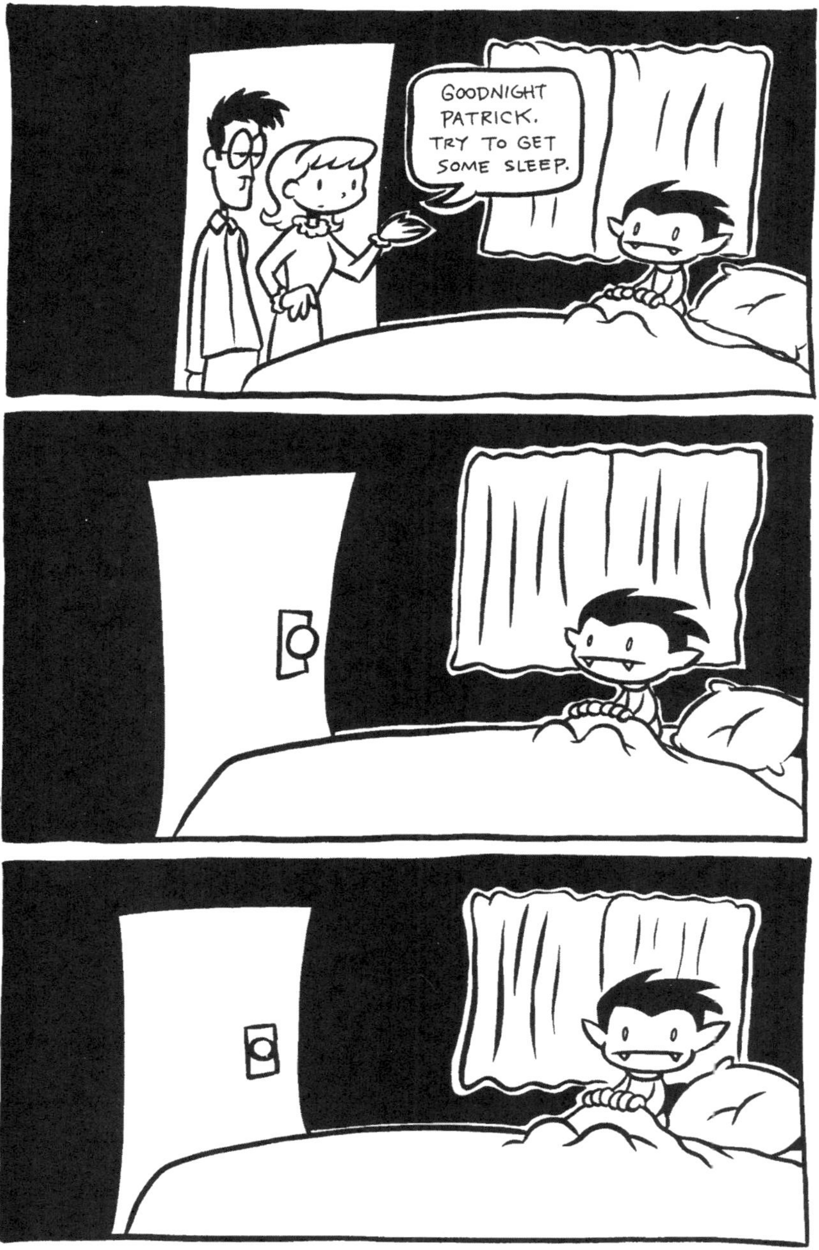
GOODNIGHT PATRICK. TRY TO GET SOME SLEEP.

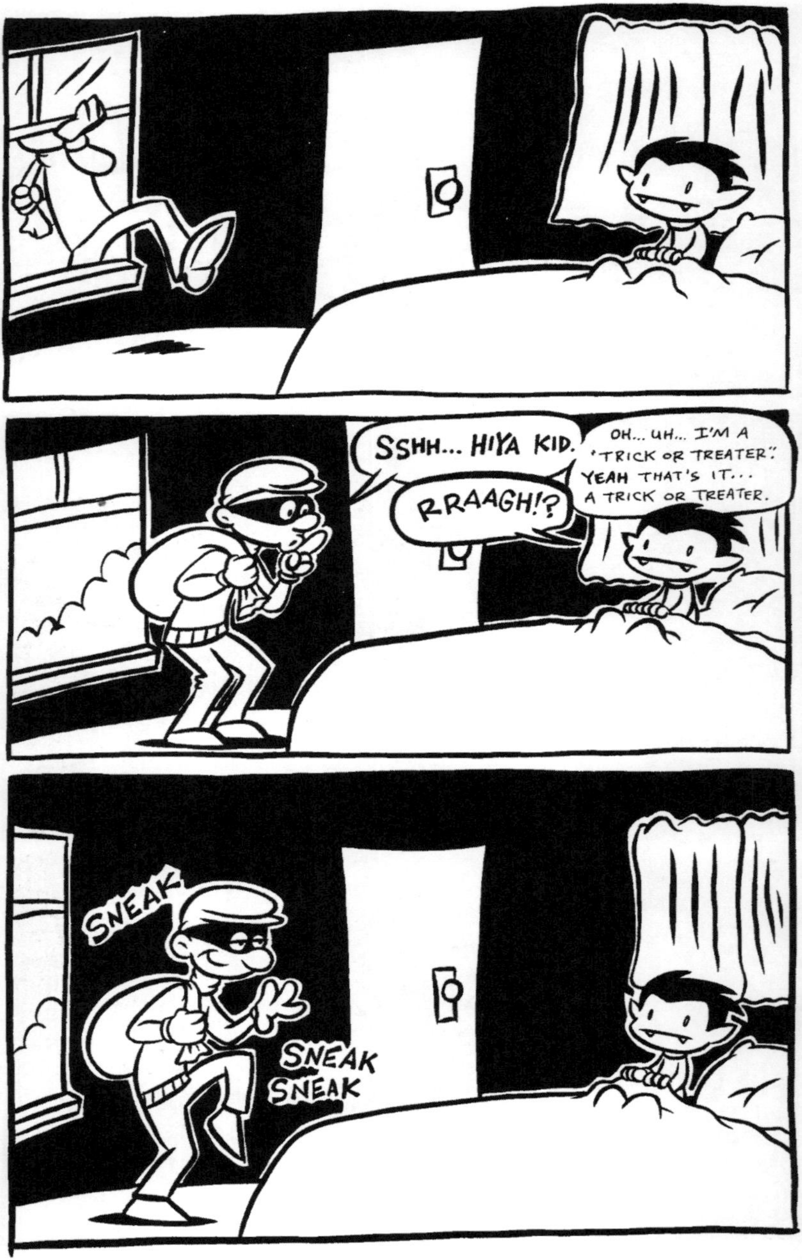
SSHH... HIYA KID.
RRAAGH!?
OH... UH... I'M A "TRICK OR TREATER". YEAH THAT'S IT... A TRICK OR TREATER.
SNEAK
SNEAK
SNEAK

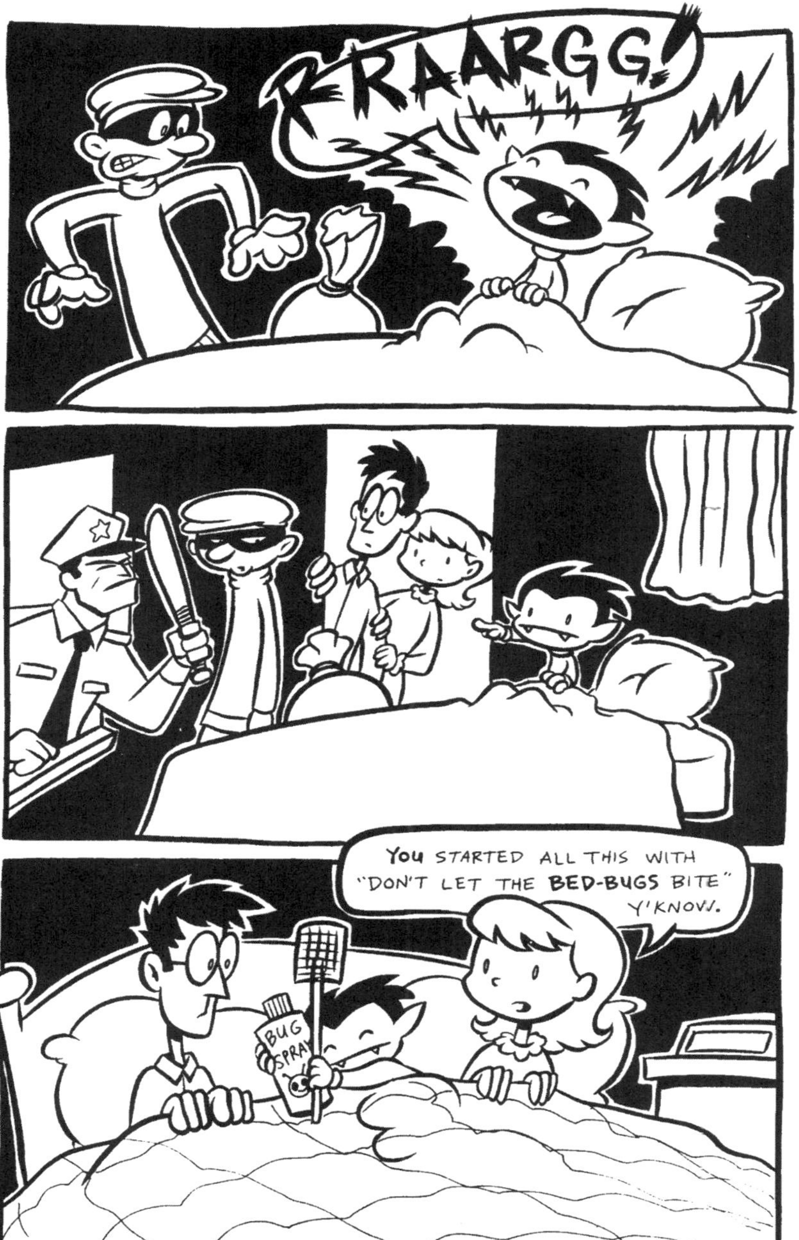
KRAARGG!
YOU STARTED ALL THIS WITH "DON'T LET THE BED-BUGS BITE" Y'KNOW.
BUG SPRAY

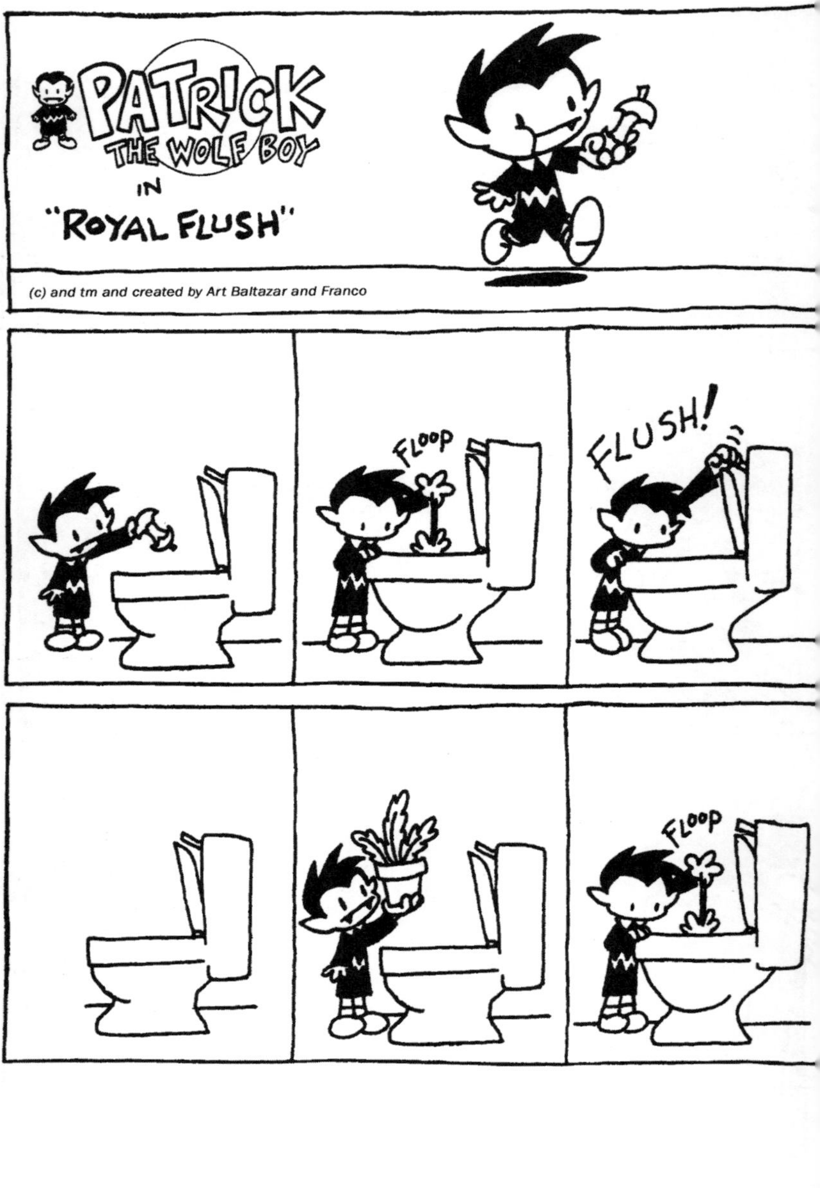
PATRICK THE WOLF BOY
IN
"ROYAL FLUSH"
(c) and tm and created by Art Baltazar and Franco
FLOOP
FLUSH!
FLOOP

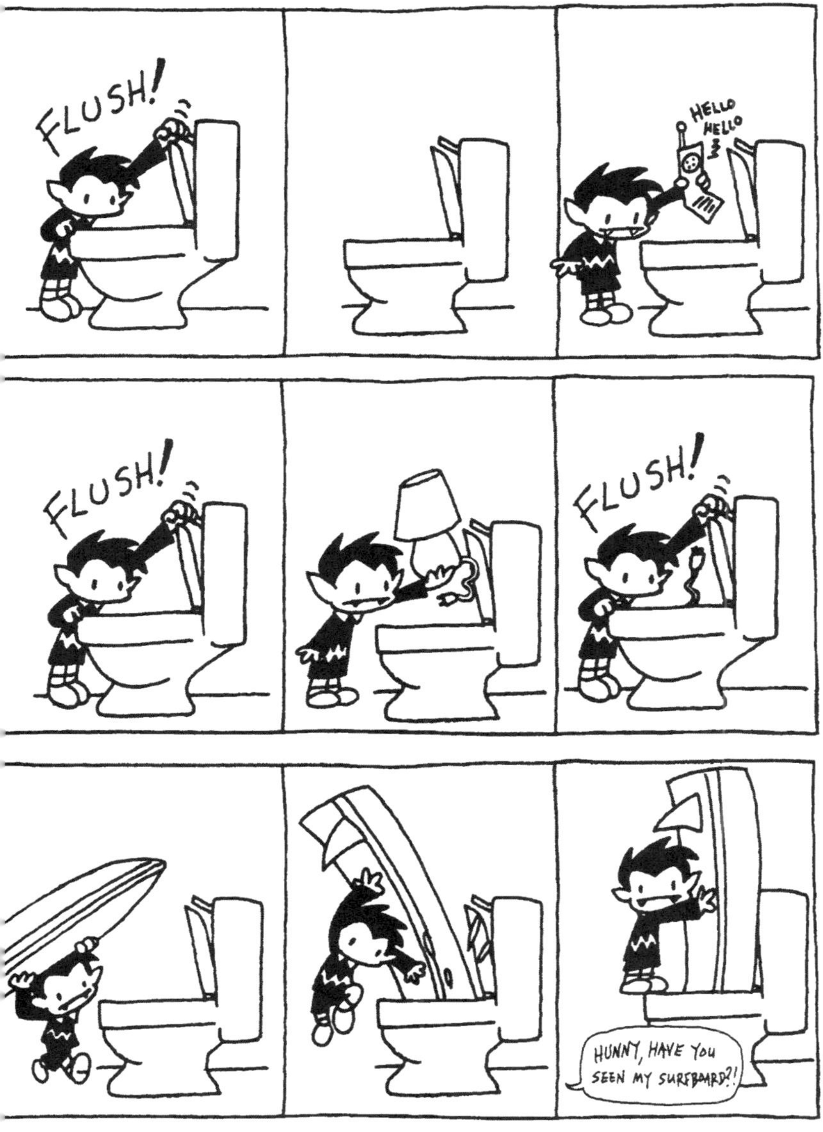
FLUSH!
HELLO
HELLO
FLUSH!
FLUSH!
HUNNY, HAVE YOU SEEN MY SURFBOARD?!

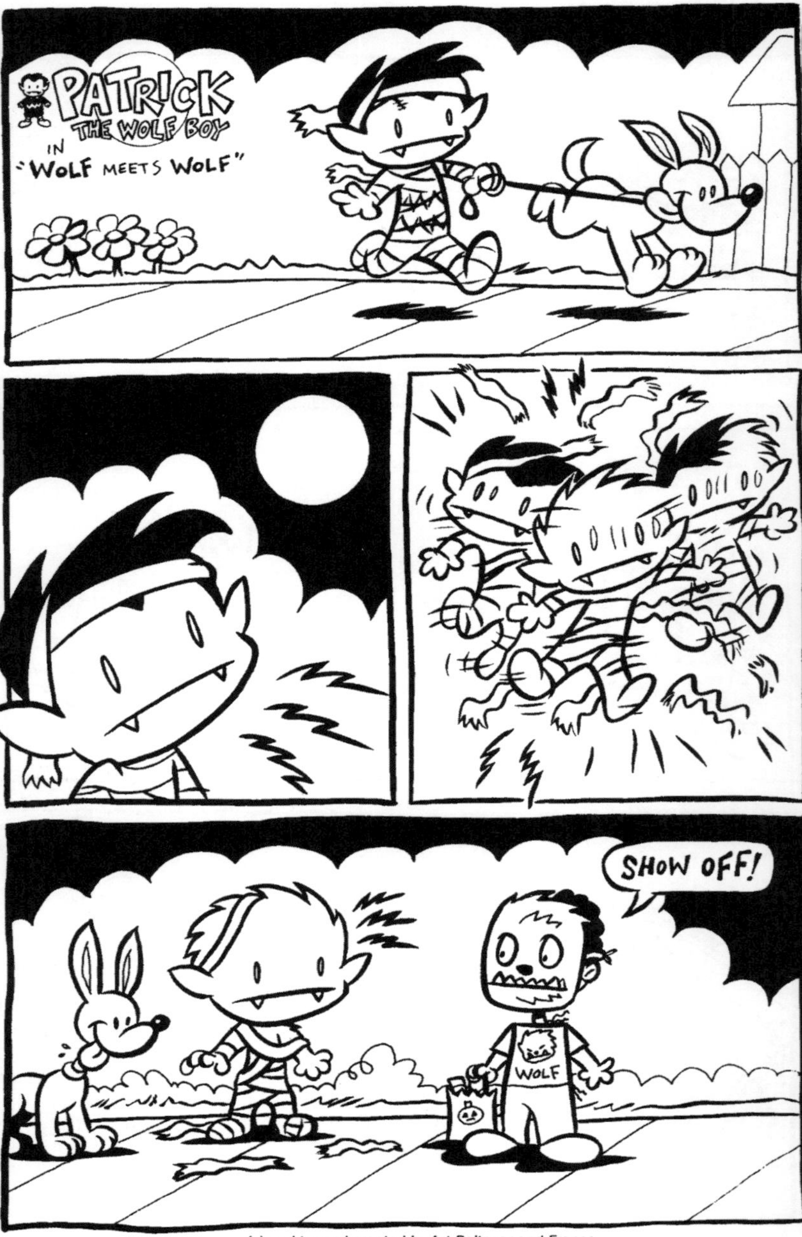
PATRICK THE WOLF BOY
IN "WOLF MEETS WOLF"
SHOW OFF!
WOLF

(c) and tm and created by Art Baltazar and Franco

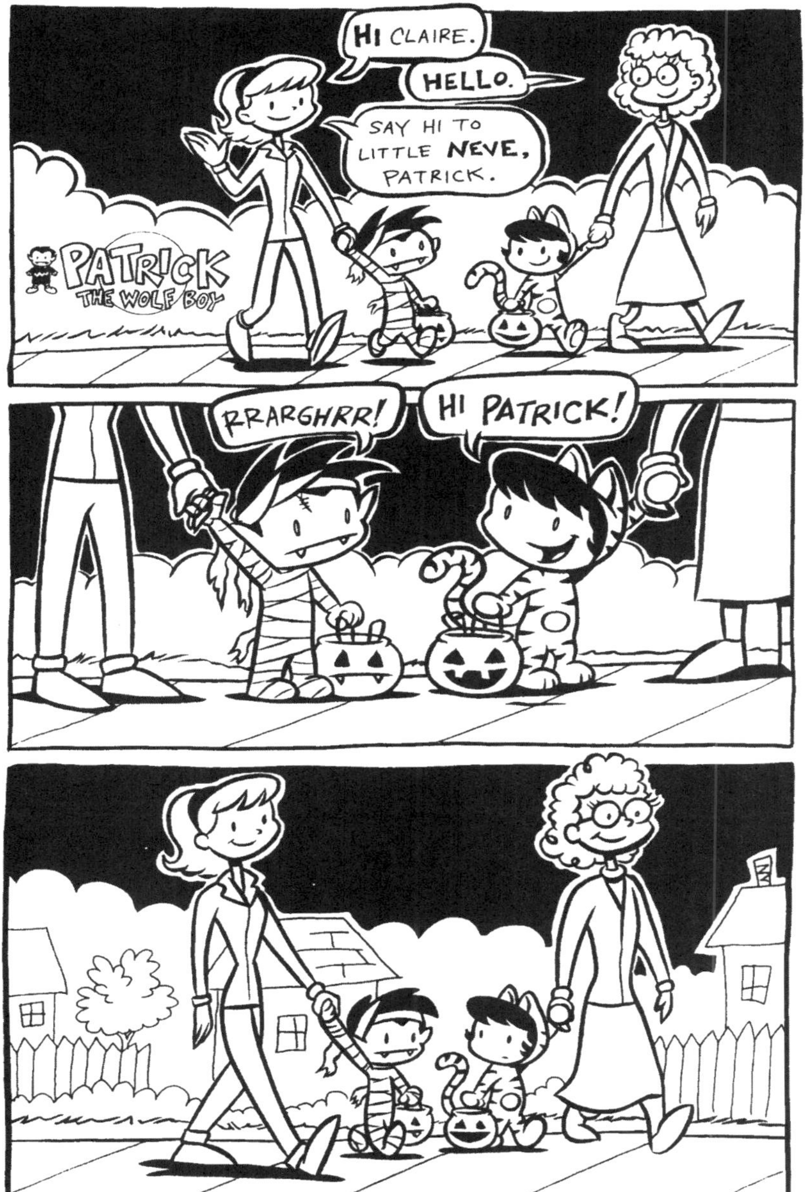
HI CLAIRE.
HELLO.
SAY HI TO LITTLE NEVE, PATRICK.
PATRICK THE WOLF BOY
RRARGHRR!
HI PATRICK!

(c) and tm and created by Art Baltazar and Franco

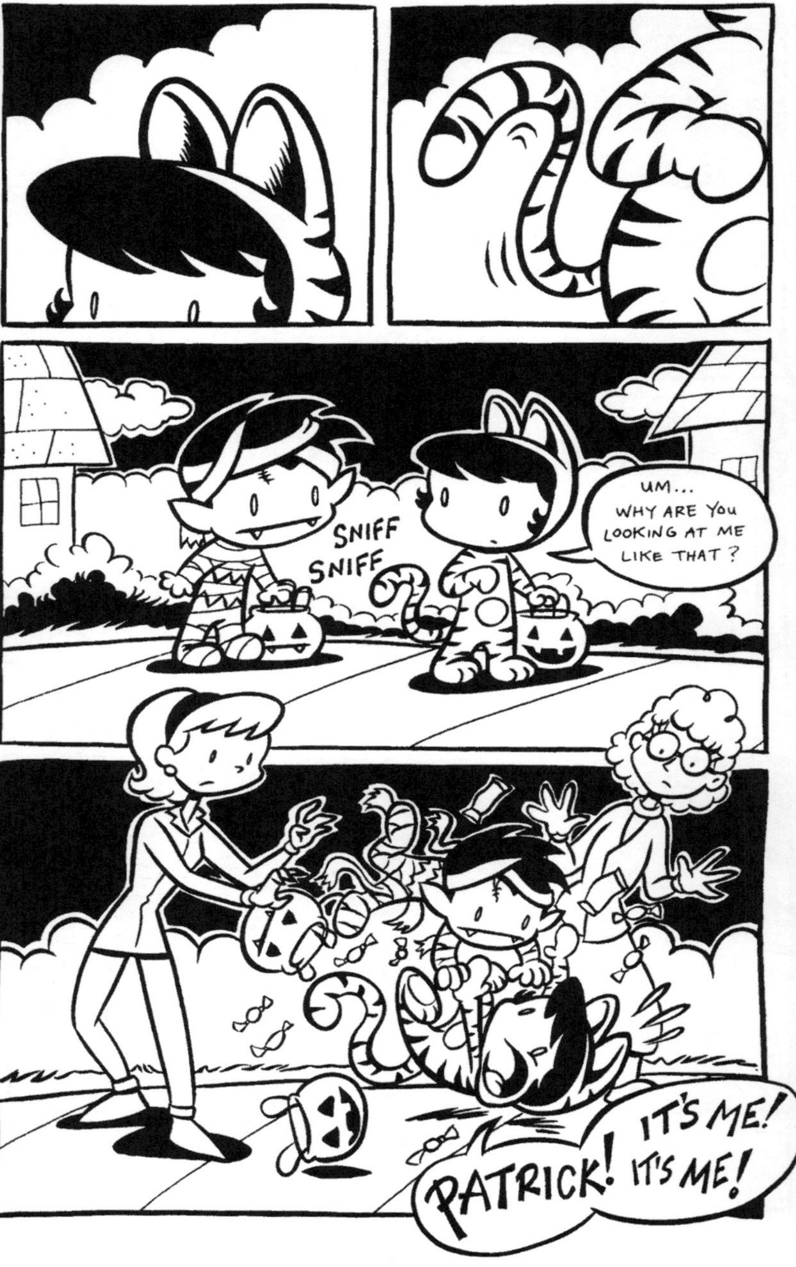
SNIFF SNIFF
UM... WHY ARE YOU LOOKING AT ME LIKE THAT?
PATRICK! IT'S ME! IT'S ME!

PATRICK
THE WOLF BOY

ANOTHER HALLOWEEN
SPECIAL
BY ART & FRANCO

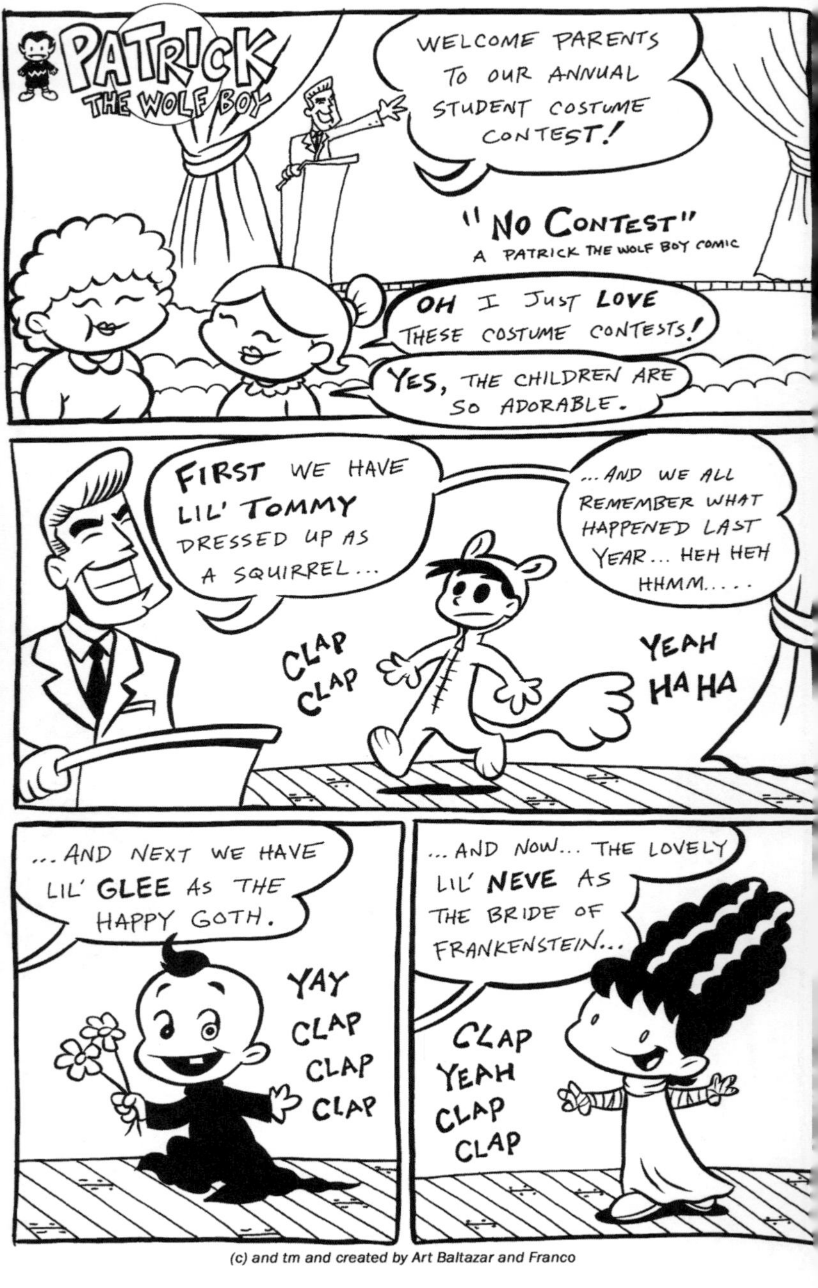
PATRICK THE WOLF BOY
WELCOME PARENTS TO OUR ANNUAL STUDENT COSTUME CONTEST!
"NO CONTEST"
A PATRICK THE WOLF BOY COMIC
OH I JUST LOVE THESE COSTUME CONTESTS!
YES, THE CHILDREN ARE SO ADORABLE.
FIRST WE HAVE LIL' TOMMY DRESSED UP AS A SQUIRREL...
...AND WE ALL REMEMBER WHAT HAPPENED LAST YEAR... HEH HEH HHMM.....
CLAP CLAP
YEAH HAHA
...AND NEXT WE HAVE LIL' GLEE AS THE HAPPY GOTH.
YAY CLAP CLAP CLAP
...AND NOW... THE LOVELY LIL' NEVE AS THE BRIDE OF FRANKENSTEIN...
CLAP YEAH CLAP CLAP

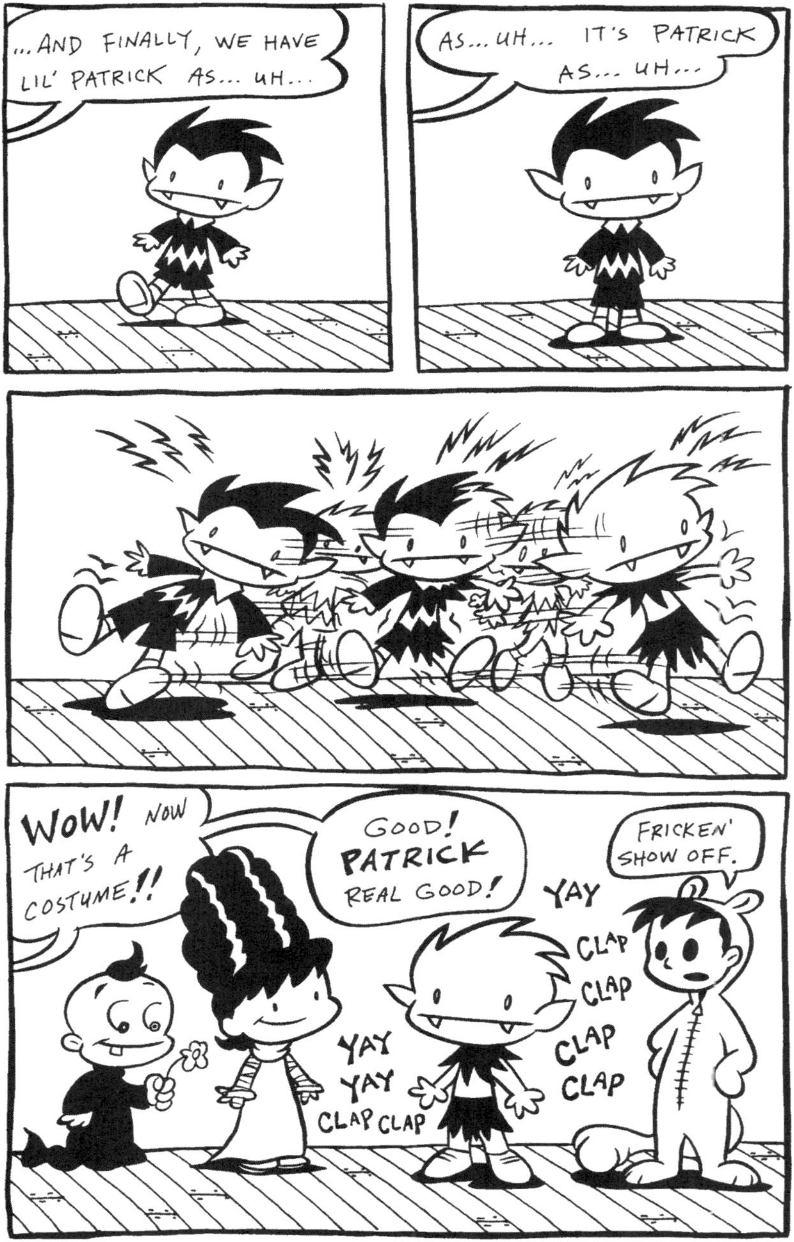
...AND FINALLY, WE HAVE LIL' PATRICK AS... UH...
AS... UH... IT'S PATRICK AS... UH...
WOW! NOW THAT'S A COSTUME!!
GOOD! PATRICK REAL GOOD!
FRICKEN' SHOW OFF.
YAY
CLAP
CLAP
CLAP
CLAP
YAY
YAY
CLAP CLAP

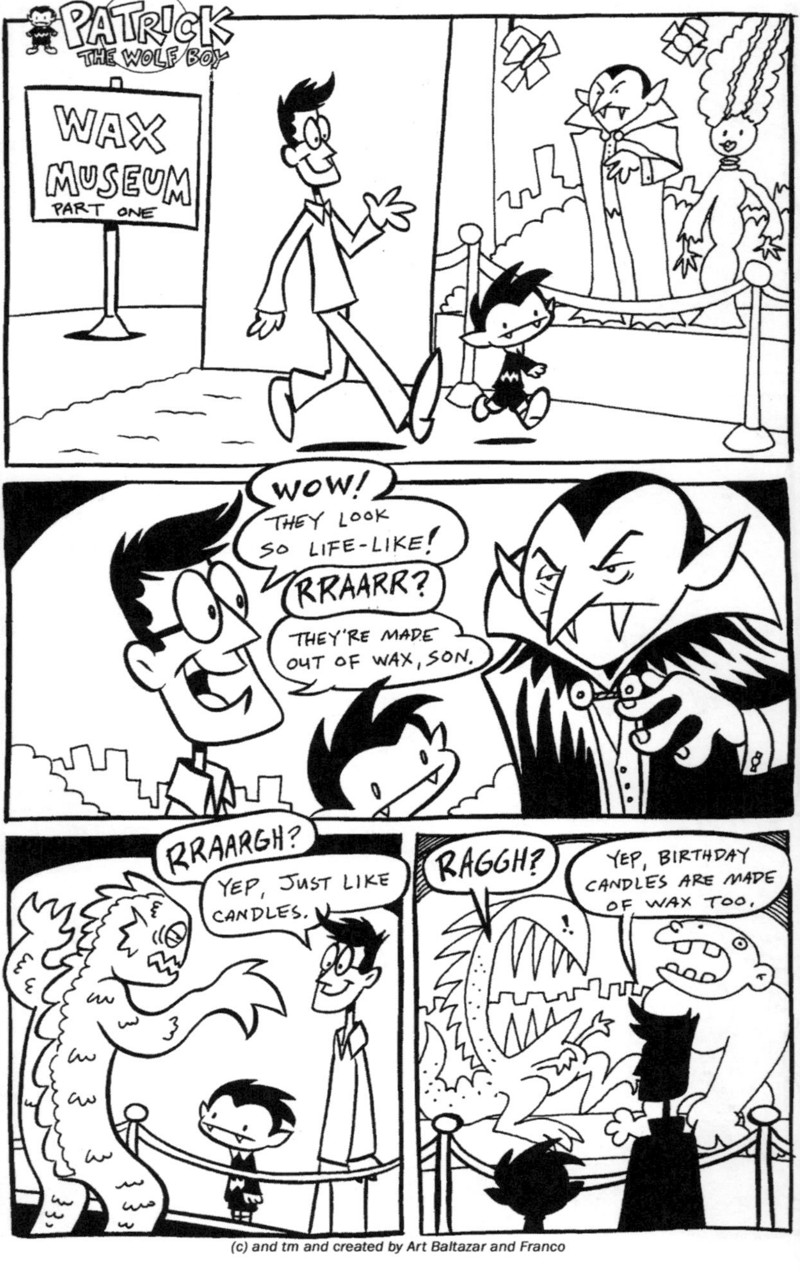
PATRICK THE WOLF BOY
WAX MUSEUM
PART ONE
WOW! THEY LOOK SO LIFE-LIKE!
RRAARR?
THEY'RE MADE OUT OF WAX, SON.
RRAARGH?
YEP, JUST LIKE CANDLES.
RAGGH?
YEP, BIRTHDAY CANDLES ARE MADE OF WAX TOO.

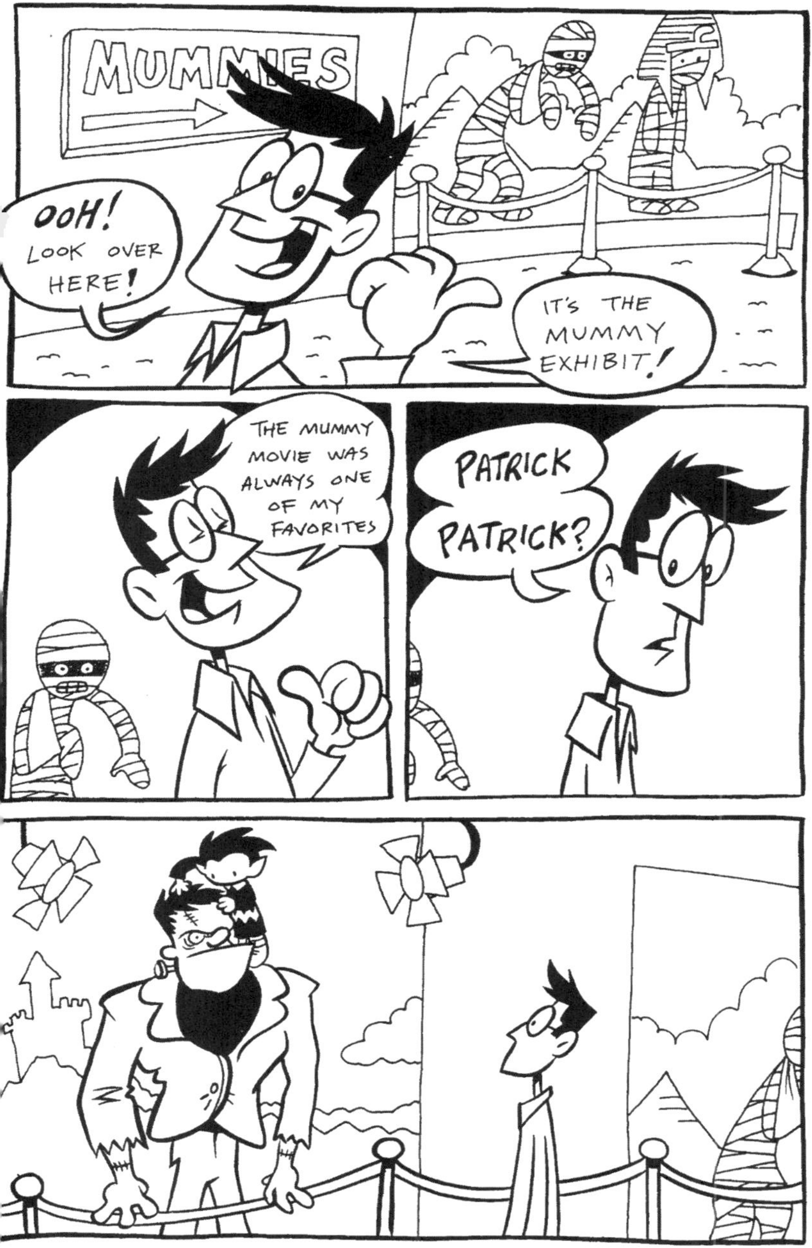
MUMMIES
OOH! LOOK OVER HERE!
IT'S THE MUMMY EXHIBIT!
THE MUMMY MOVIE WAS ALWAYS ONE OF MY FAVORITES
PATRICK
PATRICK?

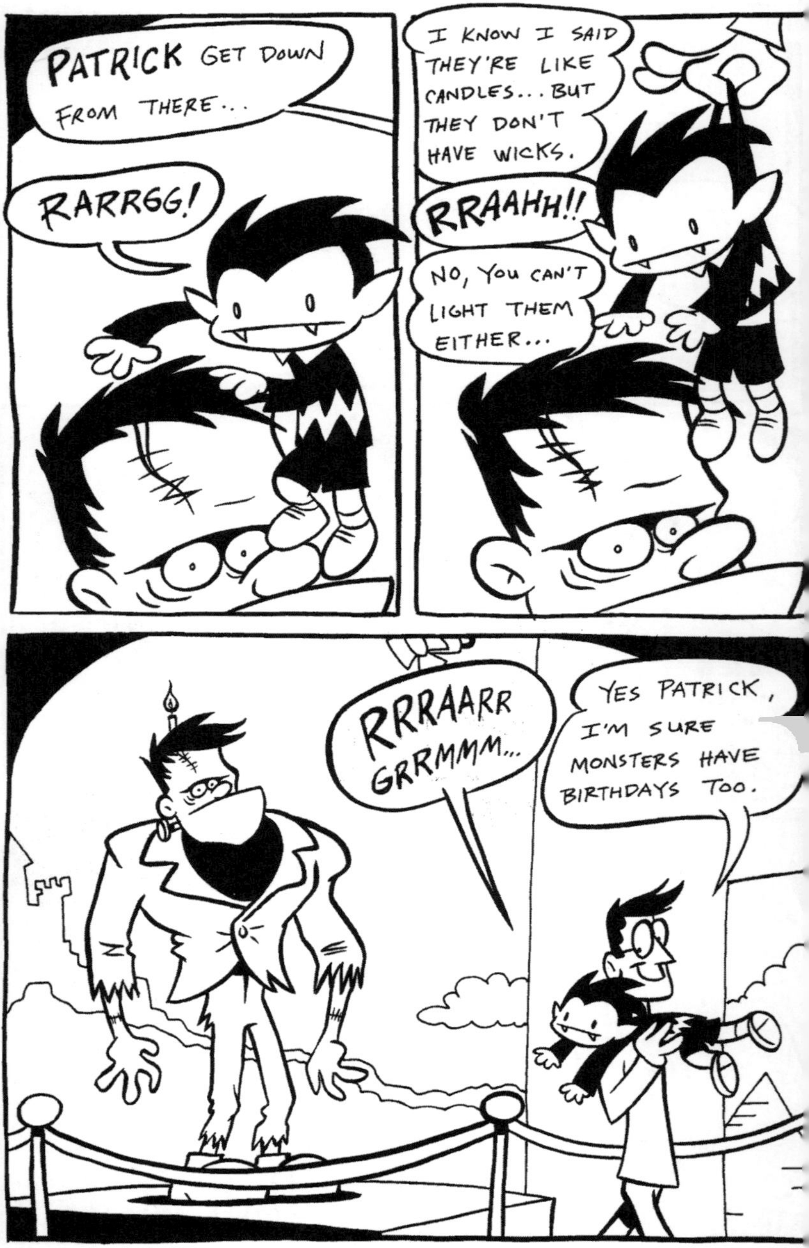
PATRICK GET DOWN FROM THERE...
RARRGG!
I KNOW I SAID THEY'RE LIKE CANDLES... BUT THEY DON'T HAVE WICKS.
RRAAHH!!
NO, YOU CAN'T LIGHT THEM EITHER...
RRRAARR GRRMMM...
YES PATRICK, I'M SURE MONSTERS HAVE BIRTHDAYS TOO.

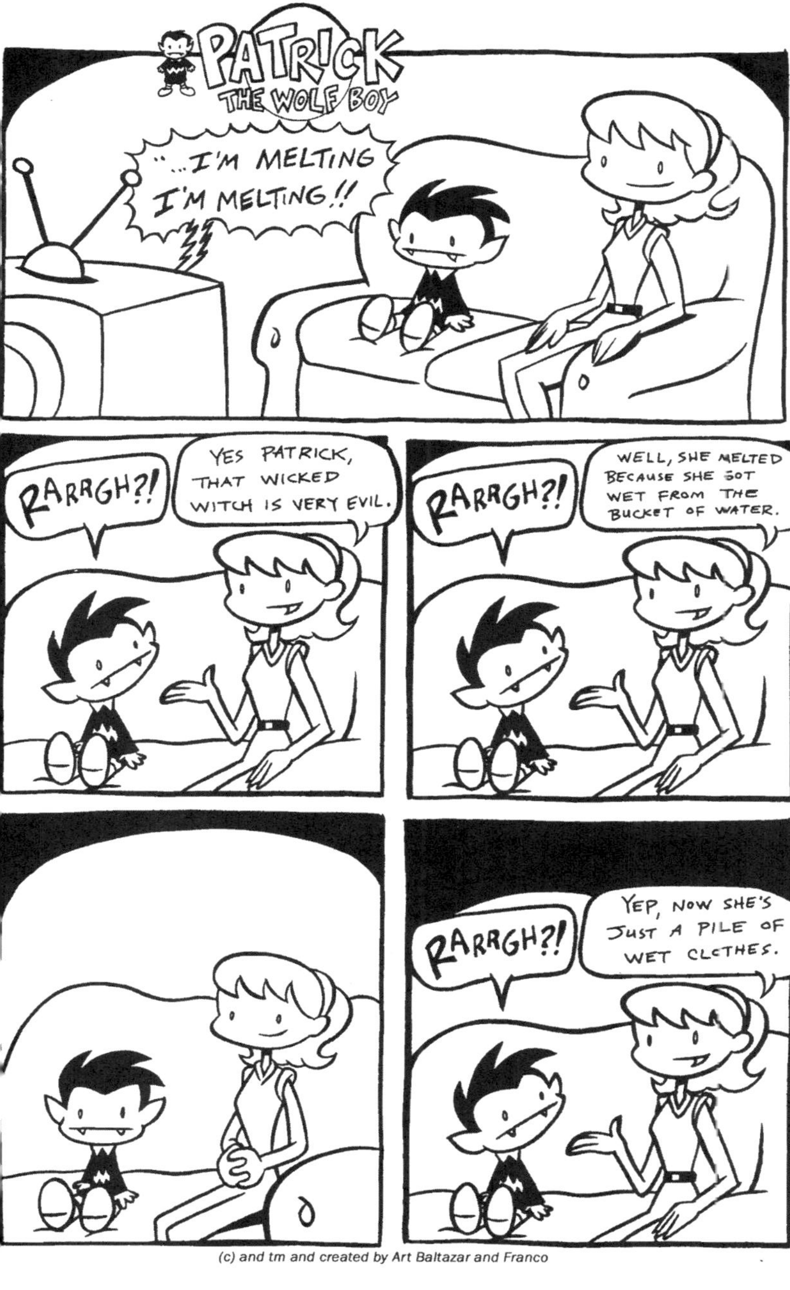
PATRICK THE WOLF BOY
"...I'M MELTING I'M MELTING!!
RARRGH?!
YES PATRICK, THAT WICKED WITCH IS VERY EVIL.
RARRGH?!
WELL, SHE MELTED BECAUSE SHE GOT WET FROM THE BUCKET OF WATER.
RARRGH?!
YEP, NOW SHE'S JUST A PILE OF WET CLOTHES.

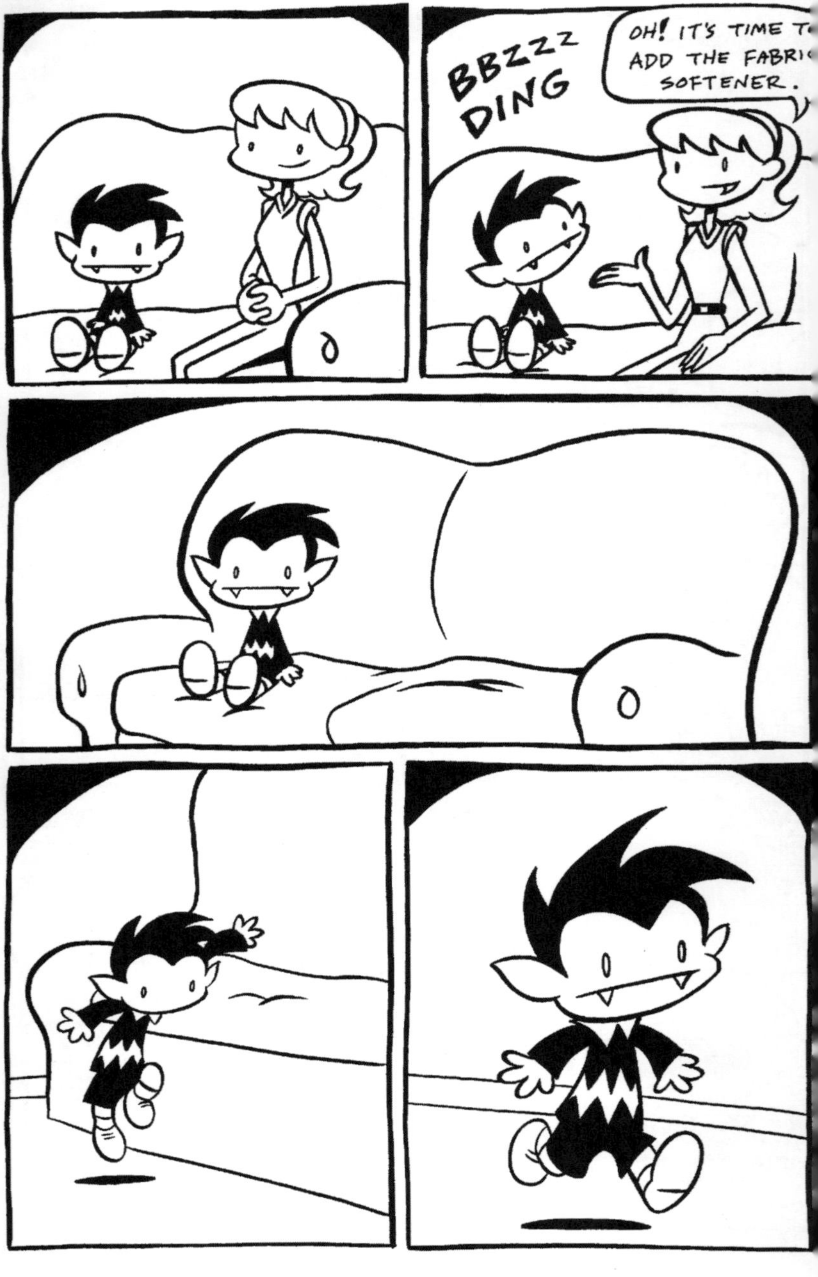
BBZZZ
DING
OH! IT'S TIME
ADD THE
SOFTENER.

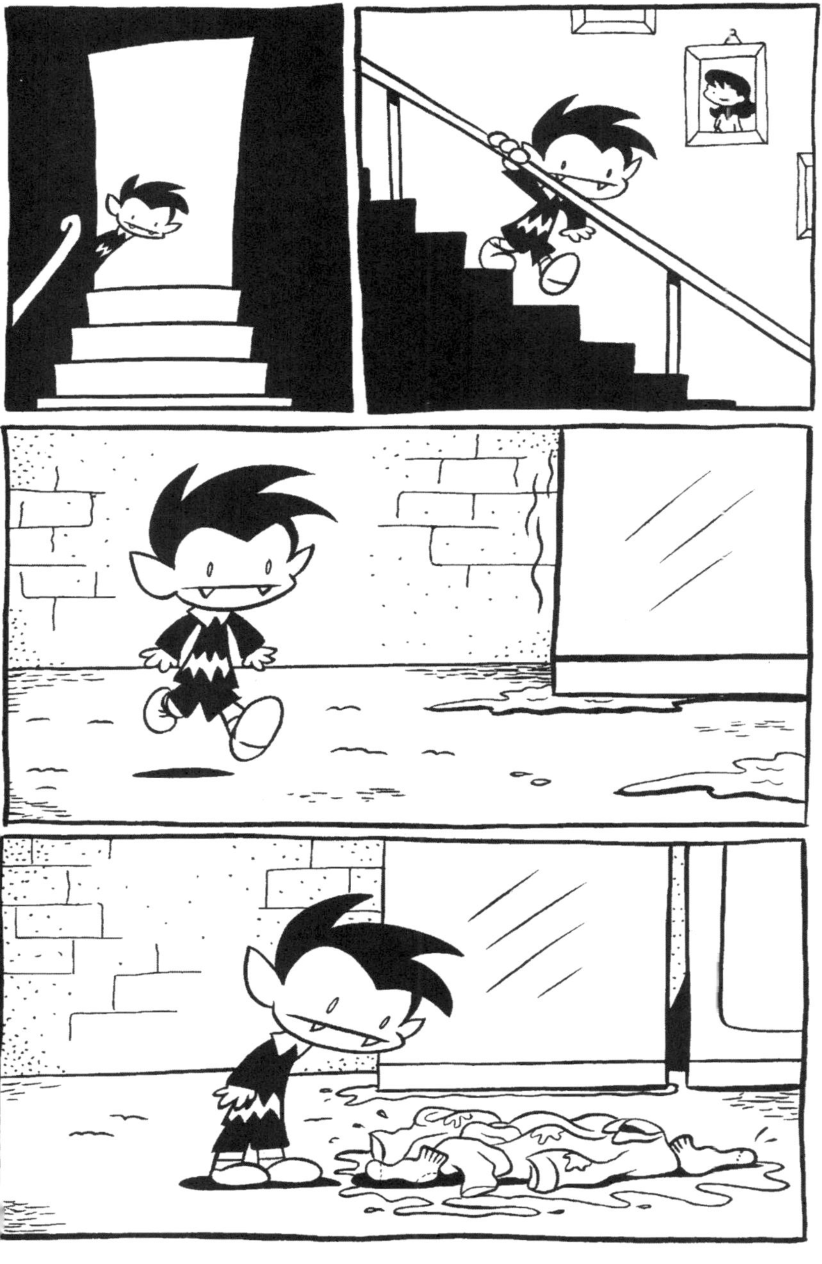

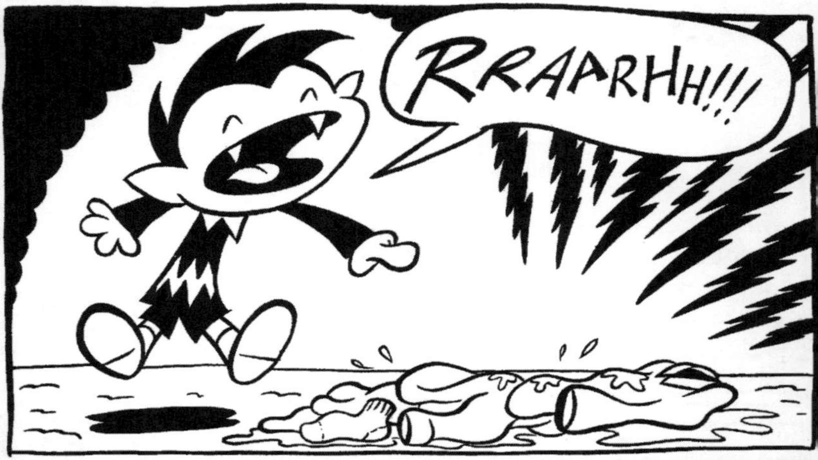
RRAARHH!!!

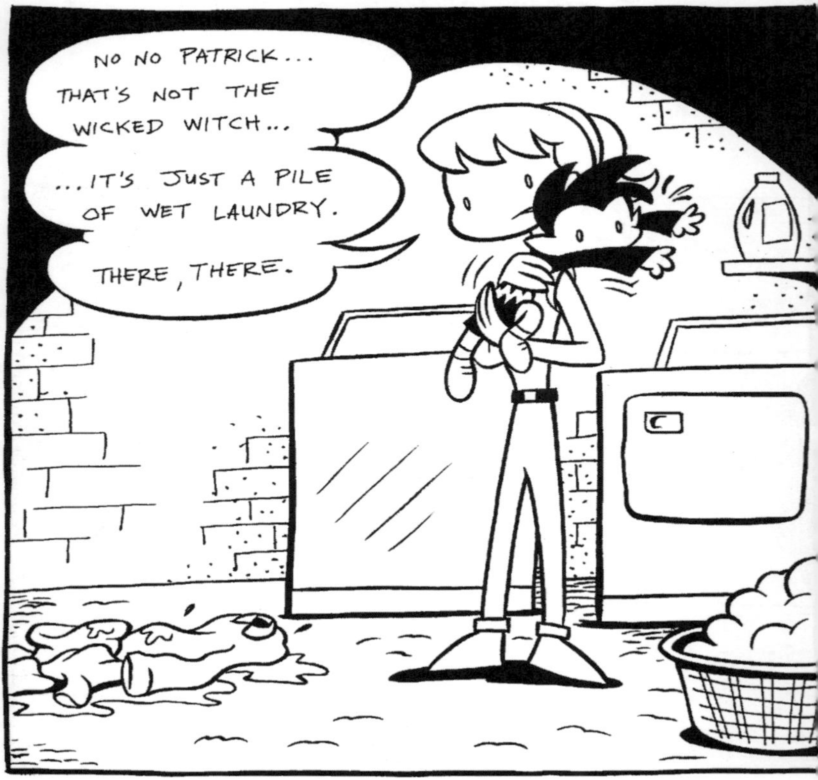
NO NO PATRICK... THAT'S NOT THE WICKED WITCH...
...IT'S JUST A PILE OF WET LAUNDRY.
THERE, THERE.

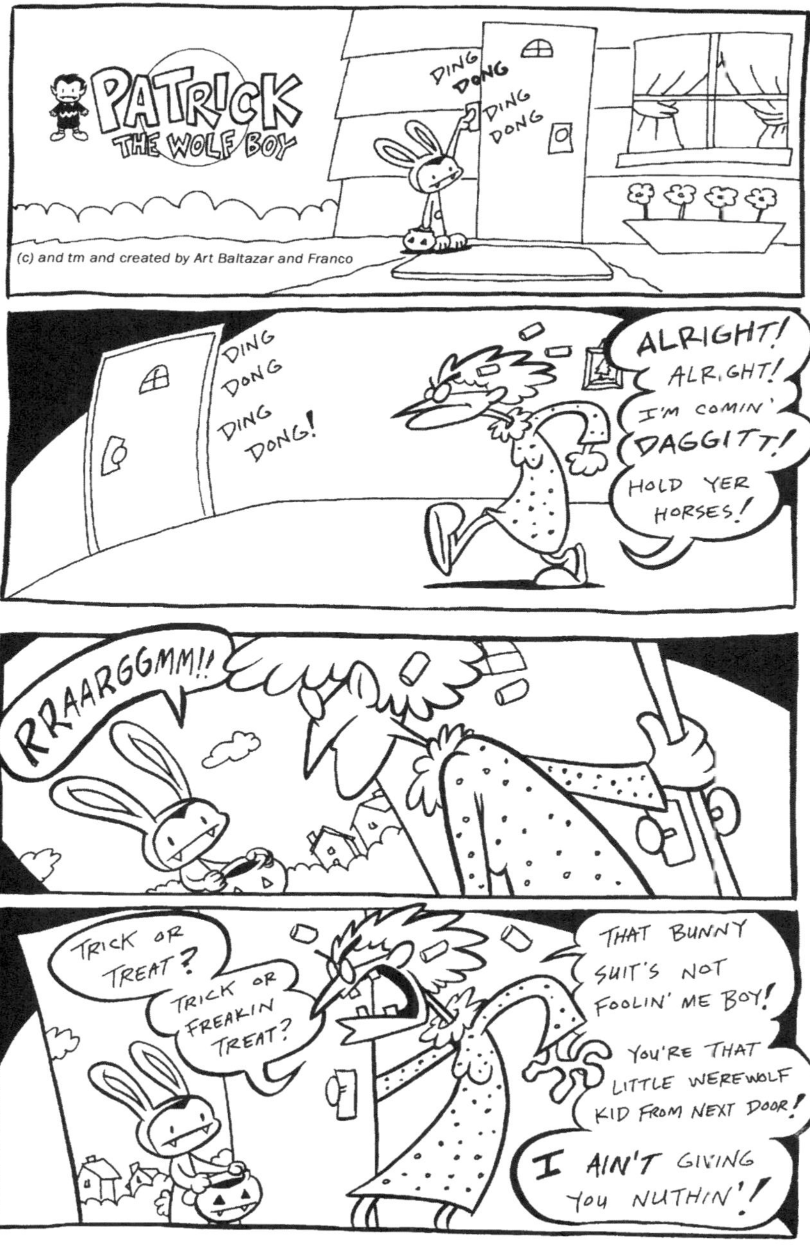
PATRICK THE WOLF BOY
DING DONG DING DONG
(c) and tm and created by Art Baltazar and Franco
DING DONG DING DONG!
ALRIGHT! ALRIGHT! I'M COMIN' DAGGITT! HOLD YER HORSES!
RRAARGGMM!!
TRICK OR TREAT?
TRICK OR FREAKIN TREAT?
THAT BUNNY SUIT'S NOT FOOLIN' ME BOY!
YOU'RE THAT LITTLE WEREWOLF KID FROM NEXT DOOR!
I AIN'T GIVING YOU NUTHIN'!

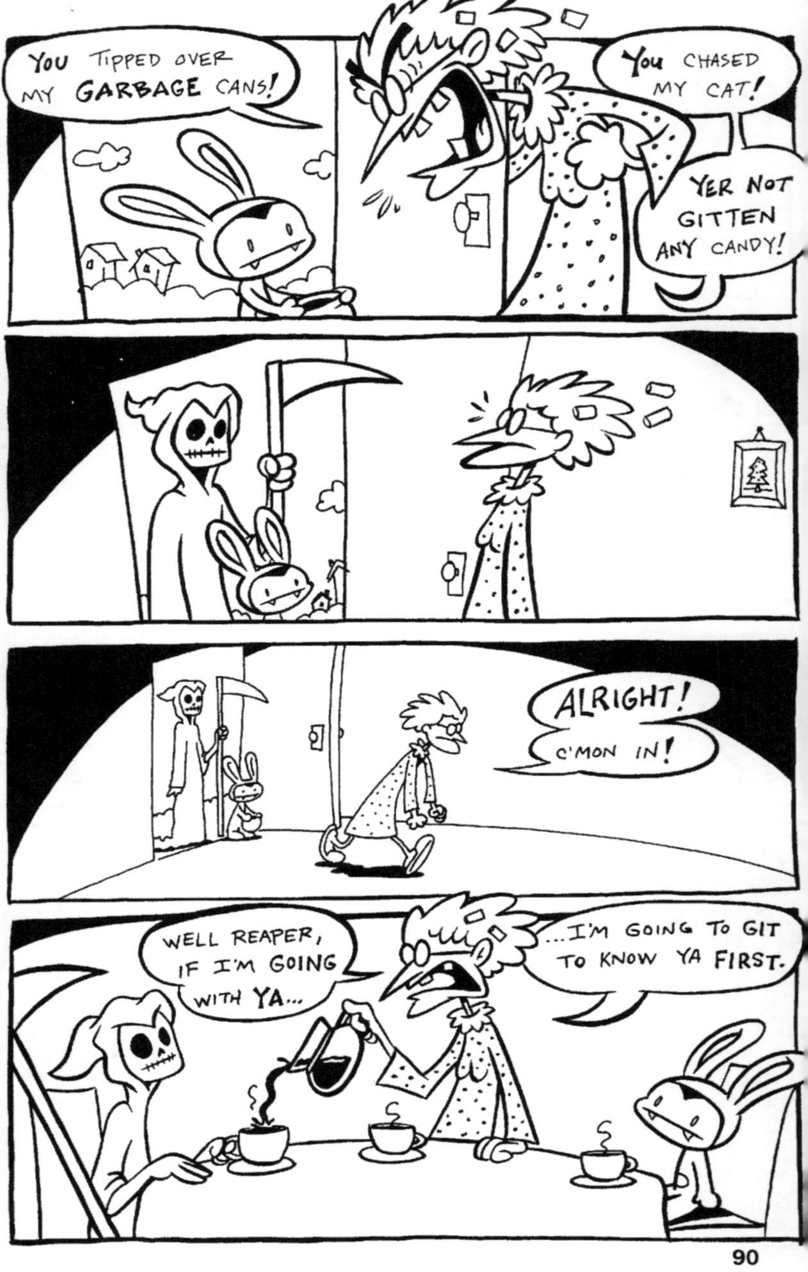
YOU TIPPED OVER MY GARBAGE CANS!
YOU CHASED MY CAT!
YER NOT GITTEN ANY CANDY!
ALRIGHT!
C'MON IN!
WELL REAPER, IF I'M GOING WITH YA...
...I'M GOING TO GIT TO KNOW YA FIRST.

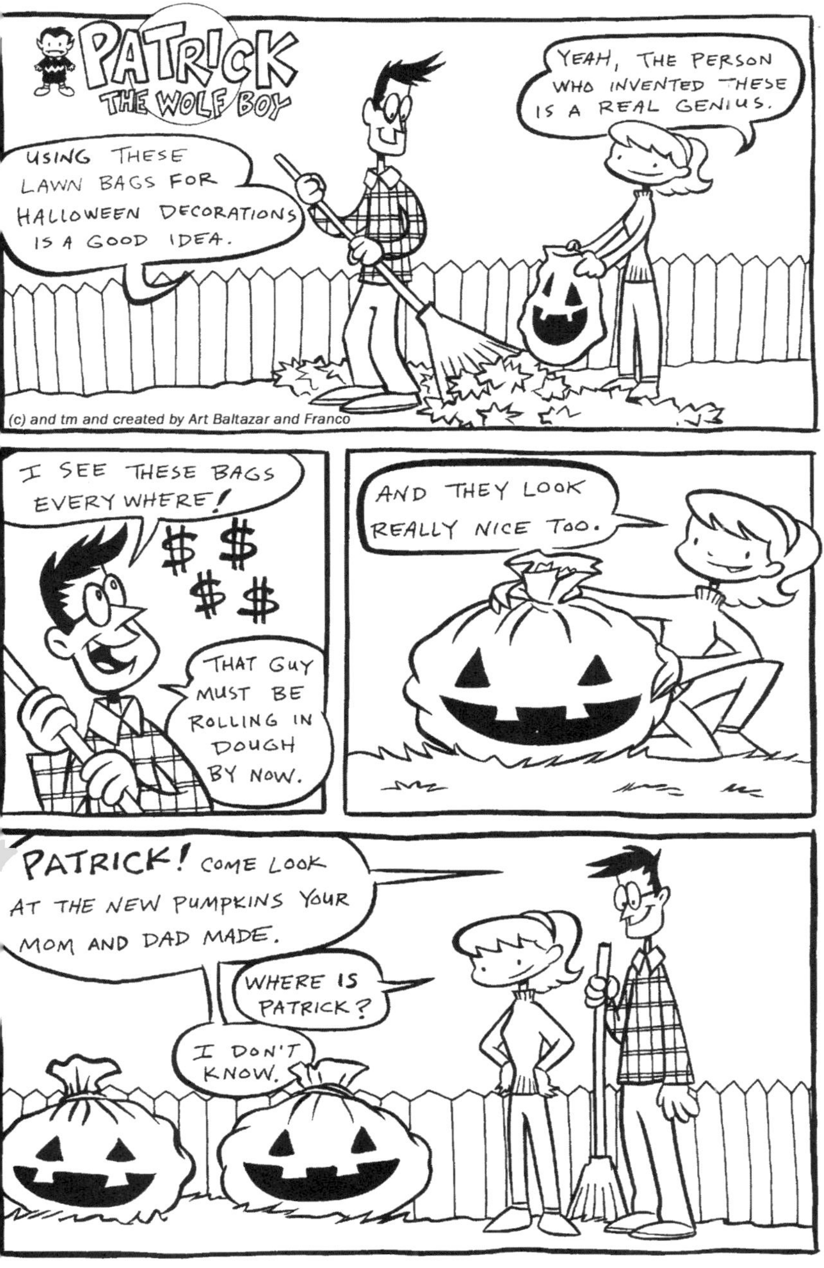
PATRICK THE WOLF BOY
USING THESE LAWN BAGS FOR HALLOWEEN DECORATIONS IS A GOOD IDEA.
YEAH, THE PERSON WHO INVENTED THESE IS A REAL GENIUS.
(c) and tm and created by Art Baltazar and Franco
I SEE THESE BAGS EVERY WHERE!
$ $ $ $
THAT GUY MUST BE ROLLING IN DOUGH BY NOW.
AND THEY LOOK REALLY NICE TOO.
PATRICK! COME LOOK AT THE NEW PUMPKINS YOUR MOM AND DAD MADE.
WHERE IS PATRICK?
I DON'T KNOW.

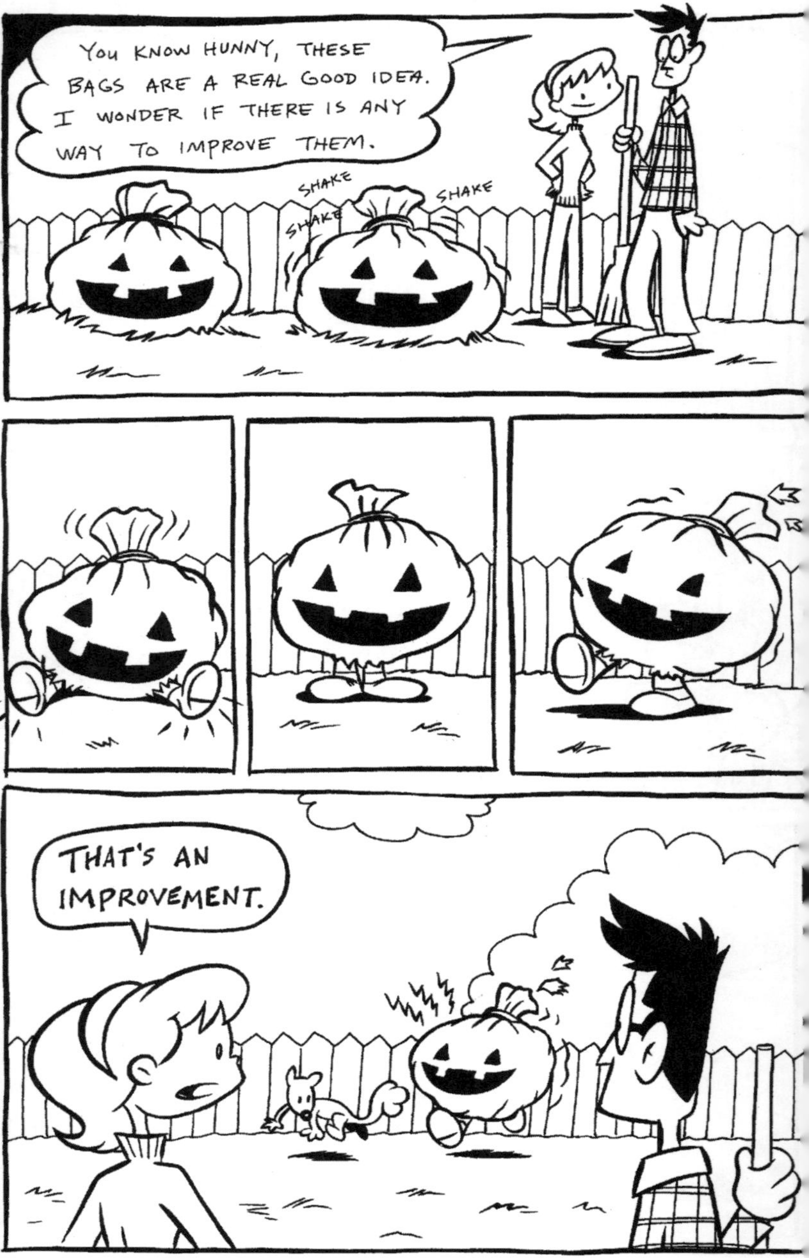
YOU KNOW HUNNY, THESE BAGS ARE A REAL GOOD IDEA. I WONDER IF THERE IS ANY WAY TO IMPROVE THEM.
SHAKE
SHAKE
SHAKE
THAT'S AN IMPROVEMENT.

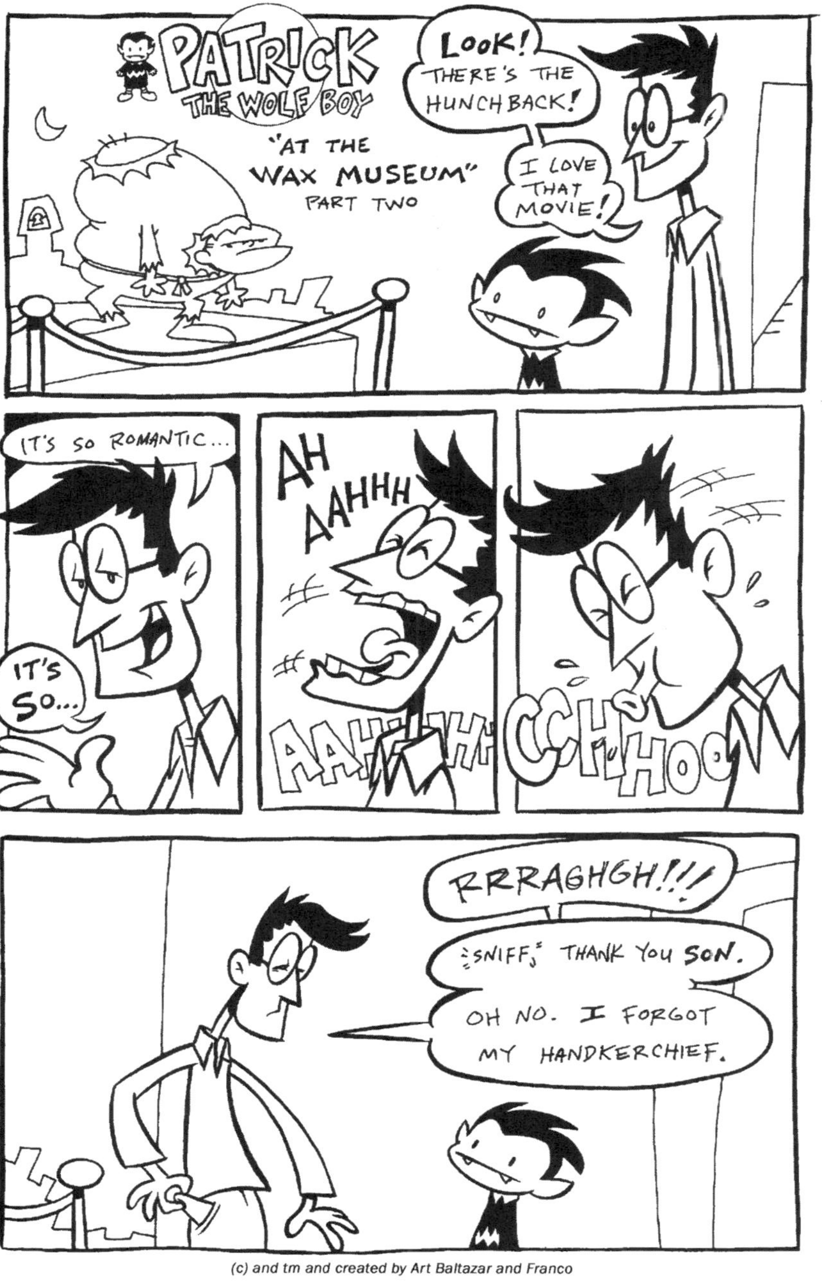

PATRICK THE WOLF BOY
"AT THE WAX MUSEUM" PART TWO
LOOK! THERE'S THE HUNCHBACK!
I LOVE THAT MOVIE!
IT'S SO ROMANTIC...
IT'S SO...
AH AAHHH
CCHOO
RRRAGHGH!!!
SNIFF THANK YOU SON.
OH NO. I FORGOT MY HANDKERCHIEF.

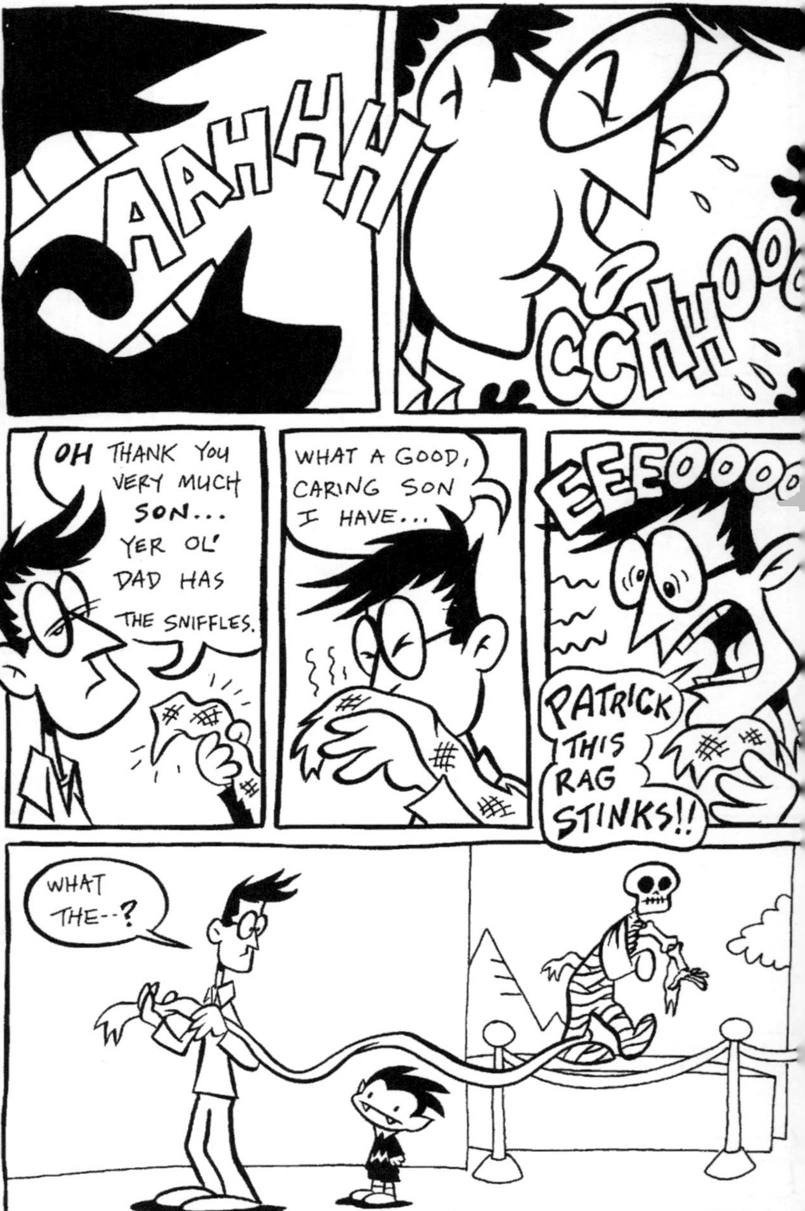

AAHHH
CCHHOOO
OH THANK YOU VERY MUCH SON... YER OL' DAD HAS THE SNIFFLES.
WHAT A GOOD, CARING SON I HAVE...
EEEOOOO
PATRICK THIS RAG STINKS!!
WHAT THE--?

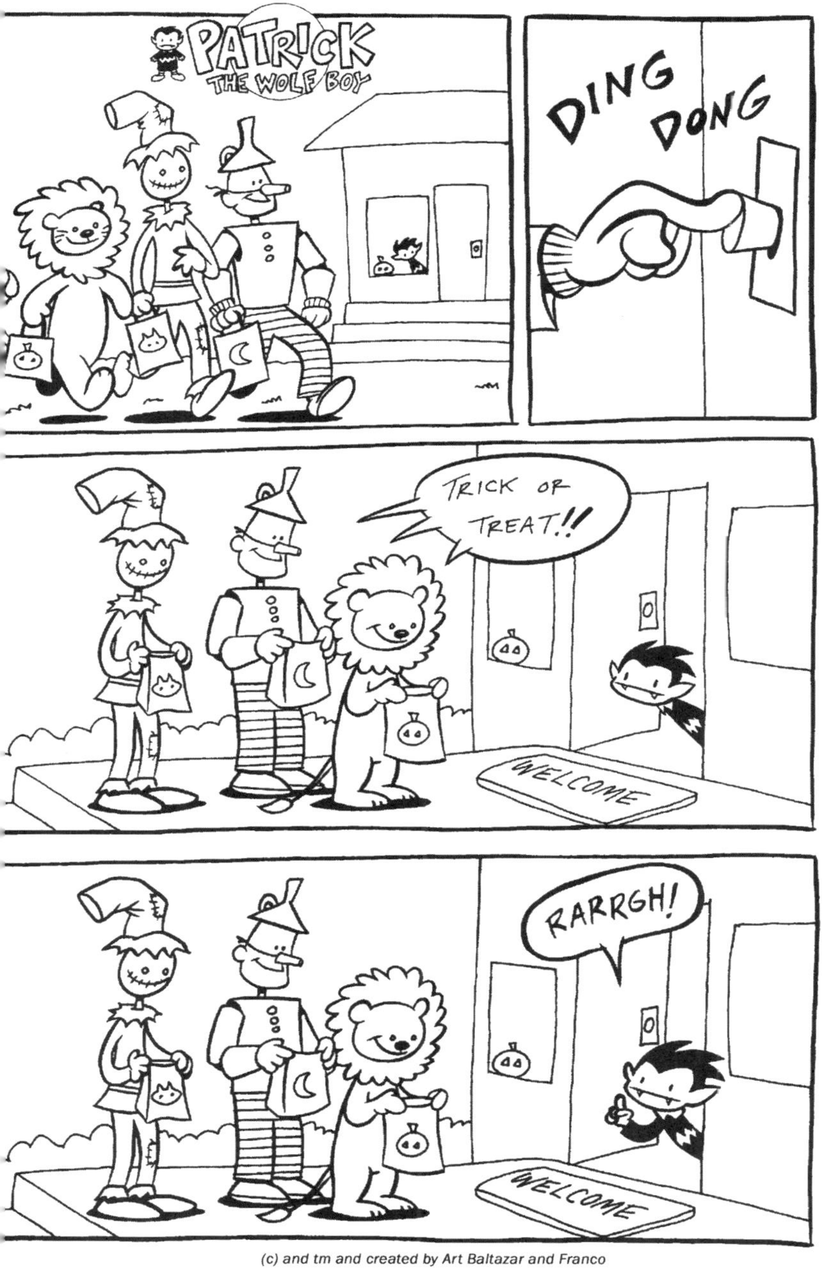
PATRICK THE WOLF BOY
DING DONG
TRICK OR TREAT!!
WELCOME
RARRGH!
WELCOME

(c) and tm and created by Art Baltazar and Franco

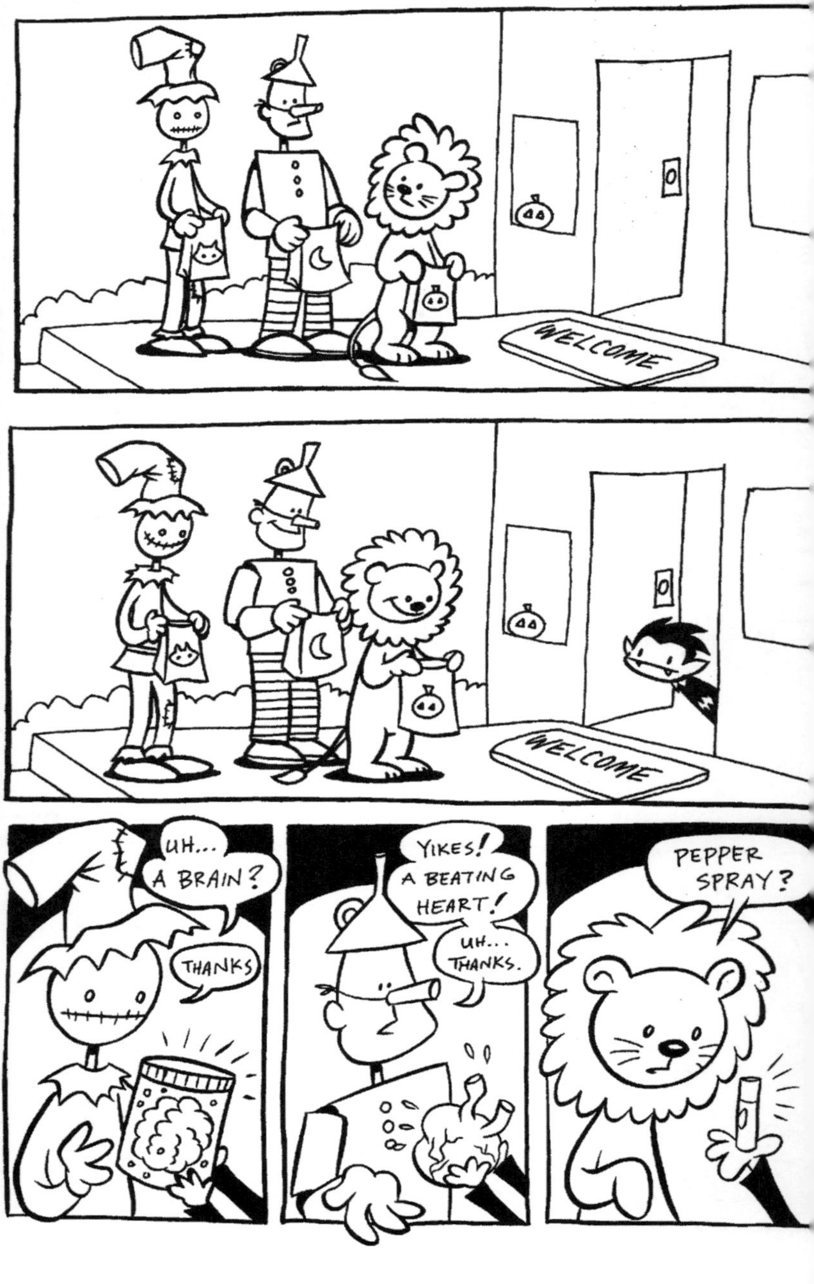
WELCOME
WELCOME
UH... A BRAIN?
THANKS
YIKES! A BEATING HEART!
UH... THANKS.
PEPPER SPRAY?

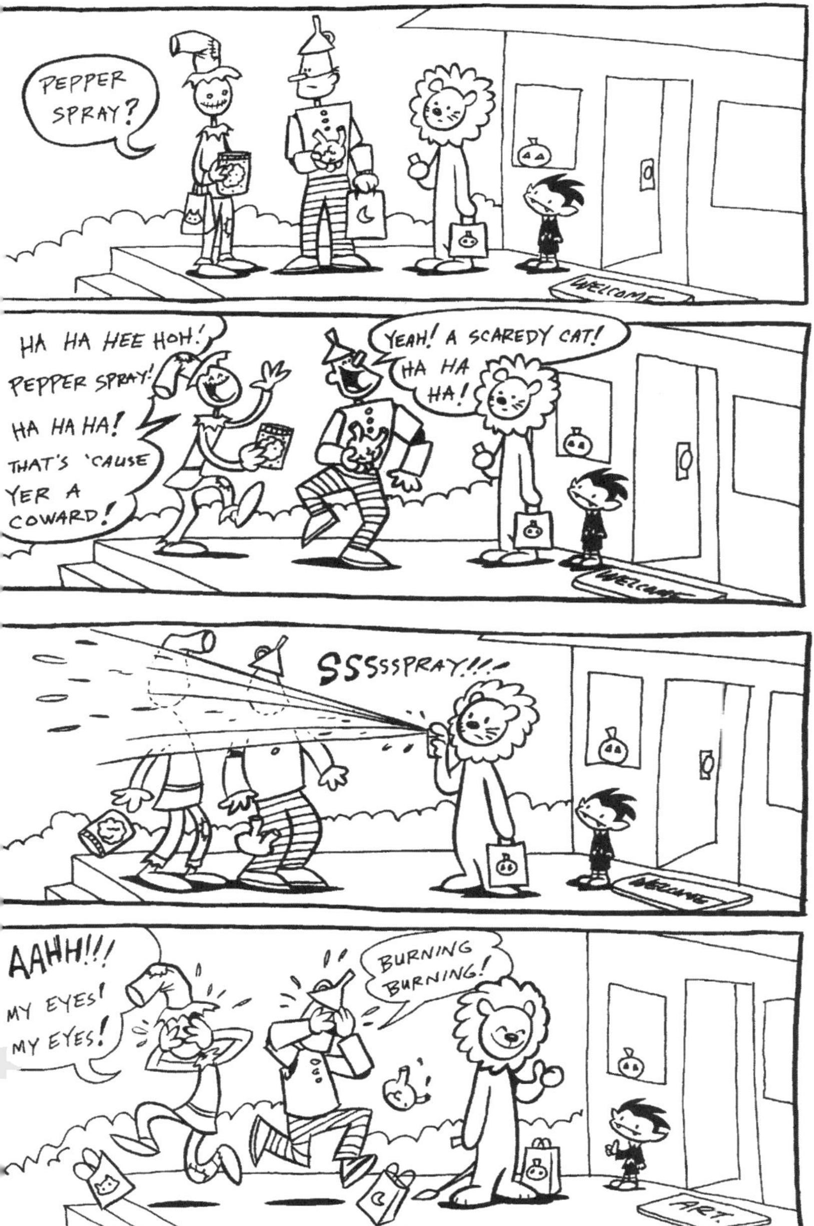

PEPPER SPRAY?
WELCOME
HA HA HEE HOH! PEPPER SPRAY! HA HA HA! THAT'S 'CAUSE YER A COWARD!
YEAH! A SCAREDY CAT!
HA HA HA!
WELCOME
SSSSSPRAY!!!
WELCOME
AAHH!!! MY EYES! MY EYES!
BURNING BURNING!
ART.

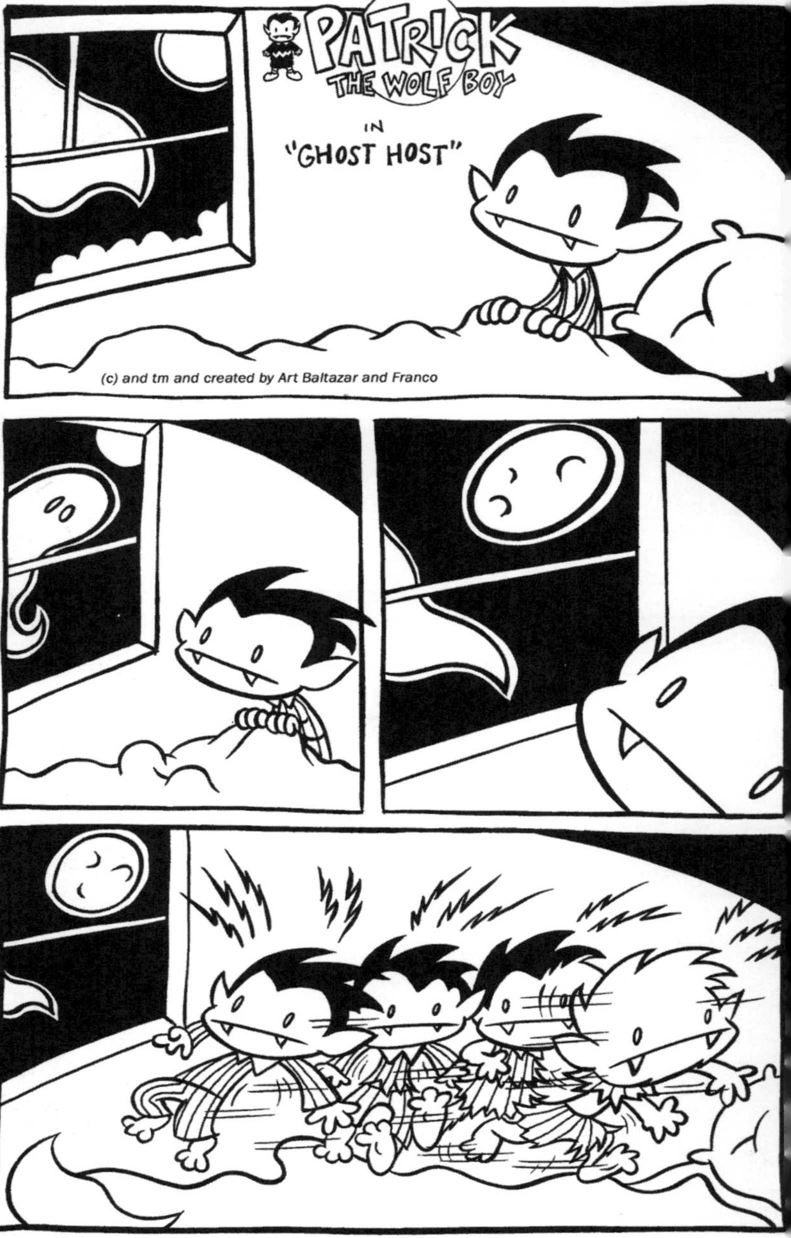
PATRICK
THE WOLF BOY
IN
"GHOST HOST"
(c) and tm and created by Art Baltazar and Franco

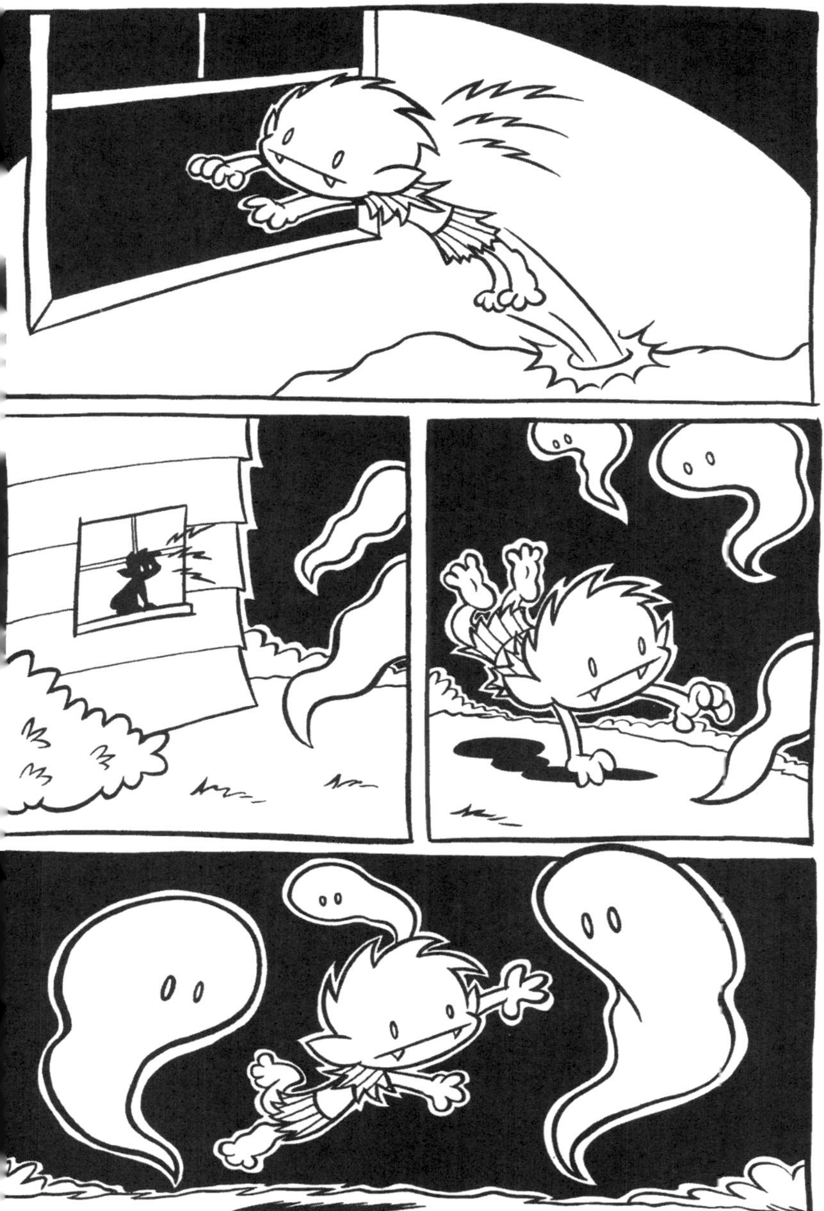

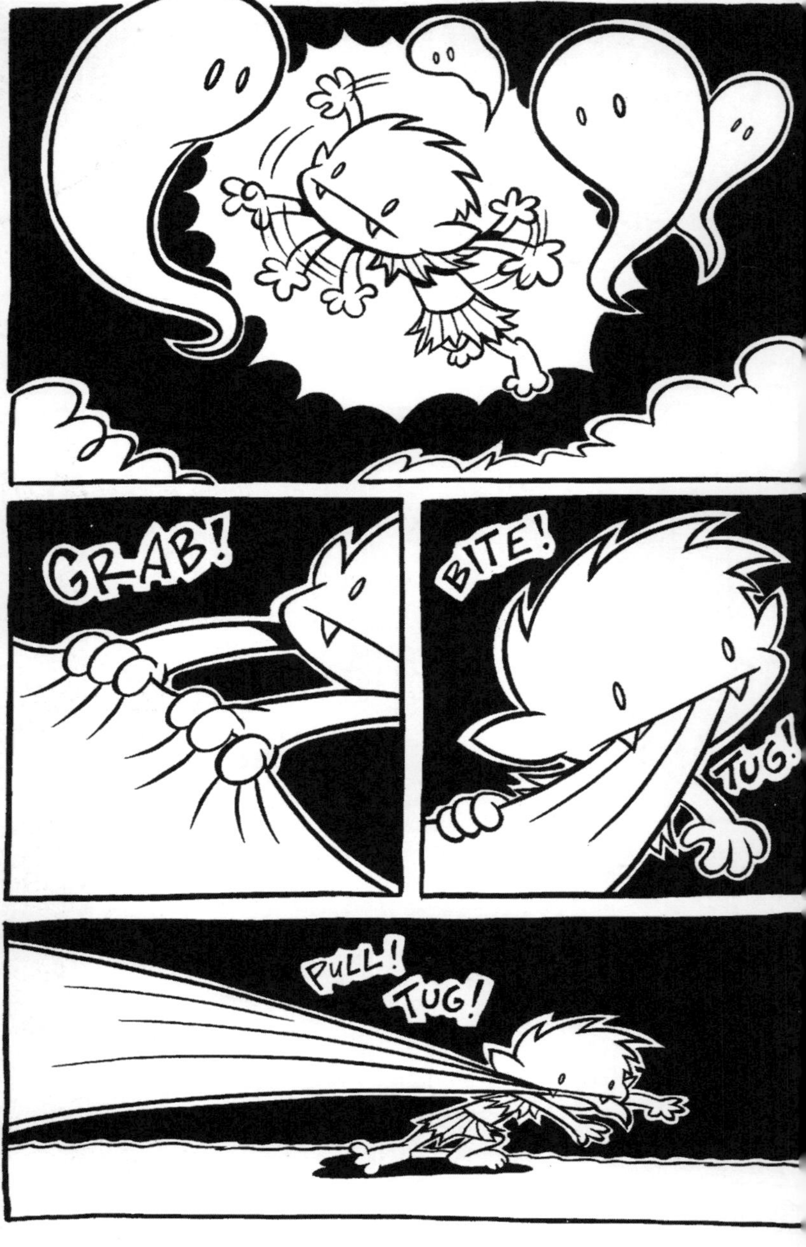
GRAB!
BITE!
TUG!
PULL!
TUG!

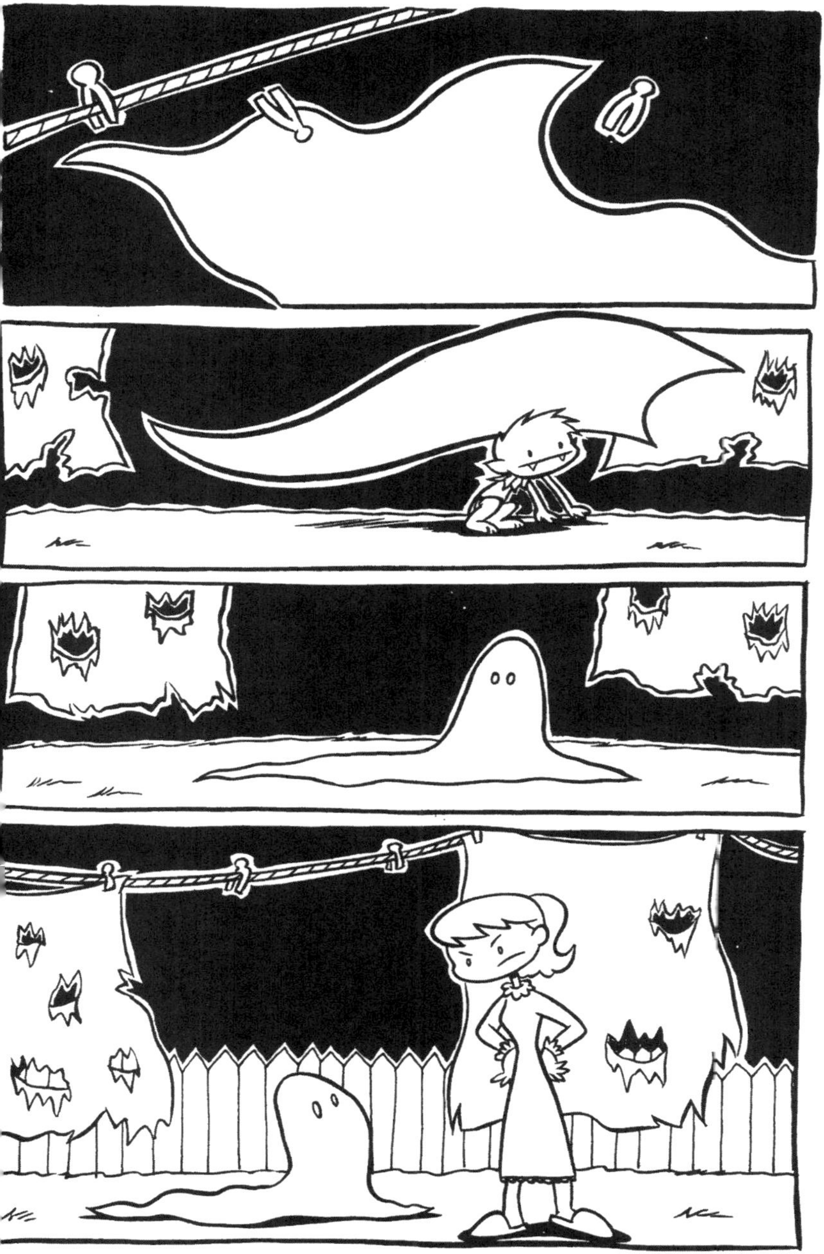

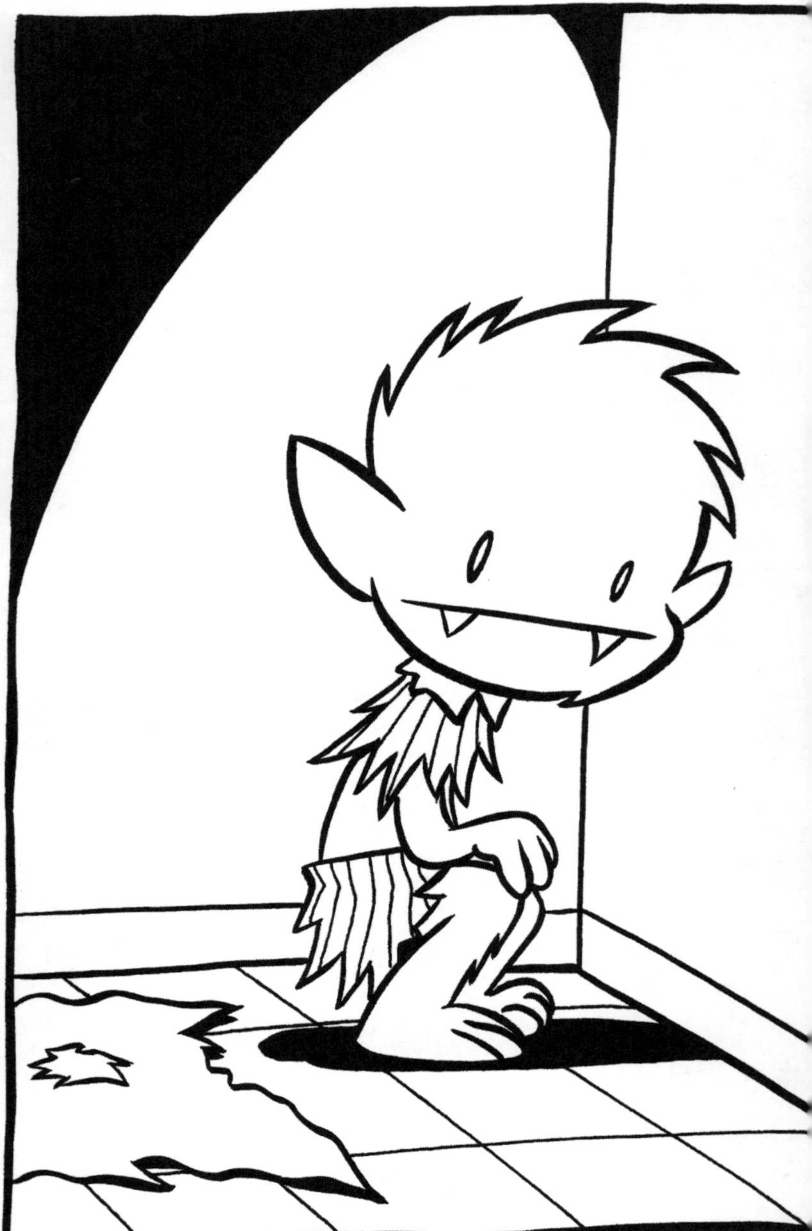

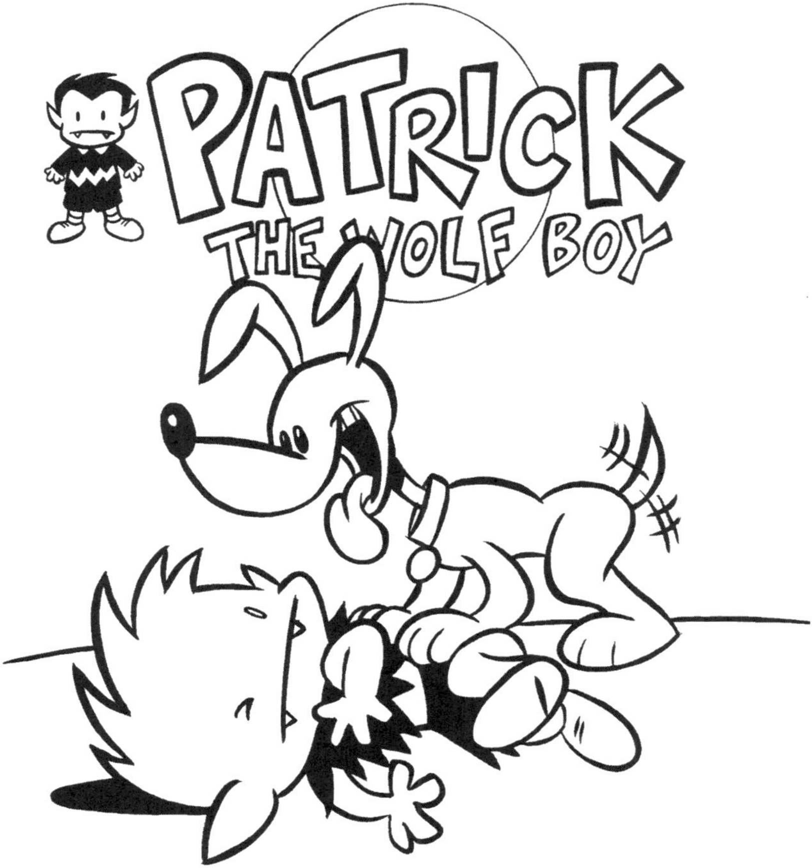
PATRICK
THE WOLF BOY

This Year's Halloween Special!

by Art Baltazar
and Franco

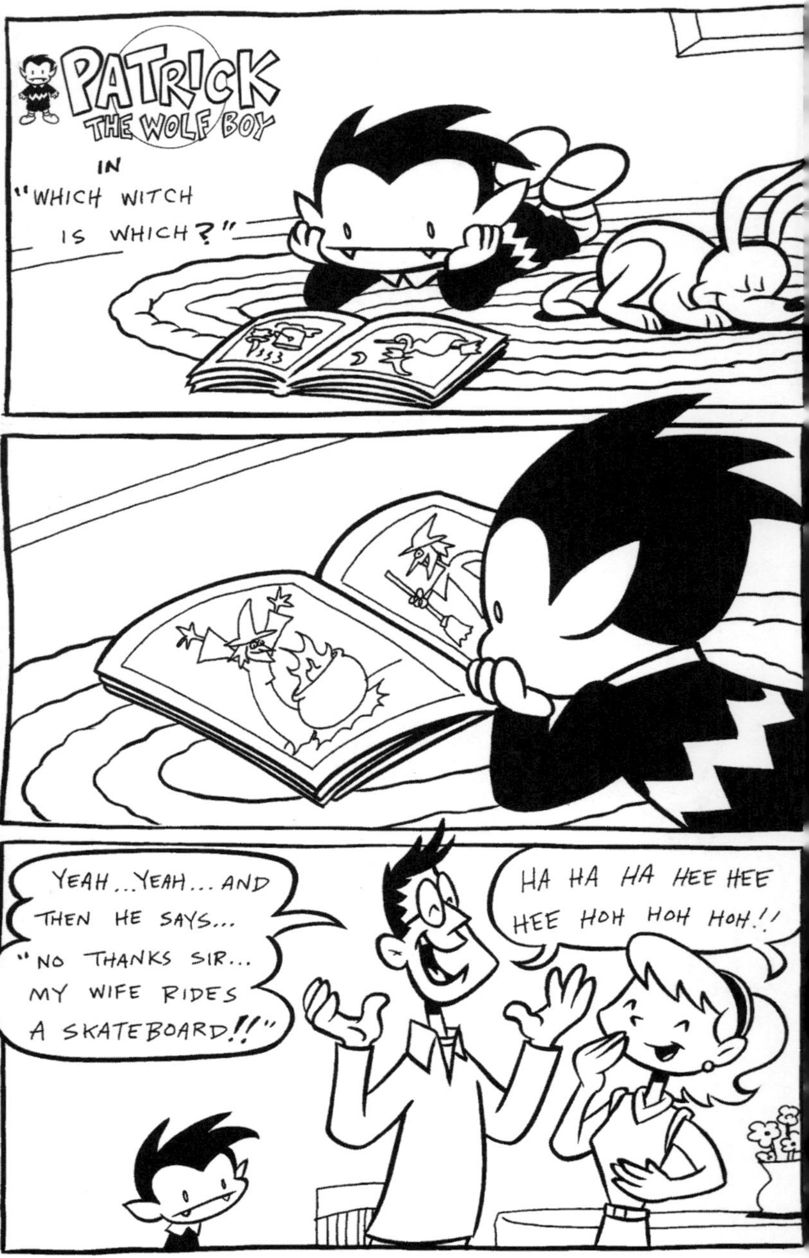
PATRICK THE WOLF BOY
IN "WHICH WITCH IS WHICH?"
YEAH...YEAH...AND THEN HE SAYS... "NO THANKS SIR... MY WIFE RIDES A SKATEBOARD!!"
HA HA HA HEE HEE HEE HOH HOH HOH!!

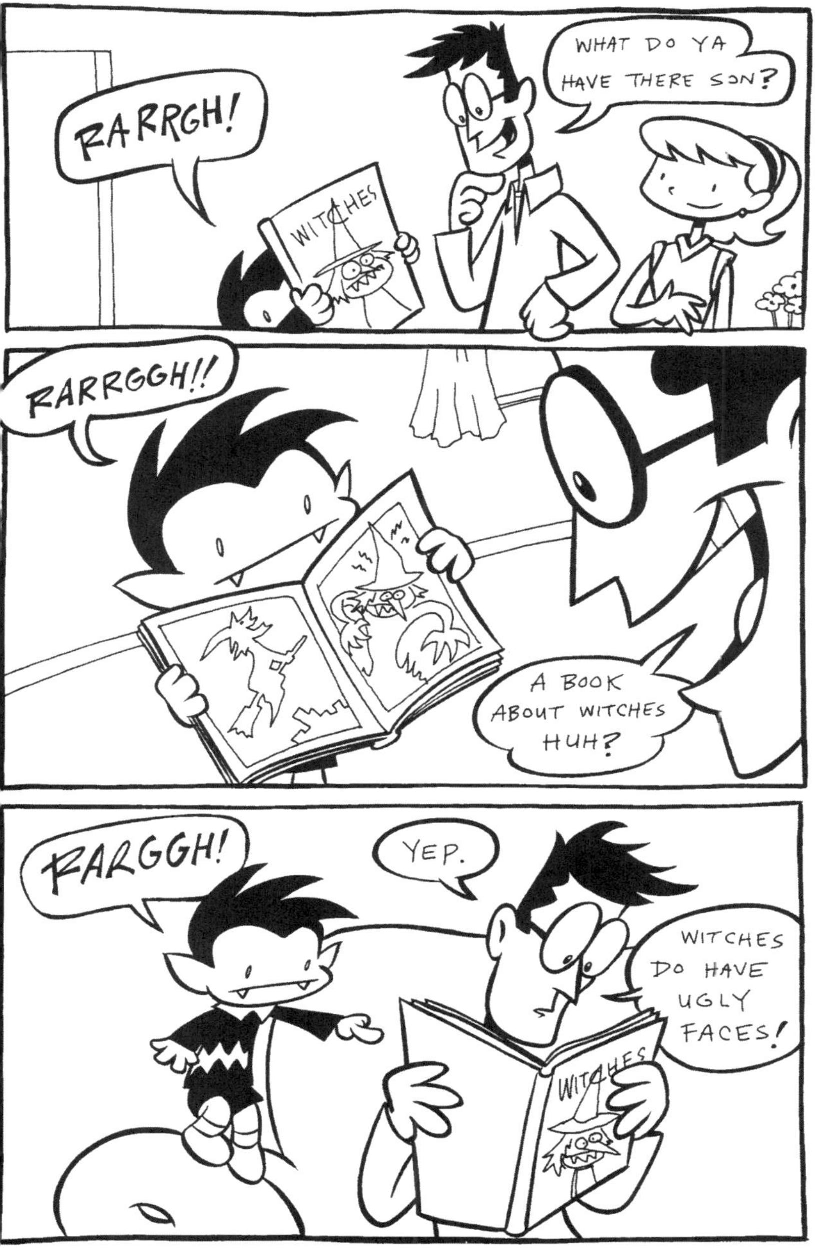
RARRGH!
WHAT DO YA HAVE THERE SON?
WITCHES
RARRGGH!!
A BOOK ABOUT WITCHES HUH?
RARGGH!
YEP.
WITCHES DO HAVE UGLY FACES!
WITCHES

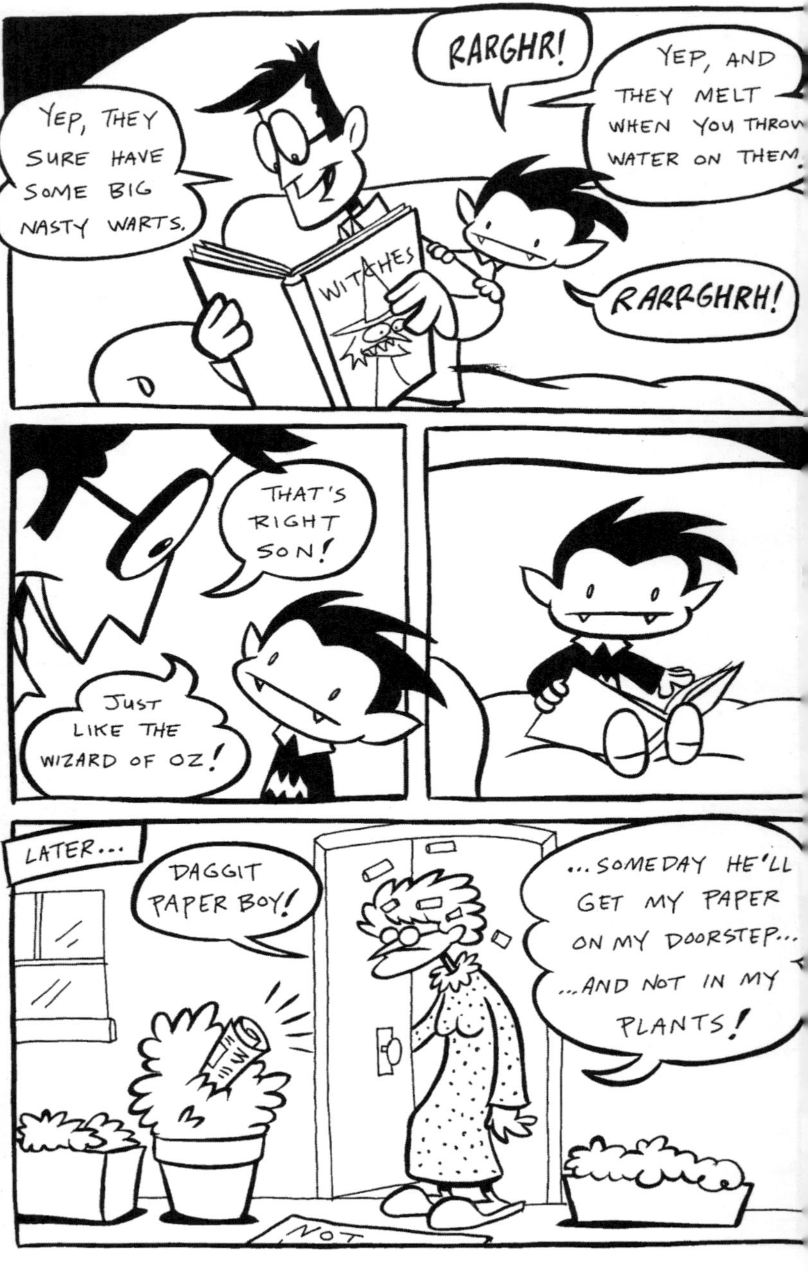
YEP, THEY SURE HAVE SOME BIG NASTY WARTS.
RARGHR!
YEP, AND THEY MELT WHEN YOU THROW WATER ON THEM.
WITCHES
RARRGHRH!
THAT'S RIGHT SON!
JUST LIKE THE WIZARD OF OZ!
LATER...
DAGGIT PAPER BOY!
...SOMEDAY HE'LL GET MY PAPER ON MY DOORSTEP...
...AND NOT IN MY PLANTS!
NOT

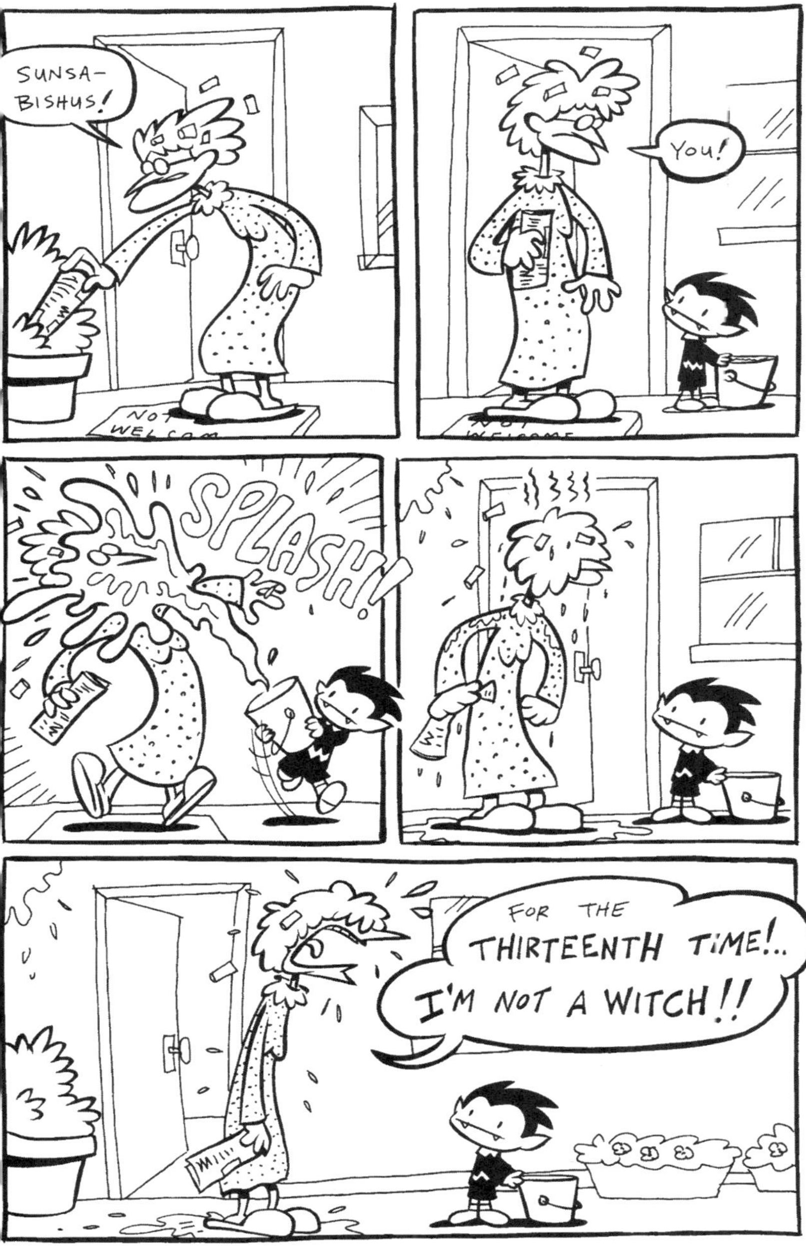
SUNSA-BISHUS!
NOT WELCOM
YOU!
NOT WELCOME
SPLASH!
FOR THE THIRTEENTH TIME!..
I'M NOT A WITCH!!

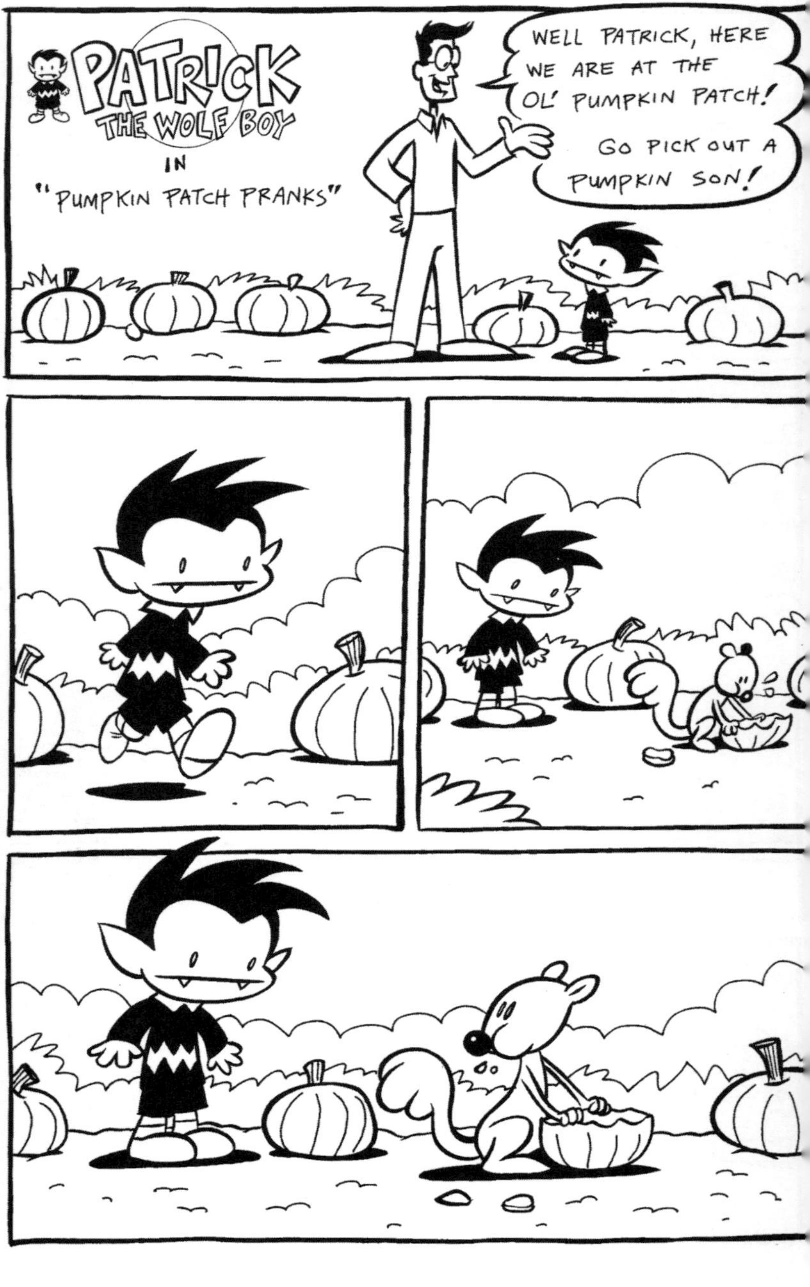
PATRICK THE WOLF BOY
IN
"PUMPKIN PATCH PRANKS"
WELL PATRICK, HERE WE ARE AT THE OL' PUMPKIN PATCH!
GO PICK OUT A PUMPKIN SON!

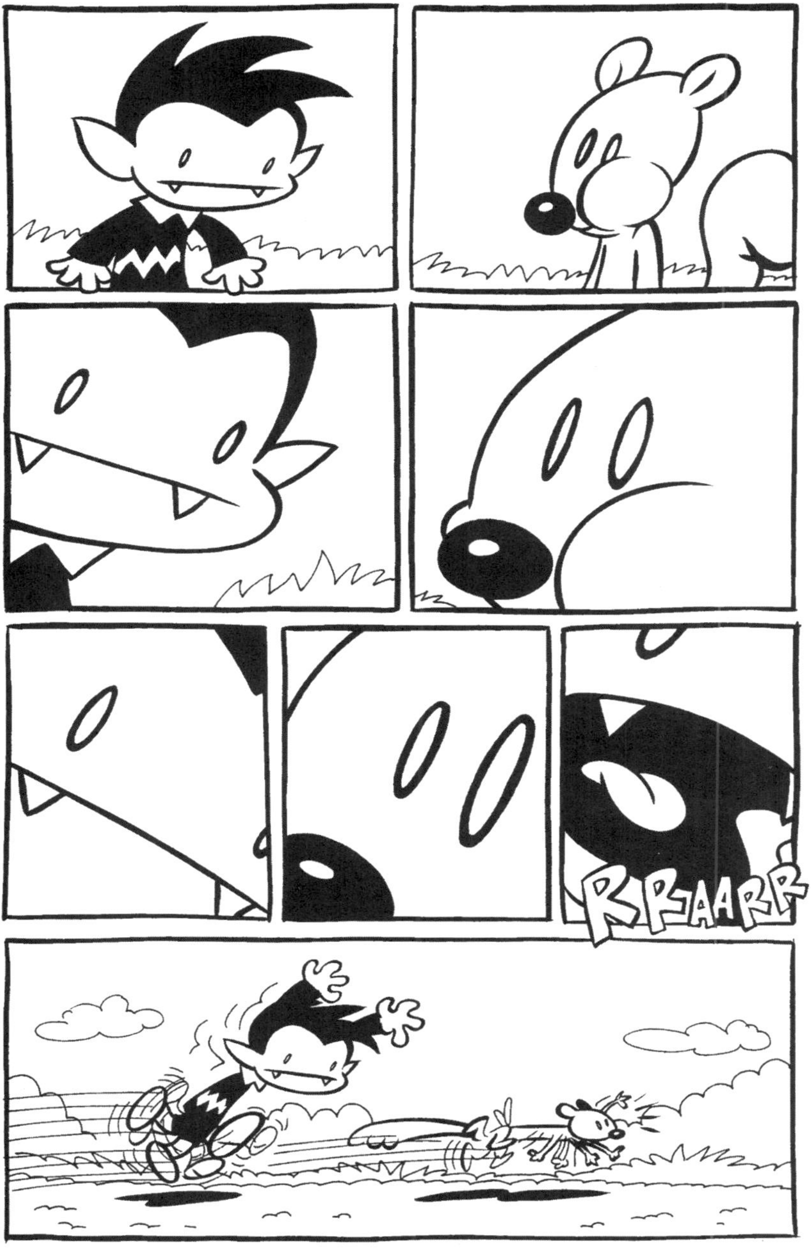
RRAARR

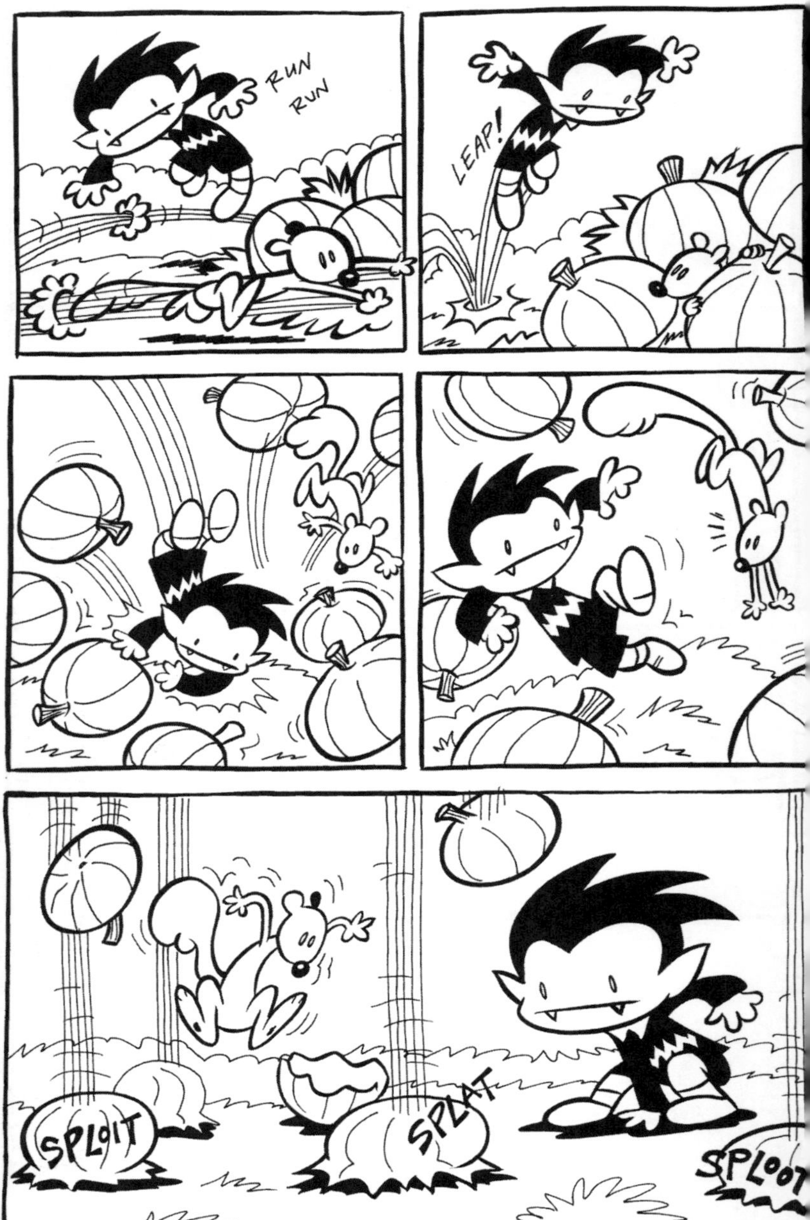
RUN
RUN
LEAP!
SPLOIT
SPLAT
SPLOOT

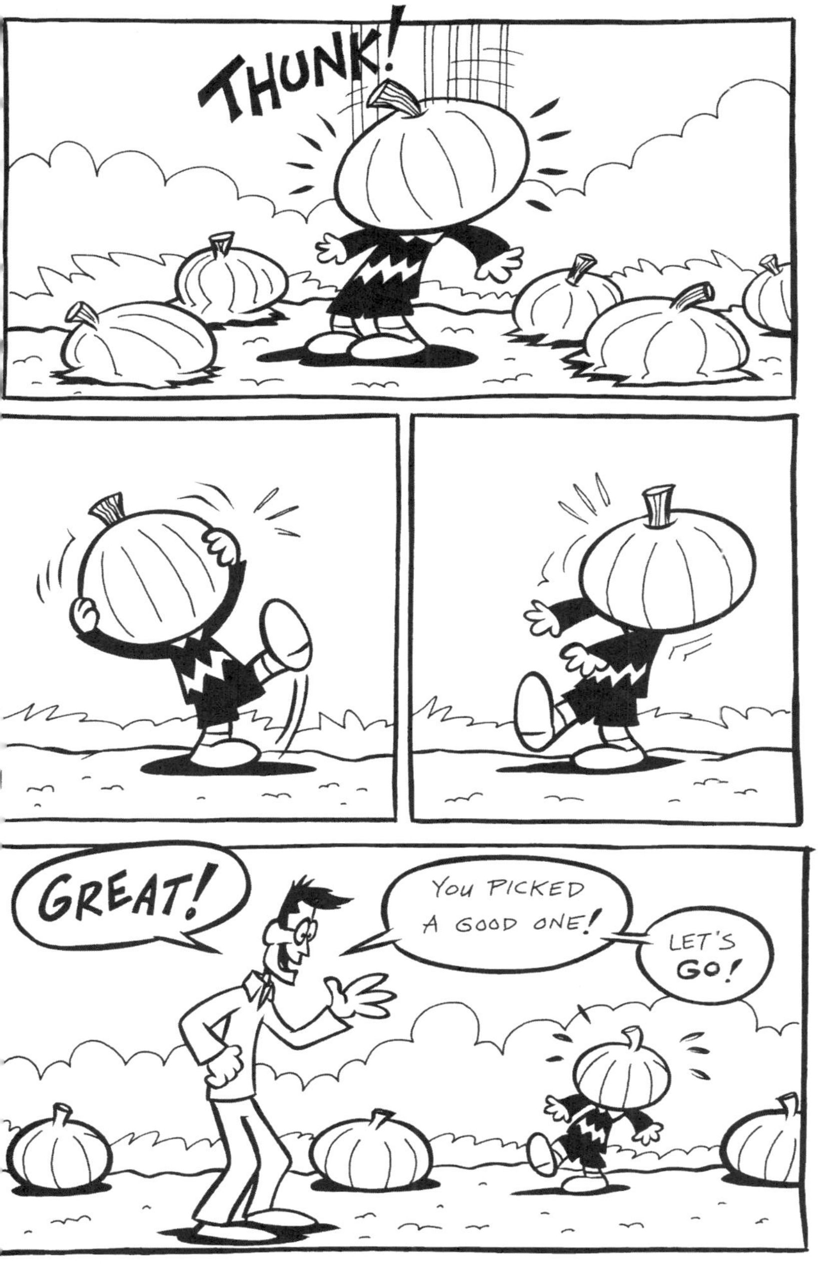
THUNK!
GREAT!
YOU PICKED A GOOD ONE!
LET'S GO!

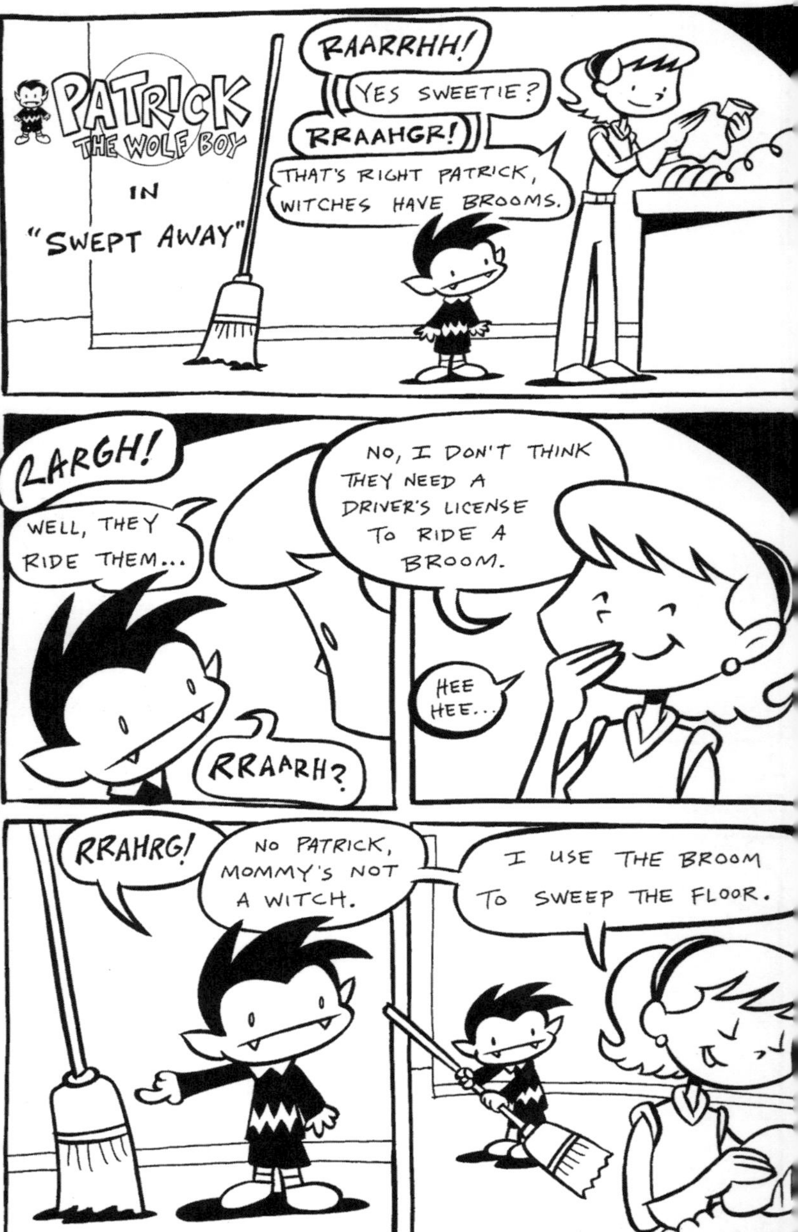
PATRICK THE WOLF BOY
IN
"SWEPT AWAY"
RAARRHH!
YES SWEETIE?
RRAAHGR!
THAT'S RIGHT PATRICK, WITCHES HAVE BROOMS.
RARGH!
WELL, THEY RIDE THEM...
NO, I DON'T THINK THEY NEED A DRIVER'S LICENSE TO RIDE A BROOM.
RRAARH?
HEE HEE...
RRAHRG!
NO PATRICK, MOMMY'S NOT A WITCH.
I USE THE BROOM TO SWEEP THE FLOOR.

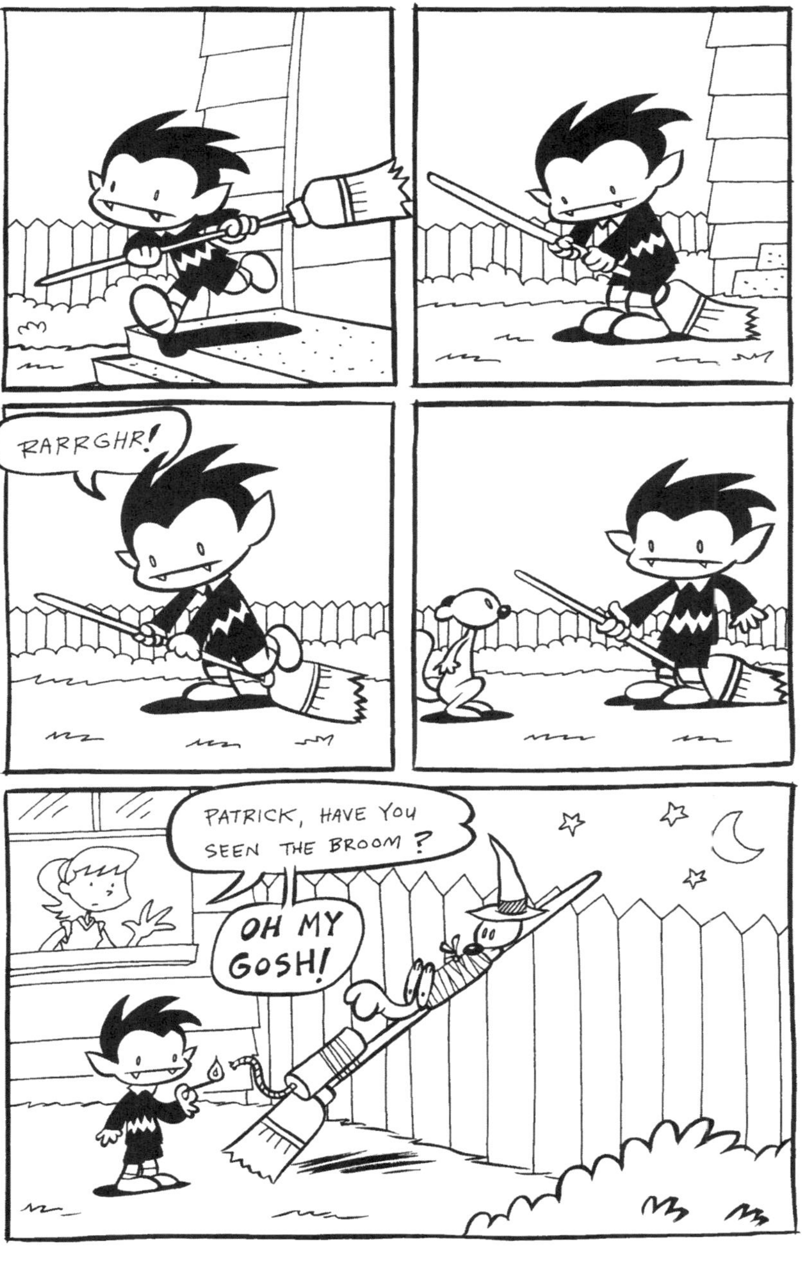
RARRGHR!
PATRICK, HAVE YOU SEEN THE BROOM?
OH MY GOSH!

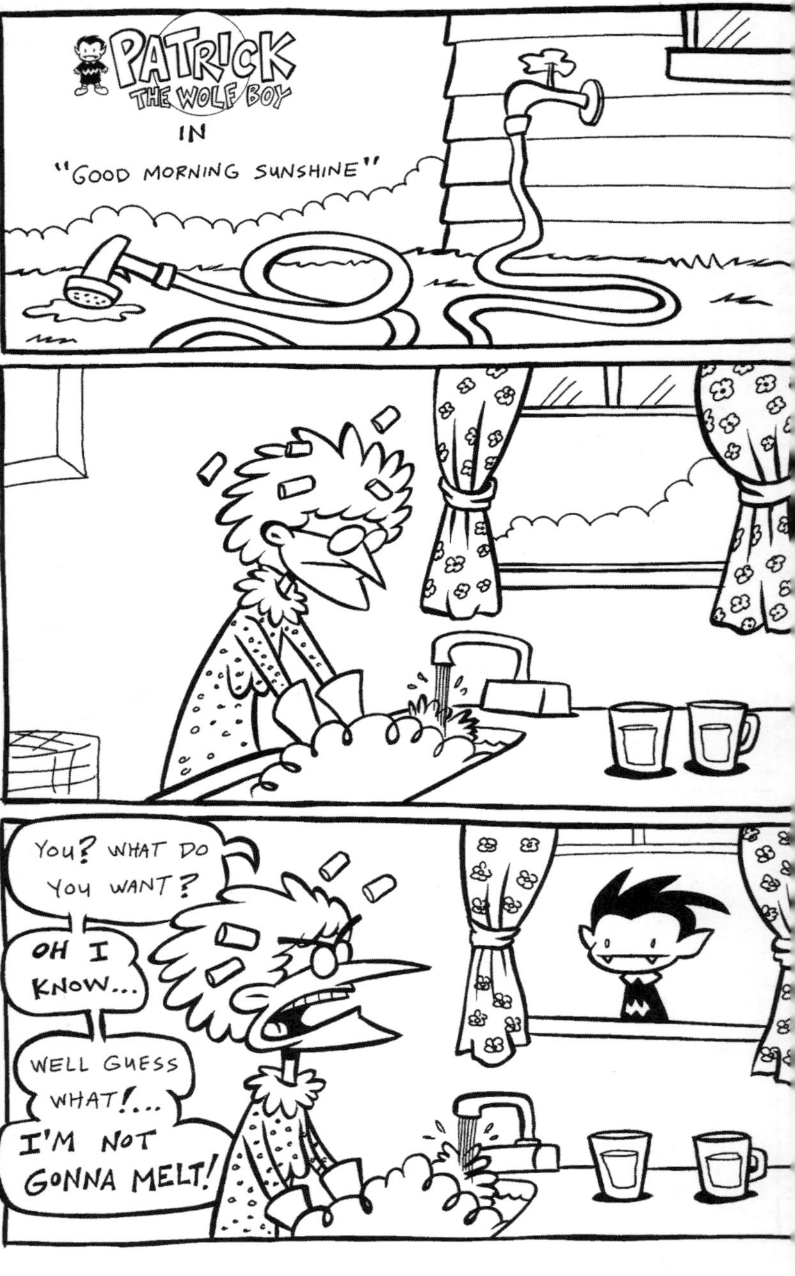
PATRICK THE WOLF BOY
IN
"GOOD MORNING SUNSHINE"
YOU? WHAT DO YOU WANT?
OH I KNOW...
WELL GUESS WHAT!...
I'M NOT GONNA MELT!

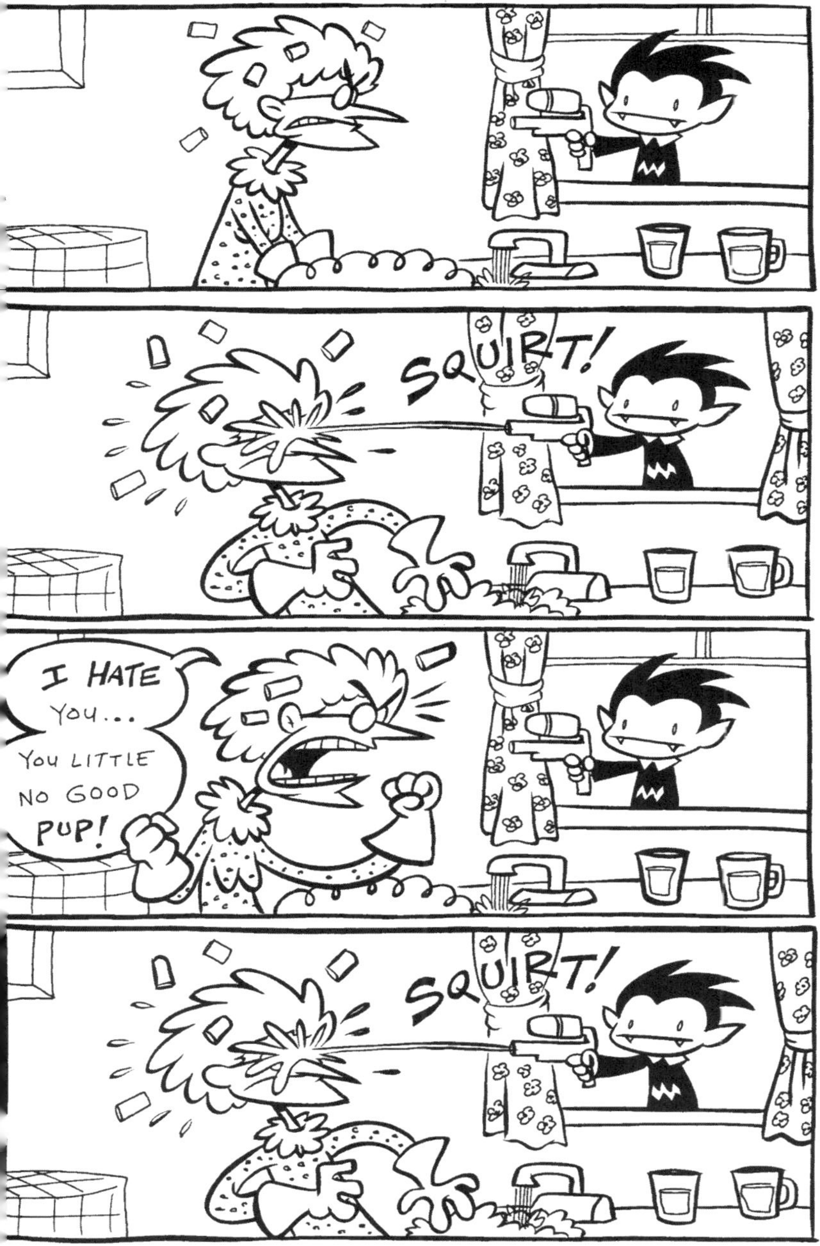
SQUIRT!
I HATE YOU... YOU LITTLE NO GOOD PUP!
SQUIRT!

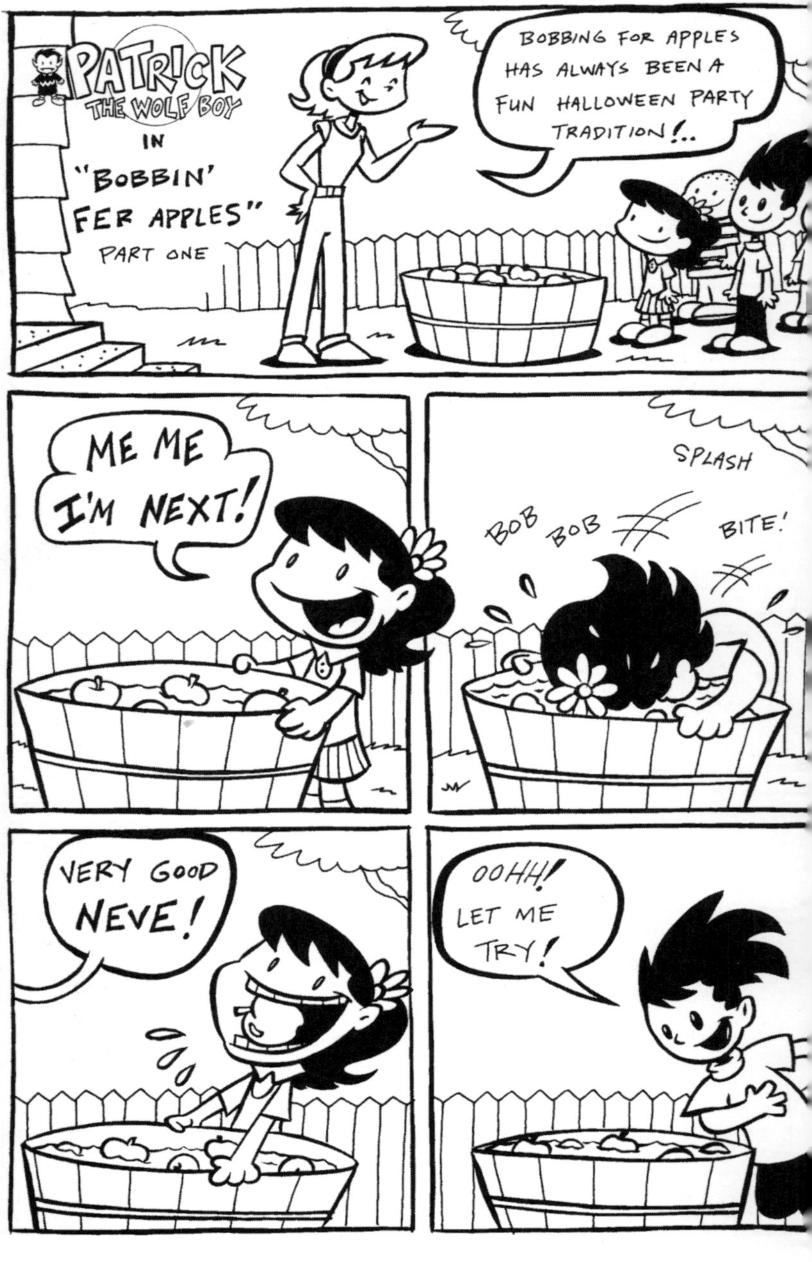

PATRICK THE WOLF BOY
IN
"BOBBIN' FER APPLES"
PART ONE
BOBBING FOR APPLES HAS ALWAYS BEEN A FUN HALLOWEEN PARTY TRADITION!..
ME ME I'M NEXT!
SPLASH
BOB BOB
BITE!
VERY GOOD NEVE!
OOHH! LET ME TRY!

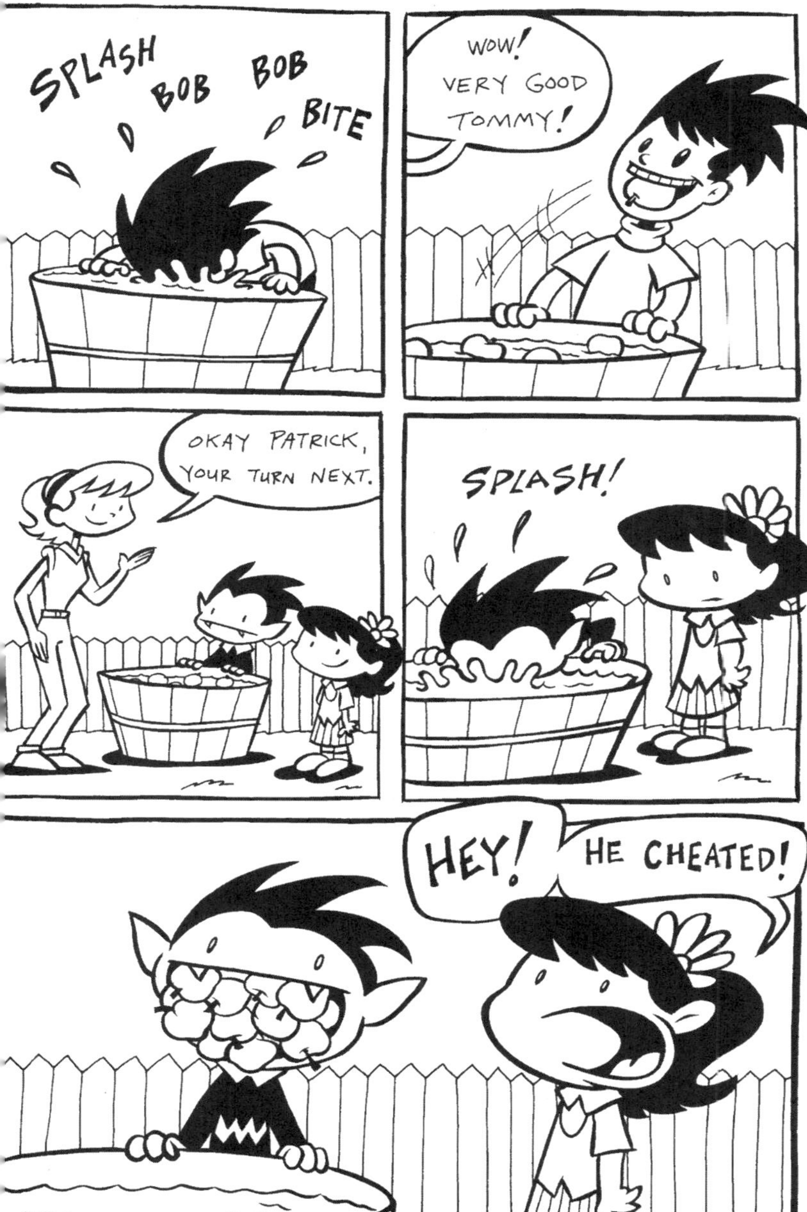
SPLASH
BOB BOB
BITE
WOW! VERY GOOD TOMMY!
OKAY PATRICK, YOUR TURN NEXT.
SPLASH!
HEY!
HE CHEATED!

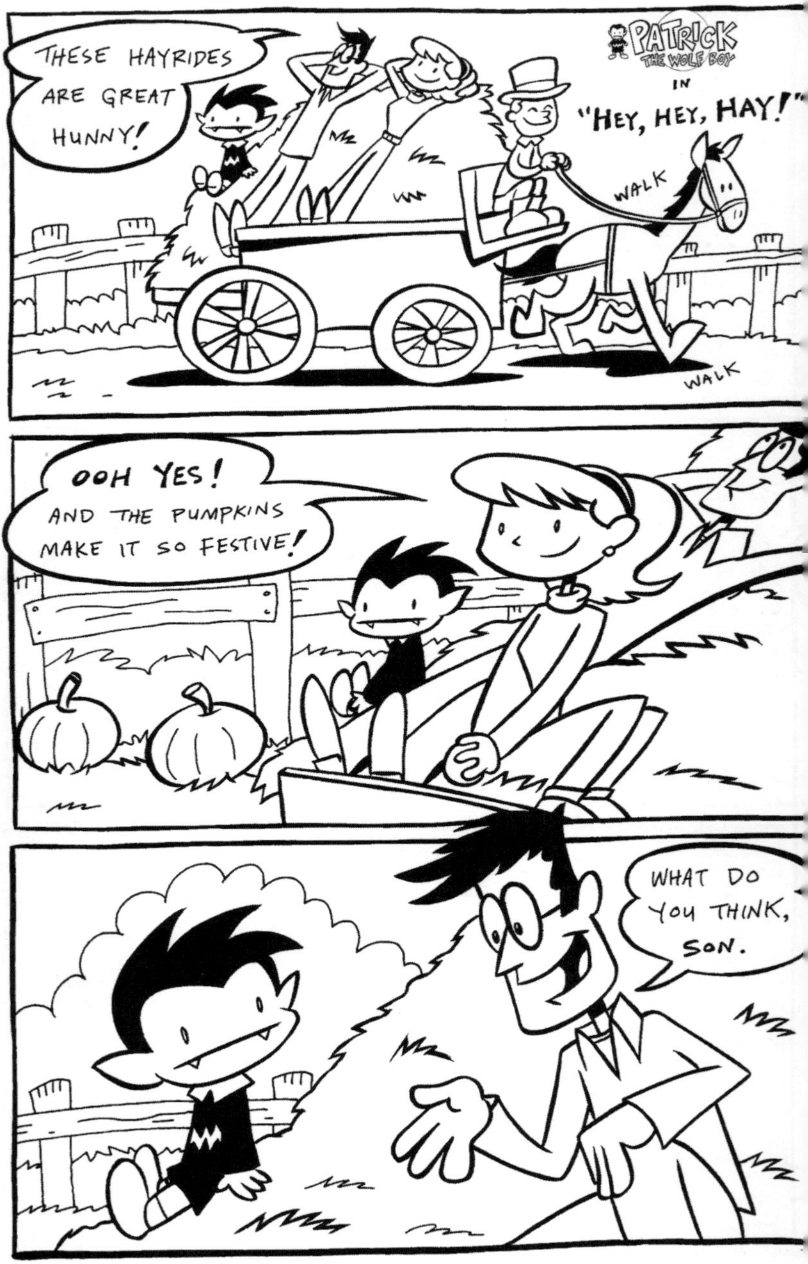
THESE HAYRIDES ARE GREAT HUNNY!
PATRICK THE WOLF BOY
IN
"HEY, HEY, HAY!"
WALK
WALK
OOH YES! AND THE PUMPKINS MAKE IT SO FESTIVE!
WHAT DO YOU THINK, SON.

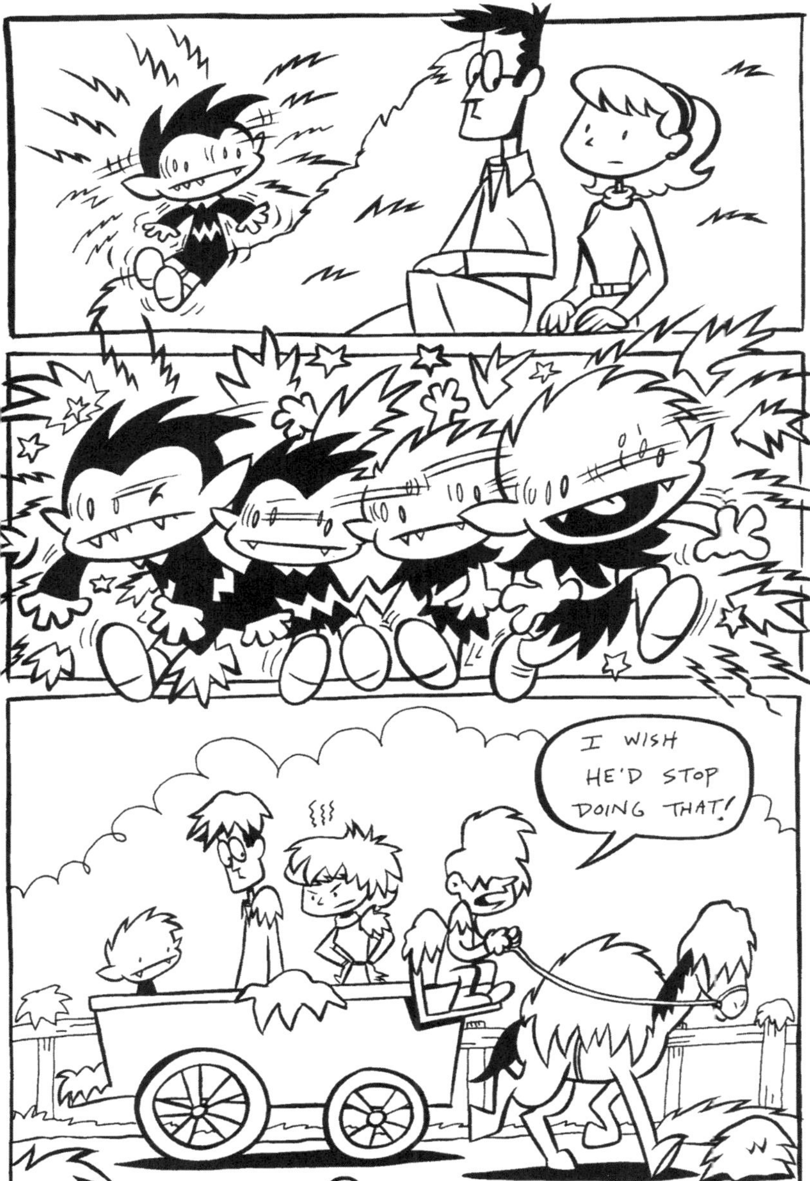
I WISH HE'D STOP DOING THAT!

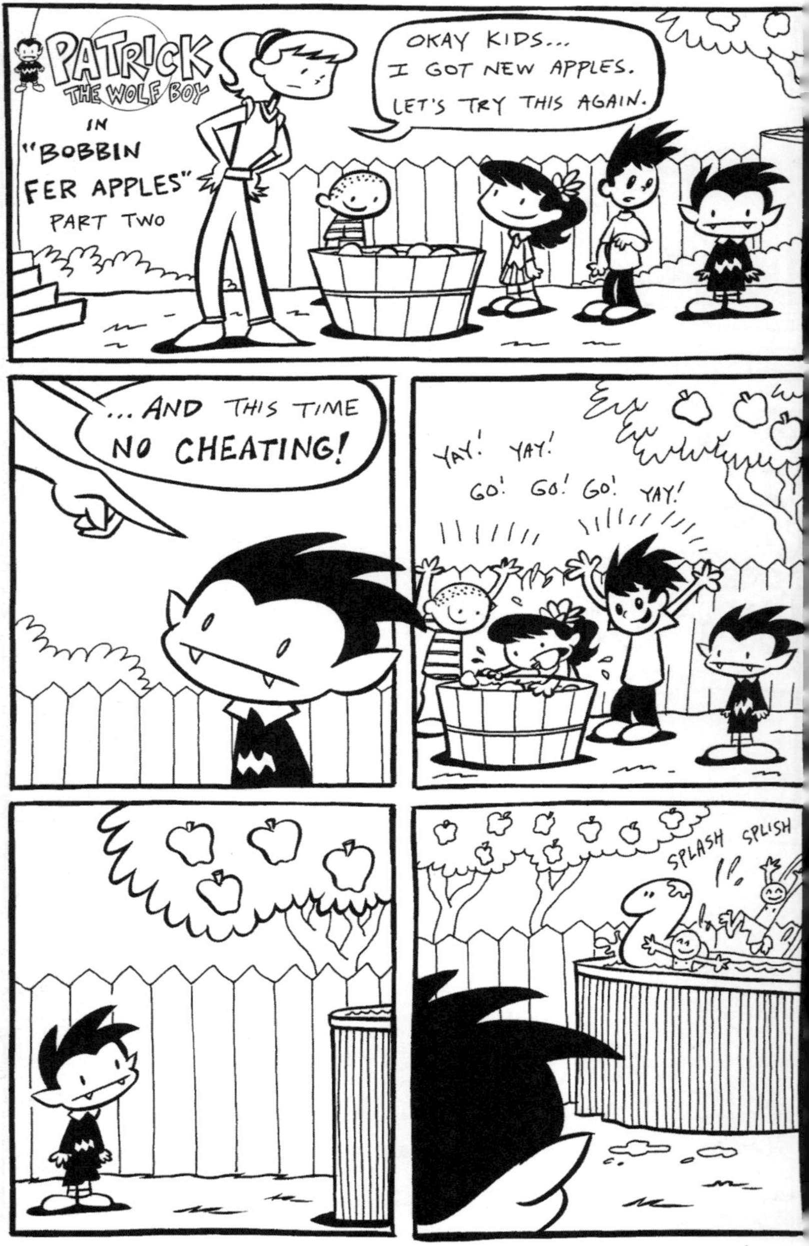
PATRICK THE WOLF BOY
IN "BOBBIN FER APPLES" PART TWO
OKAY KIDS... I GOT NEW APPLES. LET'S TRY THIS AGAIN.
...AND THIS TIME NO CHEATING!
YAY! YAY! GO! GO! GO! YAY!
SPLASH SPLISH

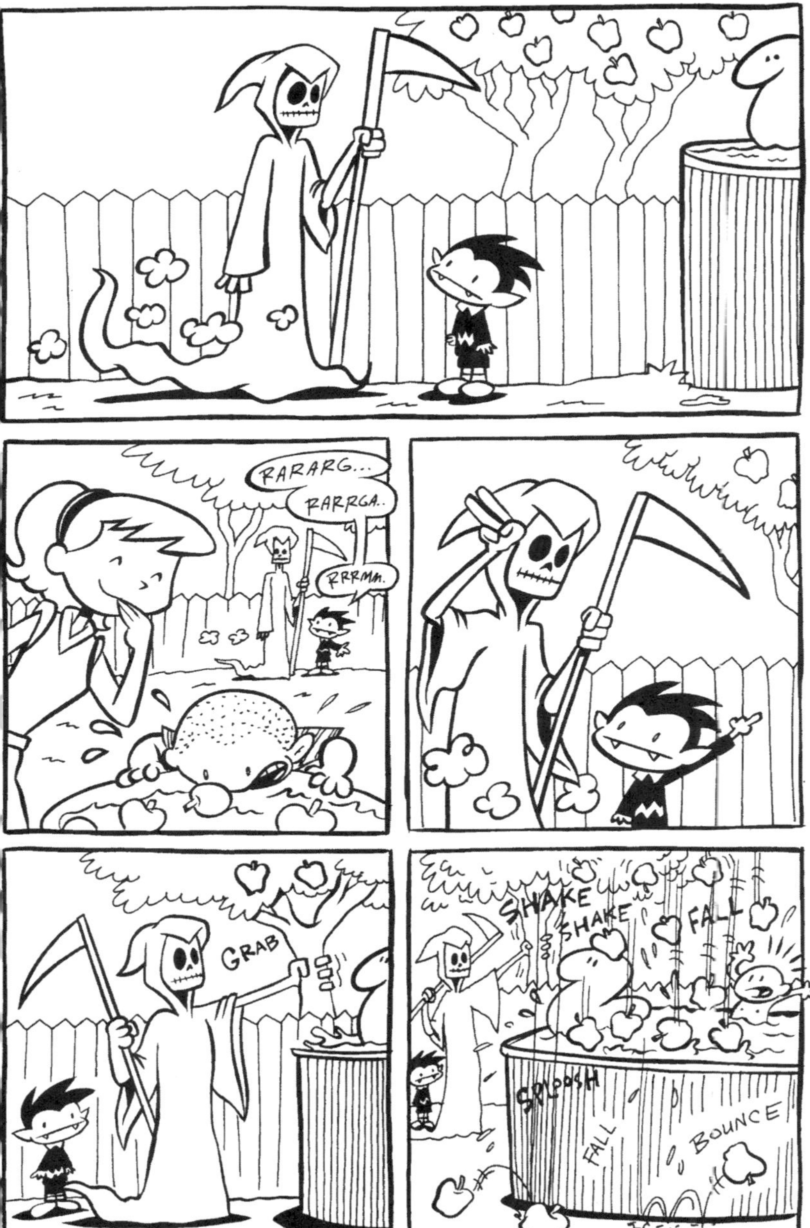

RARARG...
RARRGA..
RRRMM.
GRAB
SHAKE
SHAKE
FALL
SPLOOSH
FALL
BOUNCE

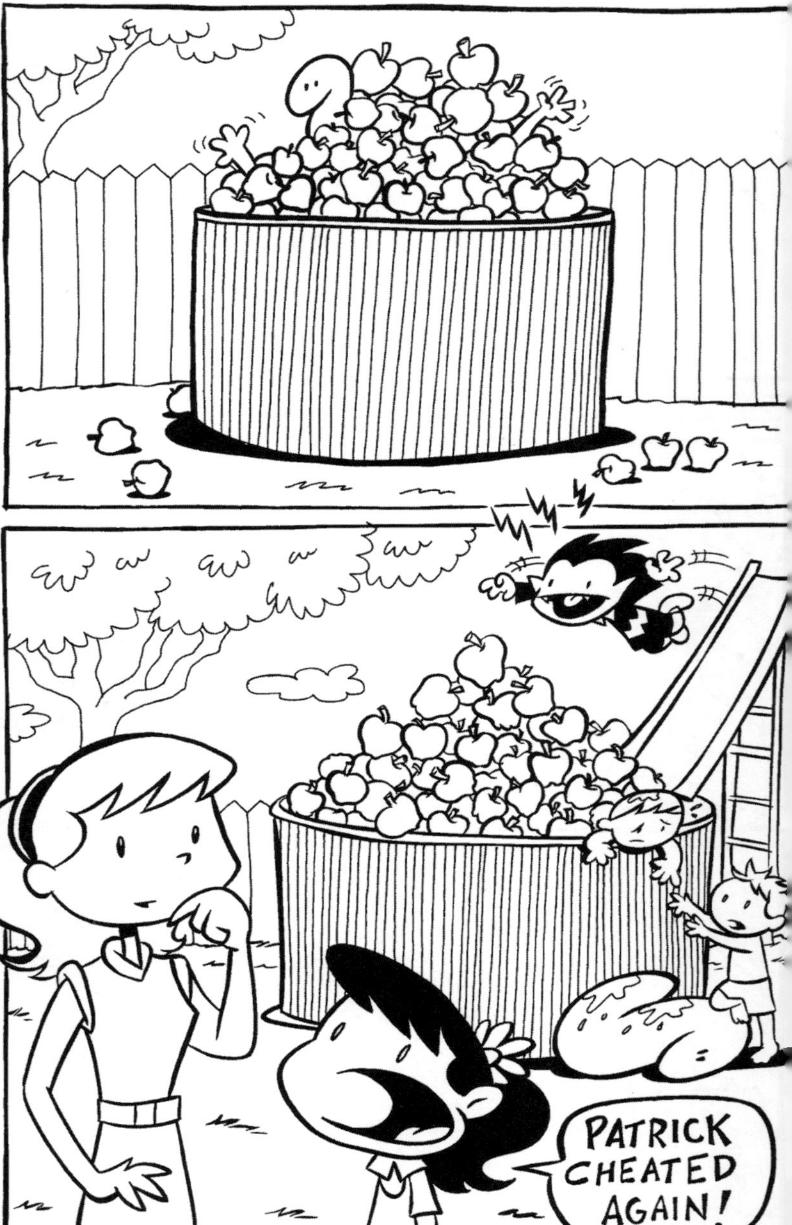
PATRICK
CHEATED
AGAIN!

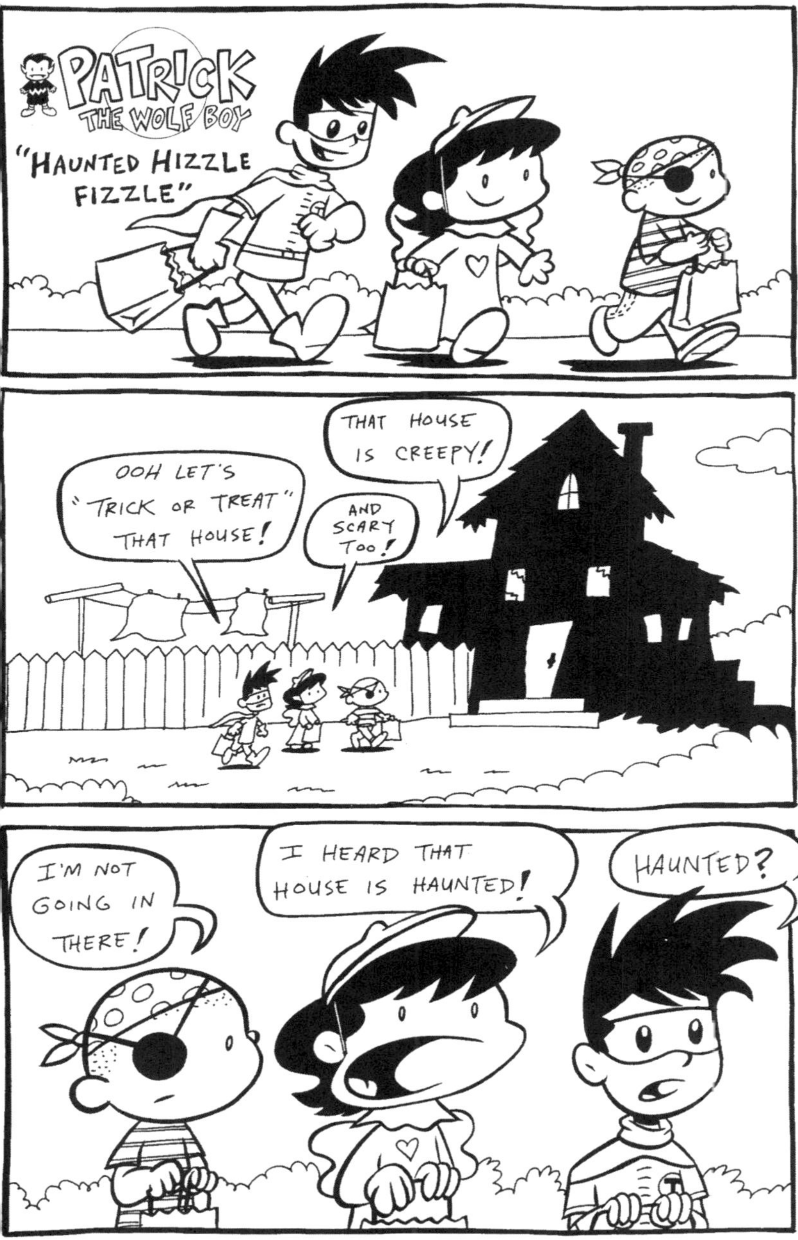
PATRICK THE WOLF BOY
"HAUNTED HIZZLE FIZZLE"
OOH LET'S "TRICK OR TREAT" THAT HOUSE!
THAT HOUSE IS CREEPY!
AND SCARY TOO!
I'M NOT GOING IN THERE!
I HEARD THAT HOUSE IS HAUNTED!
HAUNTED?

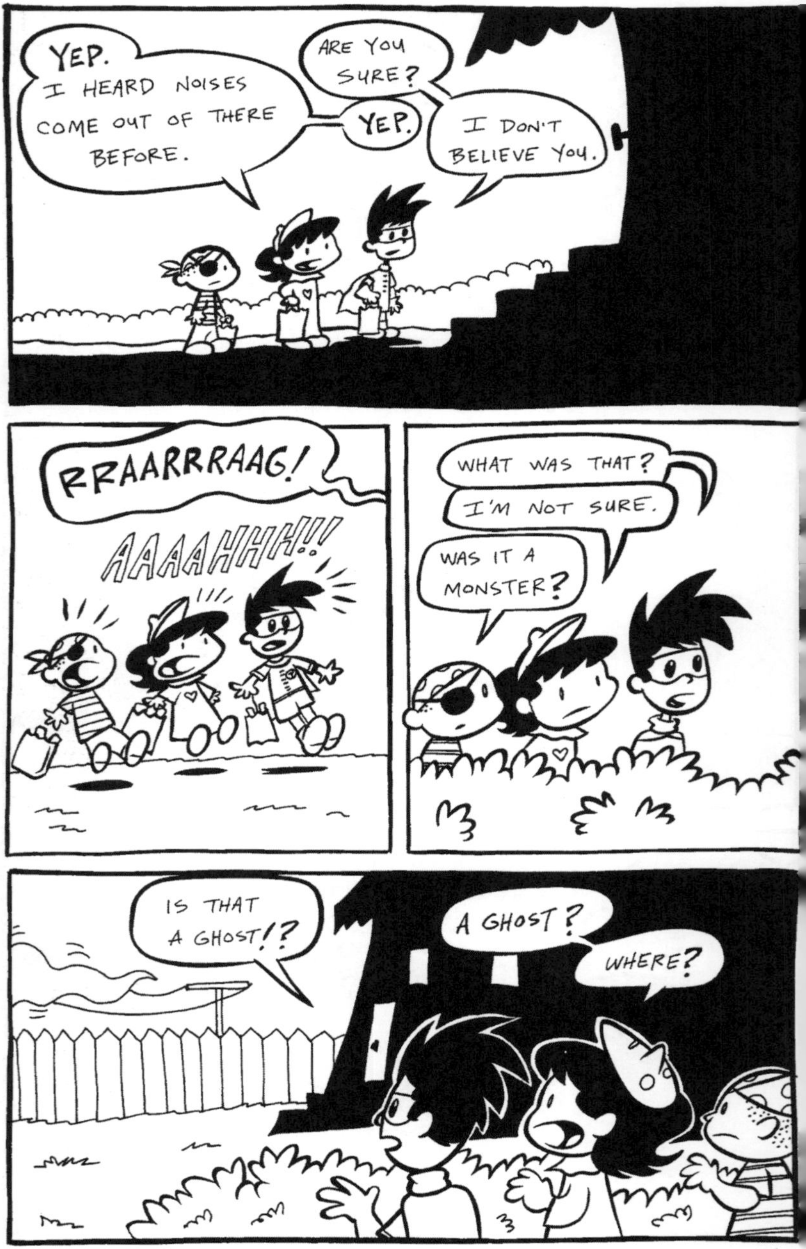
YEP.
I HEARD NOISES COME OUT OF THERE BEFORE.
ARE YOU SURE?
YEP.
I DON'T BELIEVE YOU.
RRAARRRAAG!
AAAAHHH!!
WHAT WAS THAT?
I'M NOT SURE.
WAS IT A MONSTER?
IS THAT A GHOST!?
A GHOST?
WHERE?

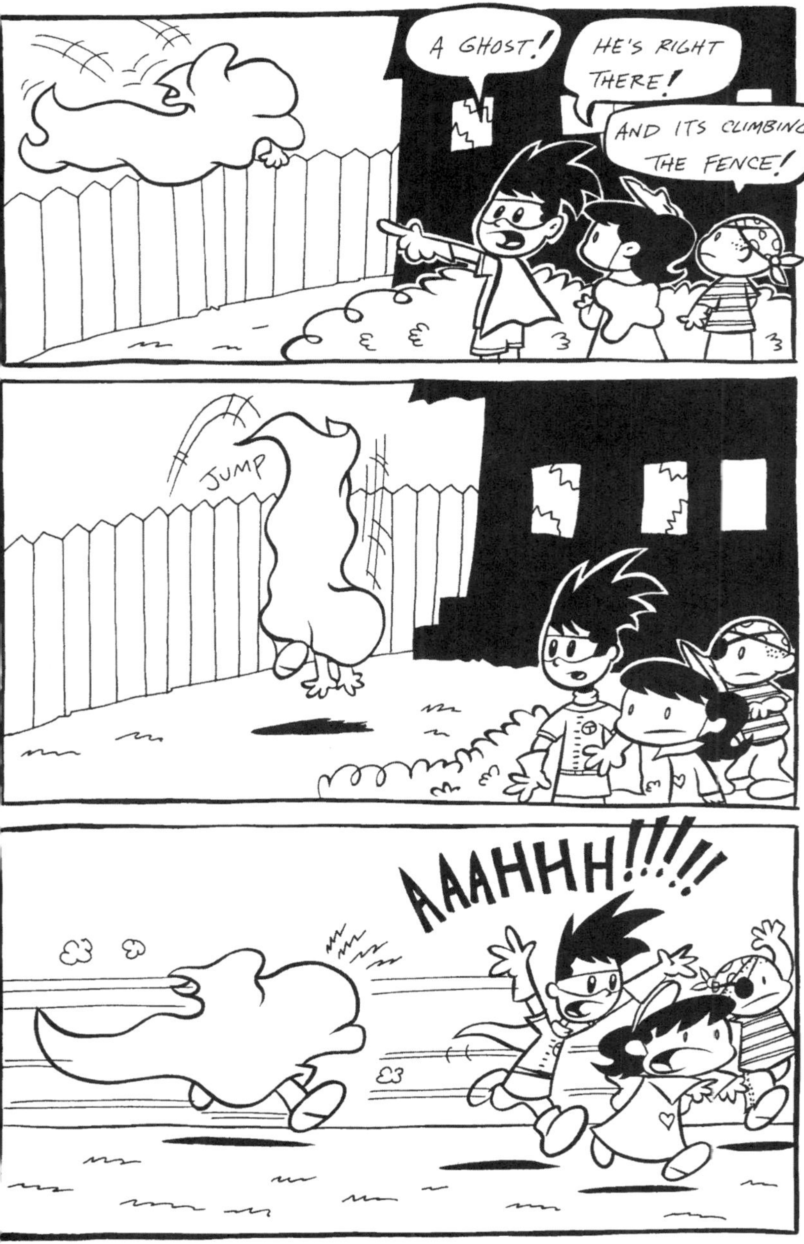
A GHOST!
HE'S RIGHT THERE!
AND ITS CLIMBING THE FENCE!
JUMP
AAAHHH!!!!!

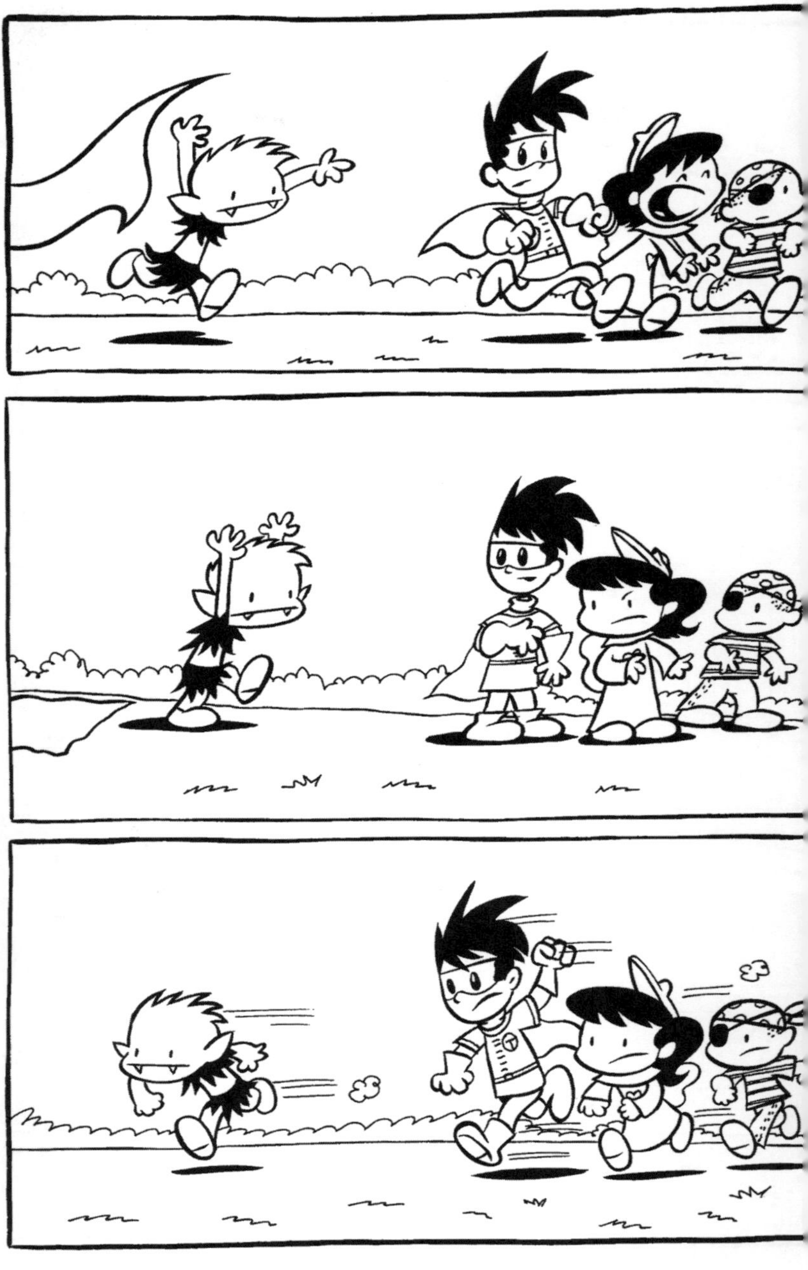

PATRICK THE WOLF BOY
IN
"EPILOGUE"
DING DONG
KNOCK
KNOCK
KNOCK
DING DONG
DING DONG
DING DONG
DING DONG
KNOCK
KNOCK
DING DONG
KNOCK KNOCK
DING DONG
DING DONG
DING
DONG
DING
DONG
DING
DONG

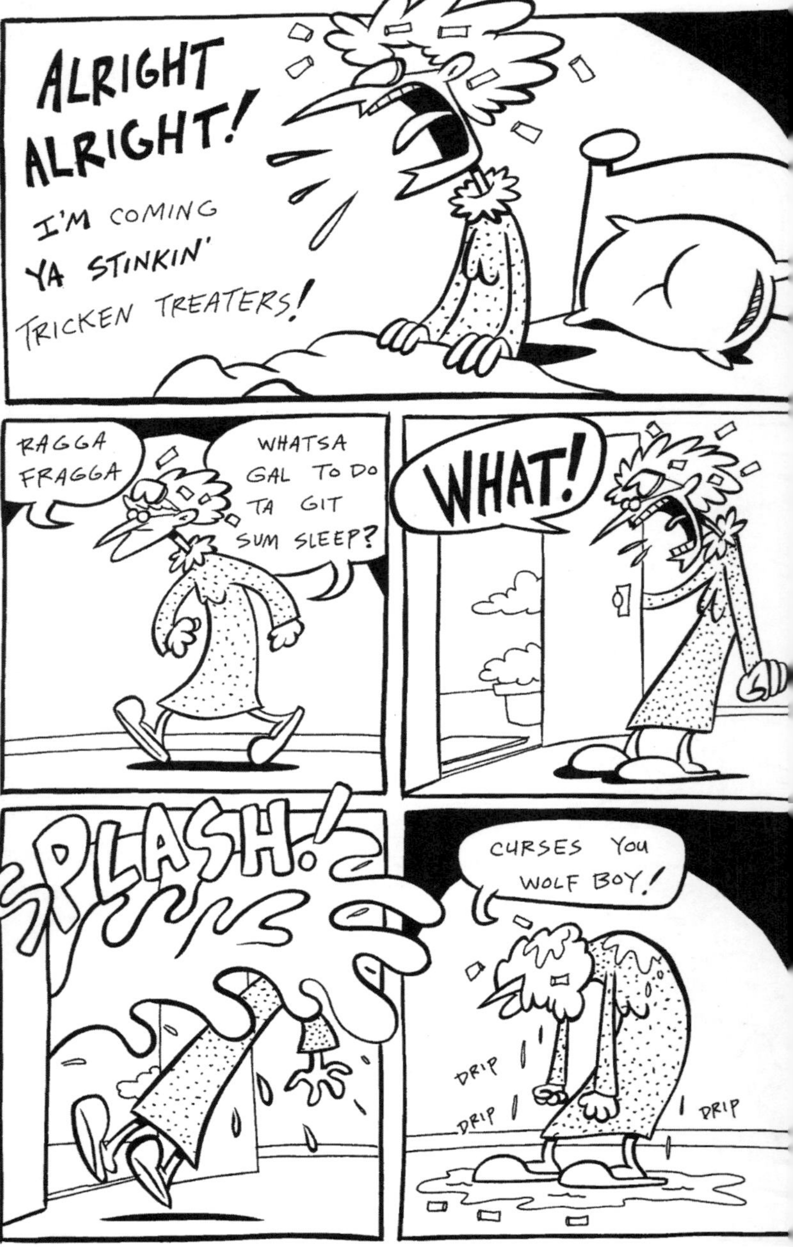
ALRIGHT ALRIGHT!
I'M COMING YA STINKIN' TRICKEN TREATERS!
RAGGA FRAGGA
WHATSA GAL TO DO TA GIT SUM SLEEP?
WHAT!
SPLASH!
CURSES YOU WOLF BOY!
DRIP
DRIP
DRIP

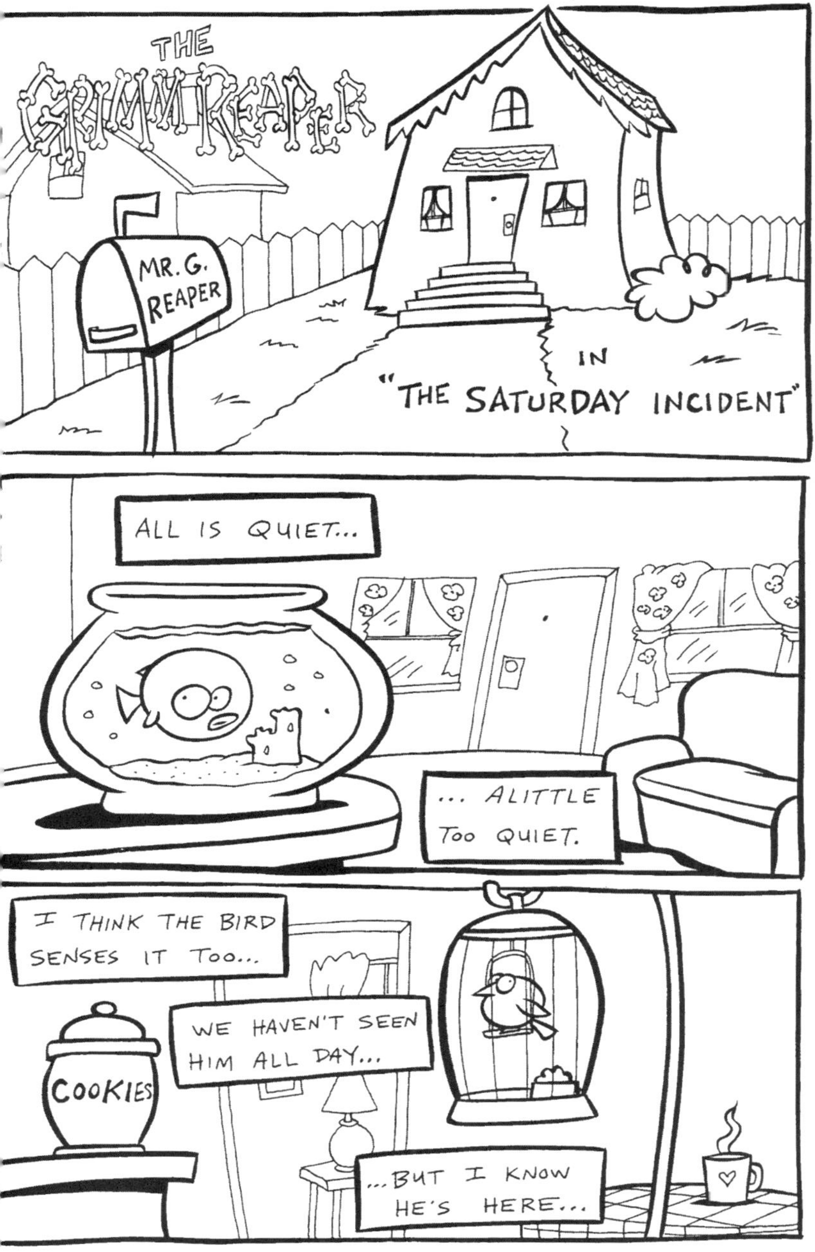
THE
GRIMM REAPER
MR. G. REAPER
IN
"THE SATURDAY INCIDENT"
ALL IS QUIET...
... ALITTLE TOO QUIET.
I THINK THE BIRD SENSES IT TOO...
WE HAVEN'T SEEN HIM ALL DAY...
COOKIES
...BUT I KNOW HE'S HERE...

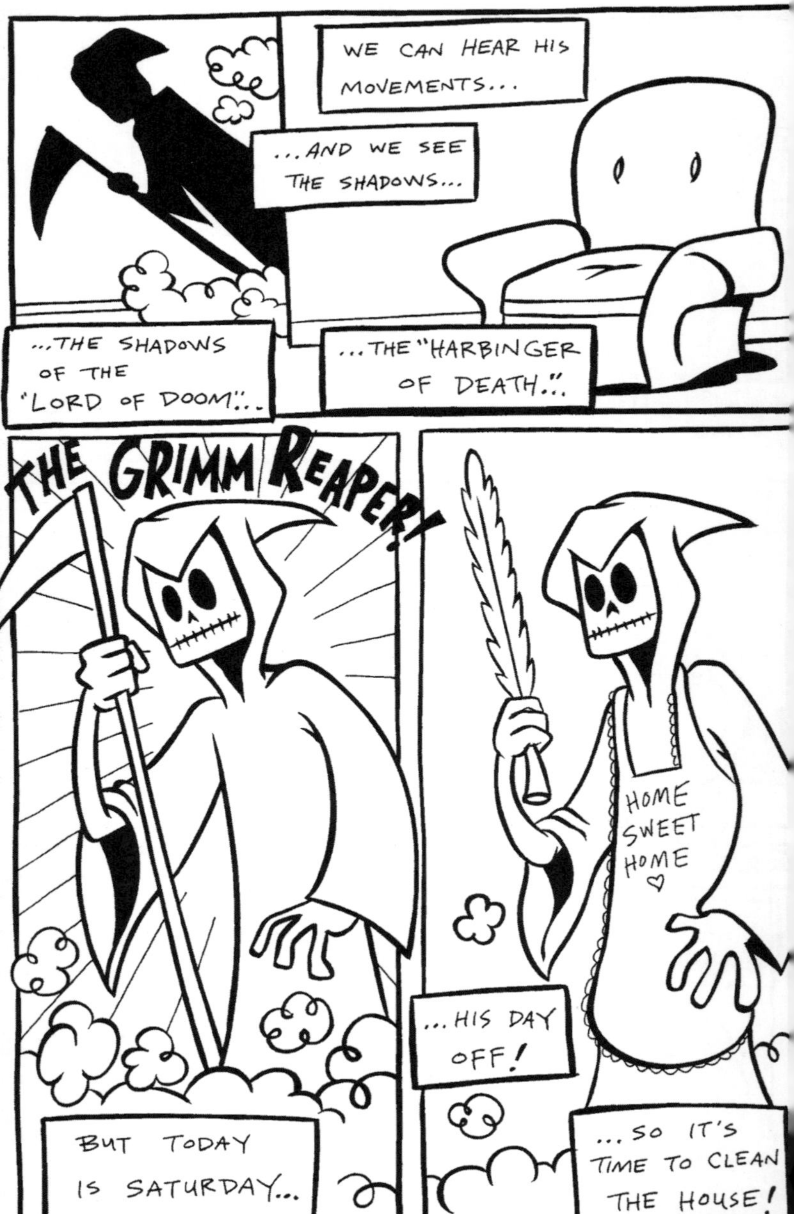
WE CAN HEAR HIS MOVEMENTS...
...AND WE SEE THE SHADOWS...
...THE SHADOWS OF THE "LORD OF DOOM"...
...THE "HARBINGER OF DEATH."...
THE GRIMM REAPER!
BUT TODAY IS SATURDAY...
...HIS DAY OFF!
HOME SWEET HOME
...SO IT'S TIME TO CLEAN THE HOUSE!

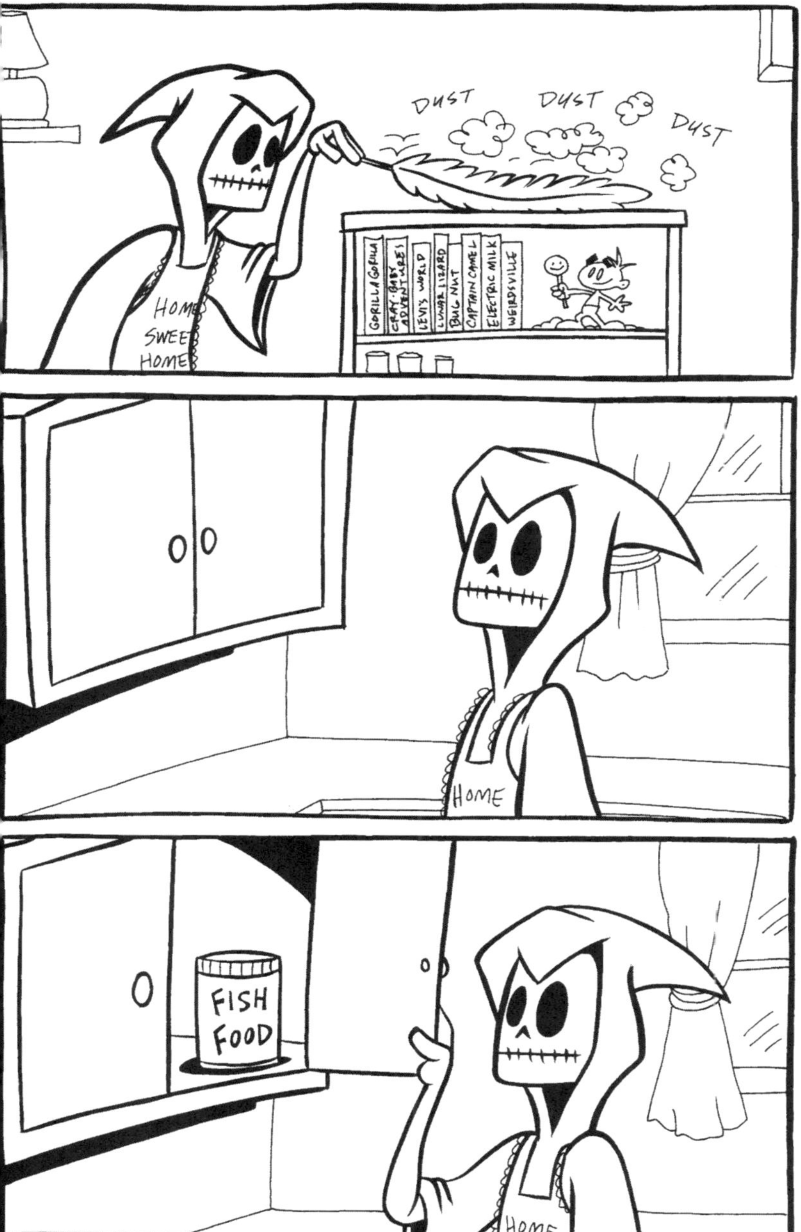
DUST
DUST
DUST
HOME SWEET HOME
GORILLA GORILLA
CRAY-BABY ADVENTURES
LEVI'S WORLD
LUNAR LIZARD
BUG NUT
CAPTAIN CAMEL
ELECTRIC MILK
WEIRDSVILLE
HOME
FISH FOOD
HOME

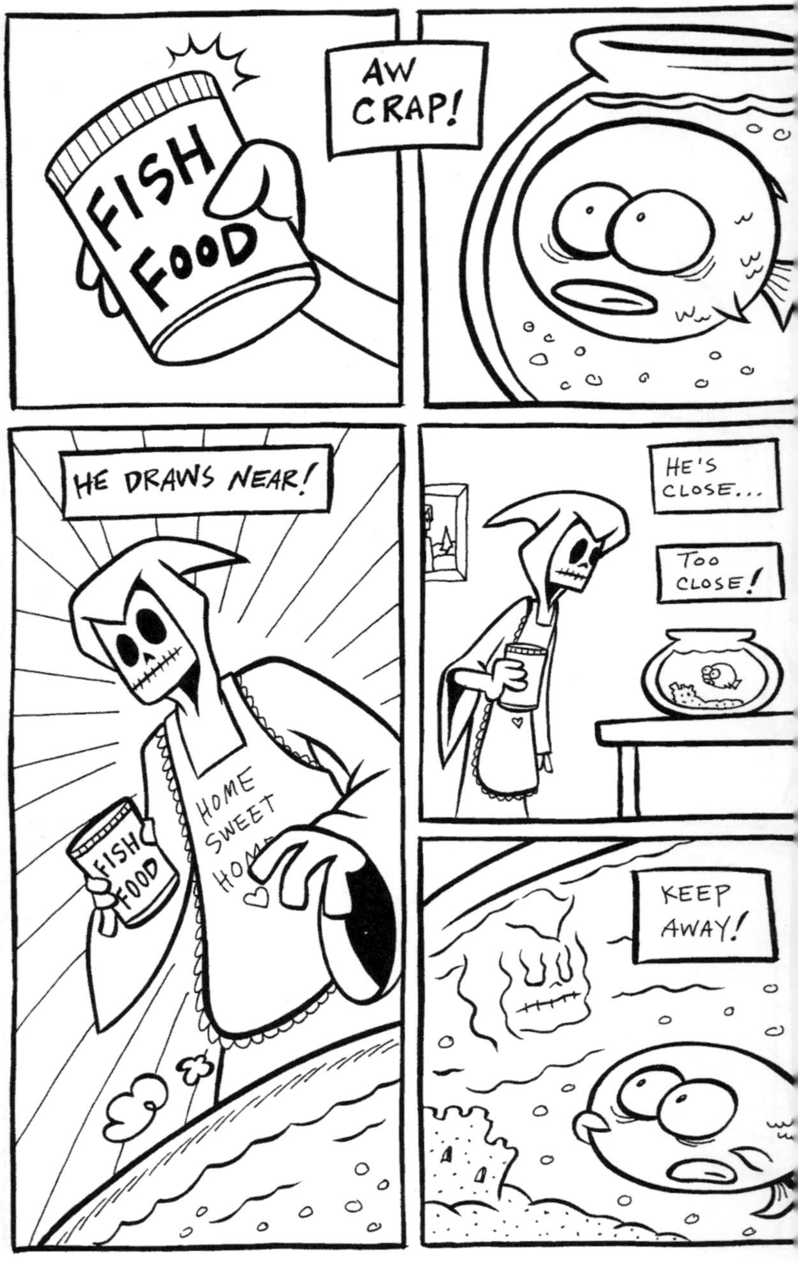
FISH FOOD
AW CRAP!
HE DRAWS NEAR!
HOME SWEET
FISH FOOD
HE'S CLOSE...
TOO CLOSE!
KEEP AWAY!

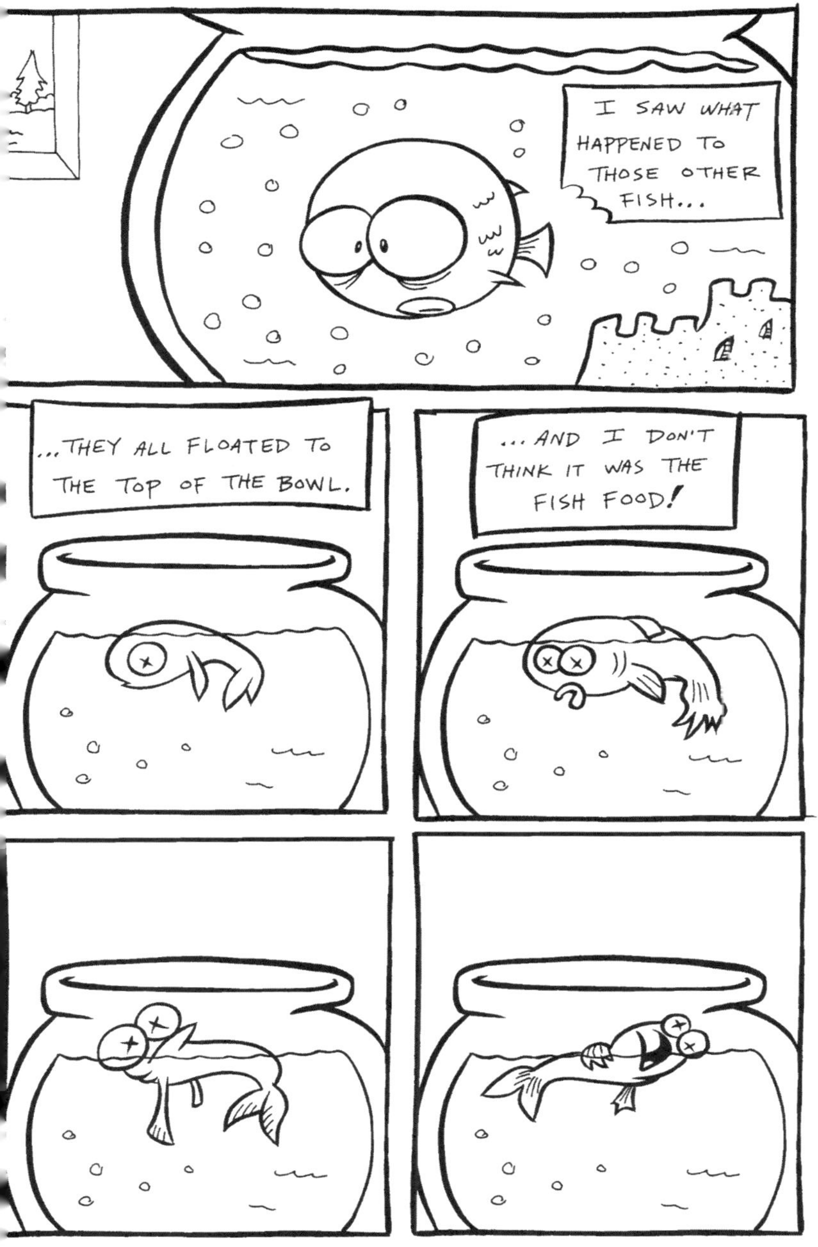
I SAW WHAT HAPPENED TO THOSE OTHER FISH...
...THEY ALL FLOATED TO THE TOP OF THE BOWL.
...AND I DON'T THINK IT WAS THE FISH FOOD!

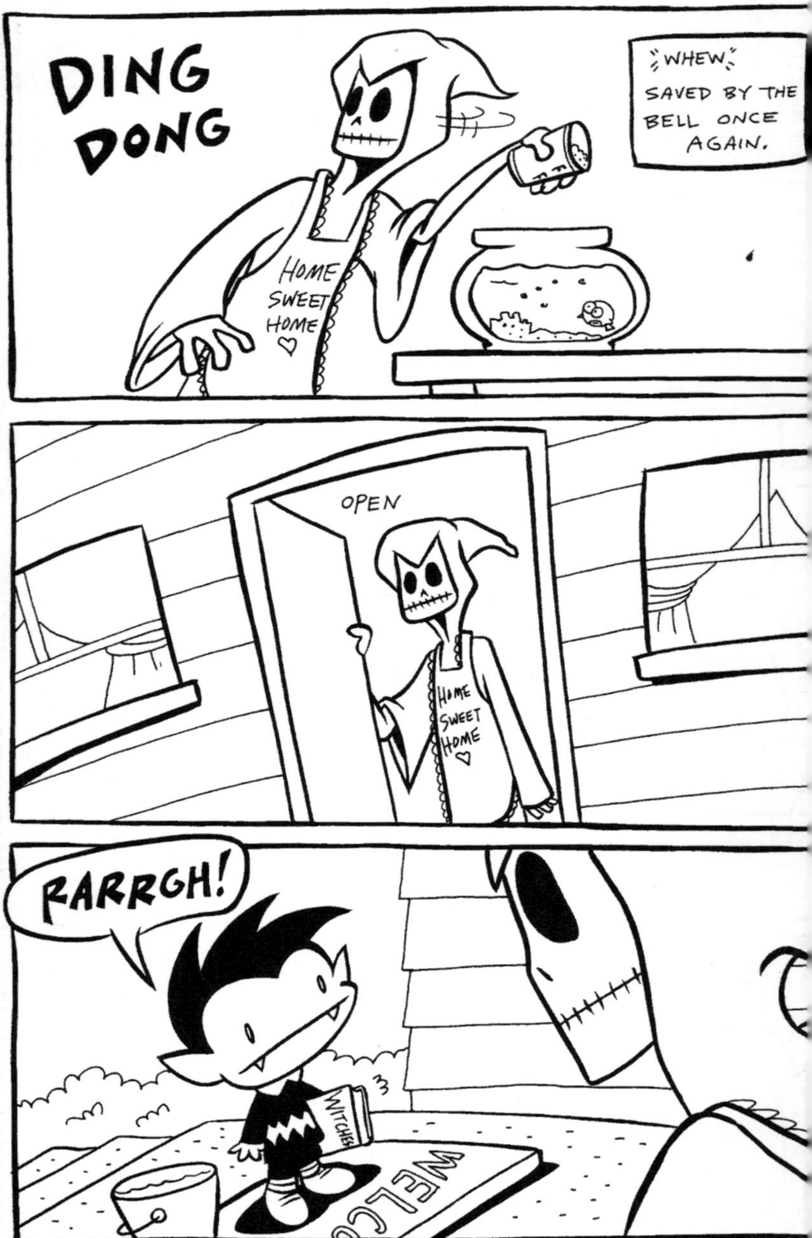
DING DONG
WHEW
SAVED BY THE BELL ONCE AGAIN.
HOME SWEET HOME
OPEN
HOME SWEET HOME
RARRGH!
WITCHES
WELC

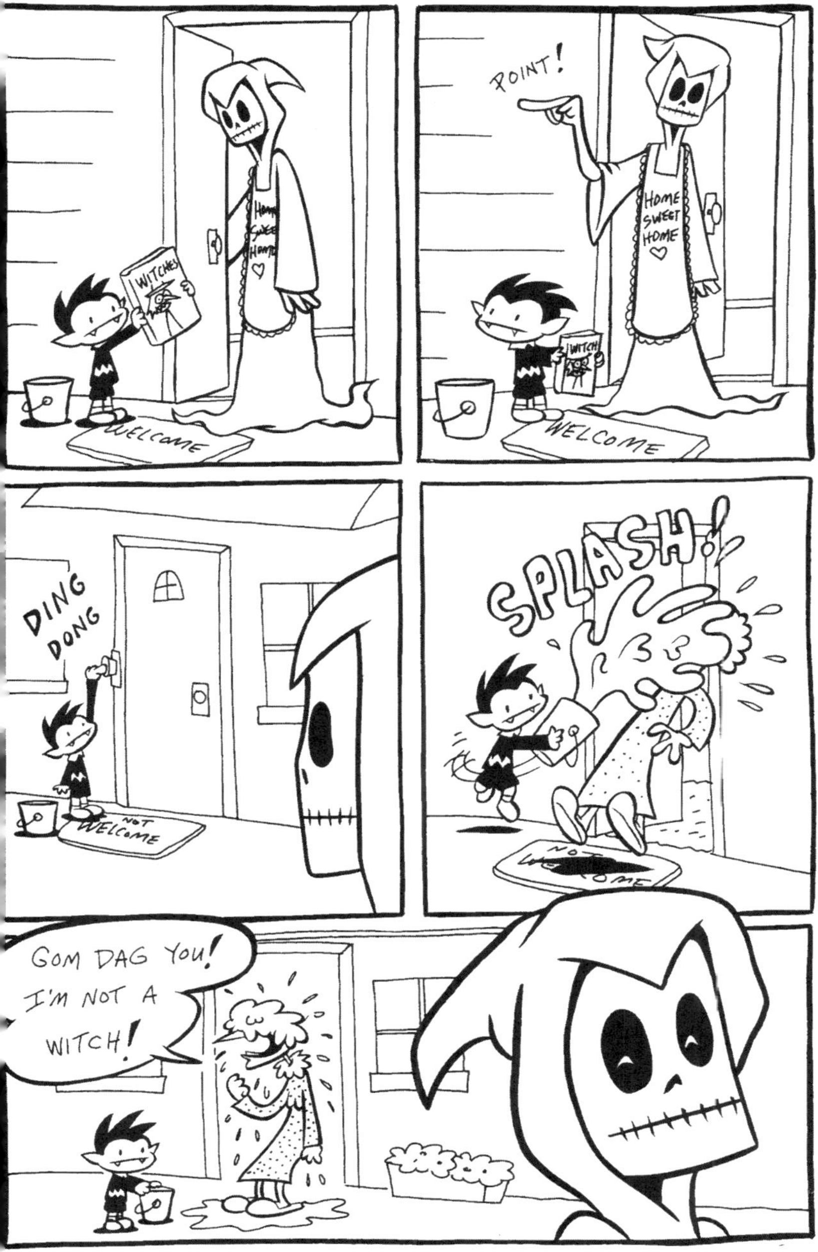

WITCHES
HOME SWEET HOME
WELCOME
POINT!
WITCH
HOME SWEET HOME
WELCOME
DING DONG
NOT WELCOME
SPLASH!
GOM DAG YOU! I'M NOT A WITCH!

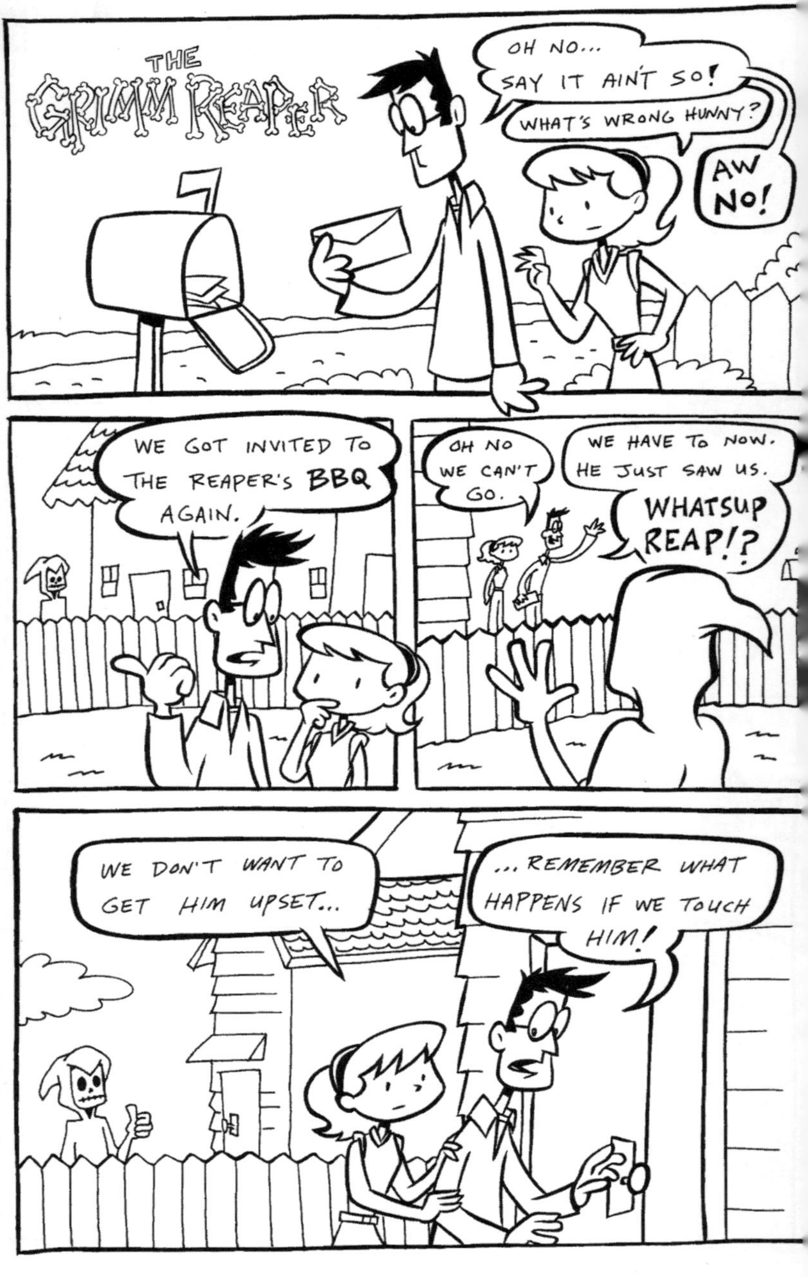
THE GRIMM REAPER
OH NO... SAY IT AIN'T SO!
WHAT'S WRONG HUNNY?
AW NO!
WE GOT INVITED TO THE REAPER'S BBQ AGAIN.
OH NO WE CAN'T GO.
WE HAVE TO NOW. HE JUST SAW US.
WHATSUP REAP!?
WE DON'T WANT TO GET HIM UPSET...
...REMEMBER WHAT HAPPENS IF WE TOUCH HIM!

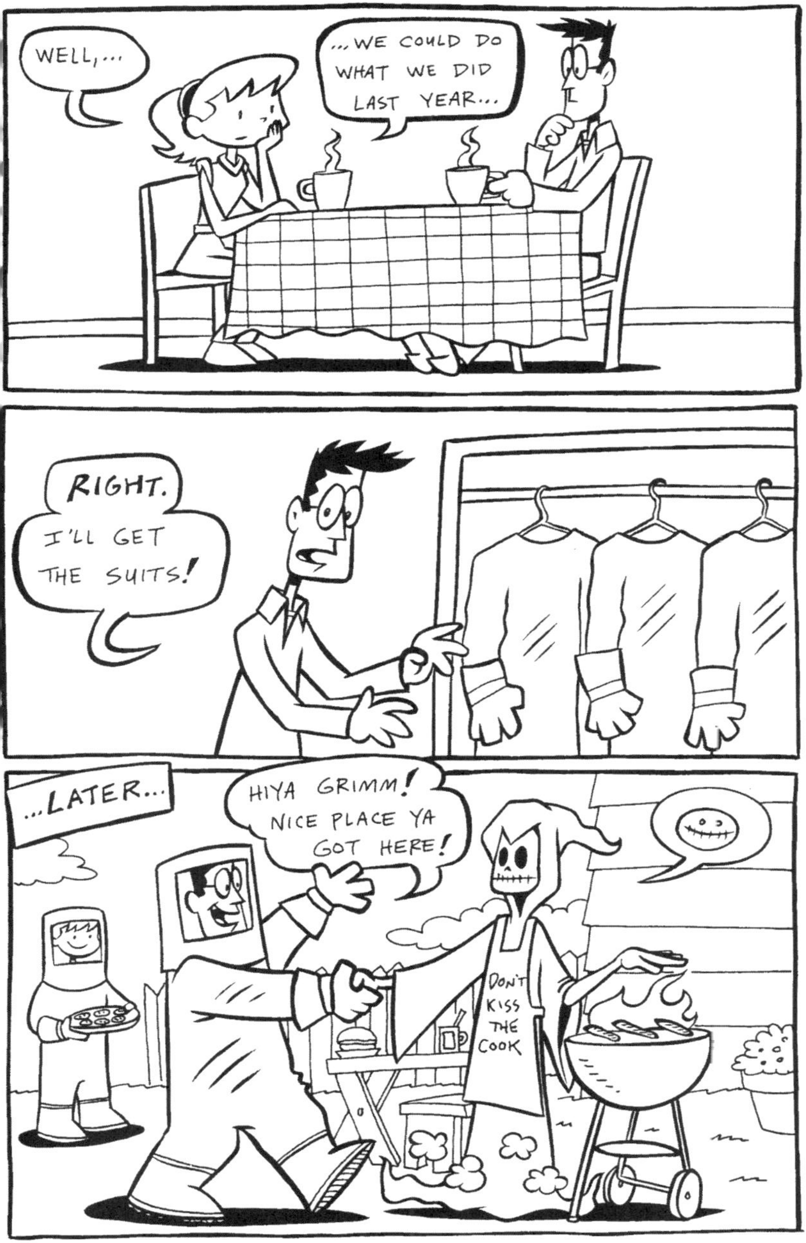
WELL,...
...WE COULD DO WHAT WE DID LAST YEAR...
RIGHT. I'LL GET THE SUITS!
...LATER...
HIYA GRIMM! NICE PLACE YA GOT HERE!
DON'T KISS THE COOK

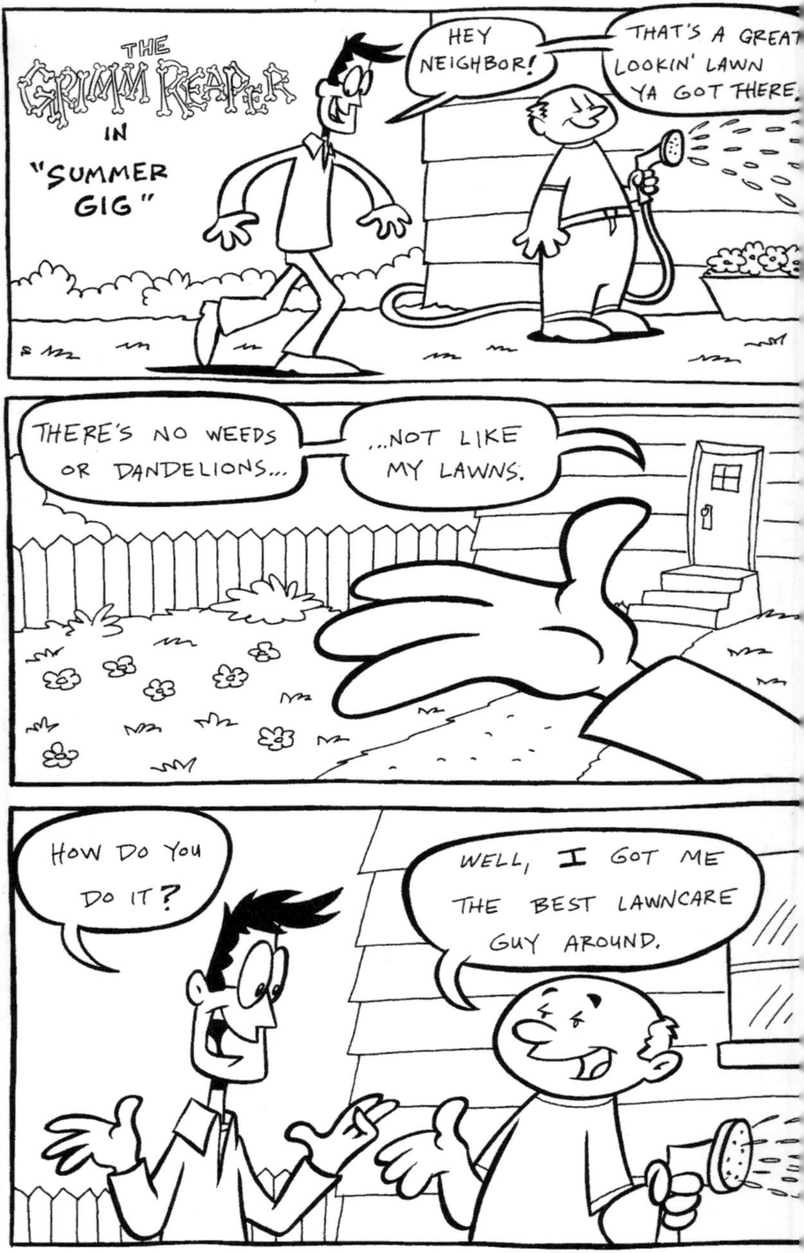
THE GRIMM REAPER IN "SUMMER GIG"
HEY NEIGHBOR!
THAT'S A GREAT LOOKIN' LAWN YA GOT THERE.
THERE'S NO WEEDS OR DANDELIONS...
...NOT LIKE MY LAWNS.
HOW DO YOU DO IT?
WELL, I GOT ME THE BEST LAWNCARE GUY AROUND.

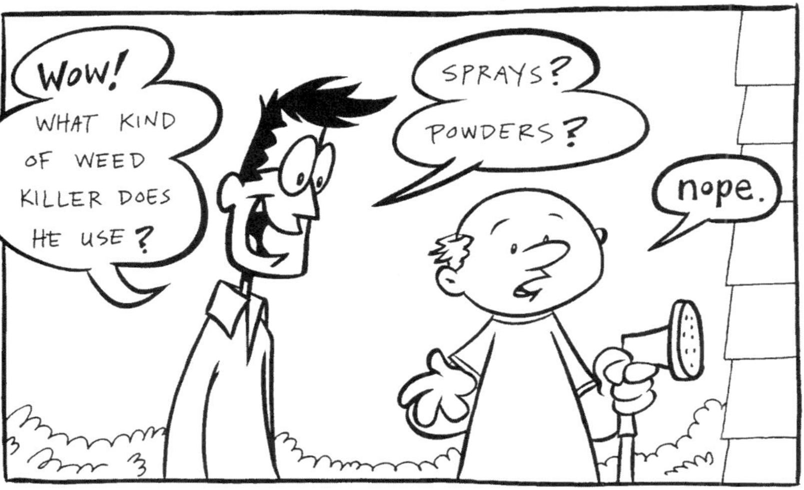
WOW! WHAT KIND OF WEED KILLER DOES HE USE?
SPRAYS? POWDERS?
nope.

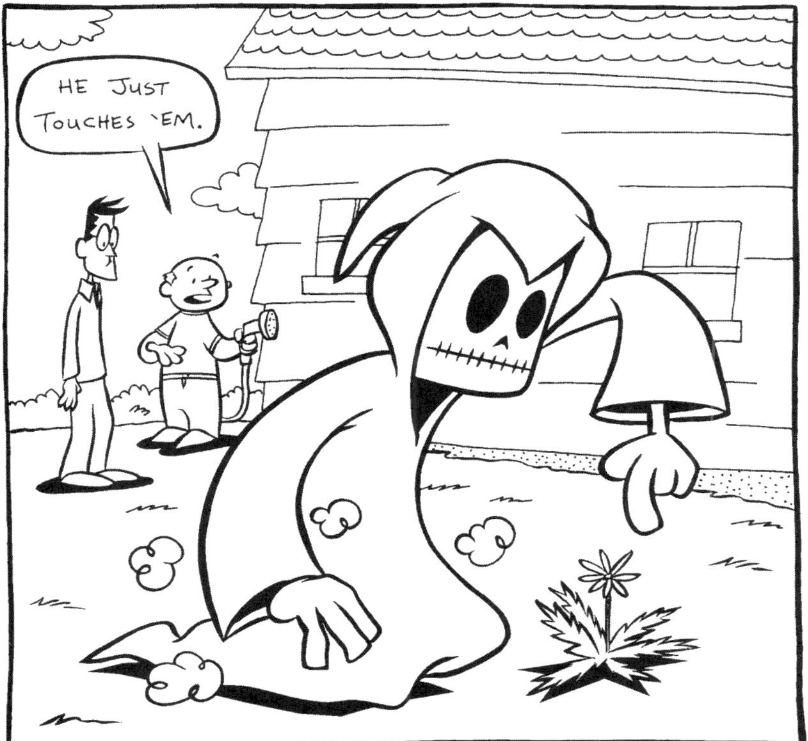
HE JUST TOUCHES 'EM.

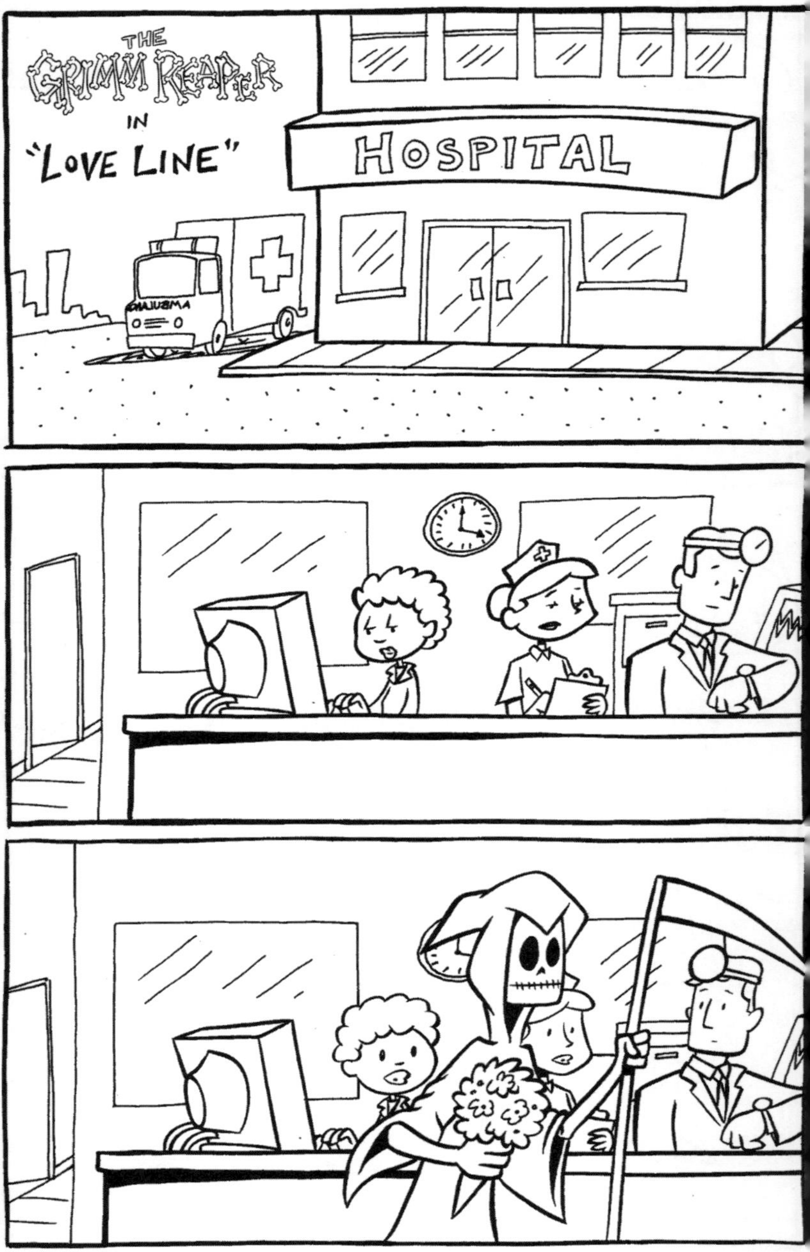
THE GRIMM REAPER IN "LOVE LINE"
HOSPITAL
AMBULANCE

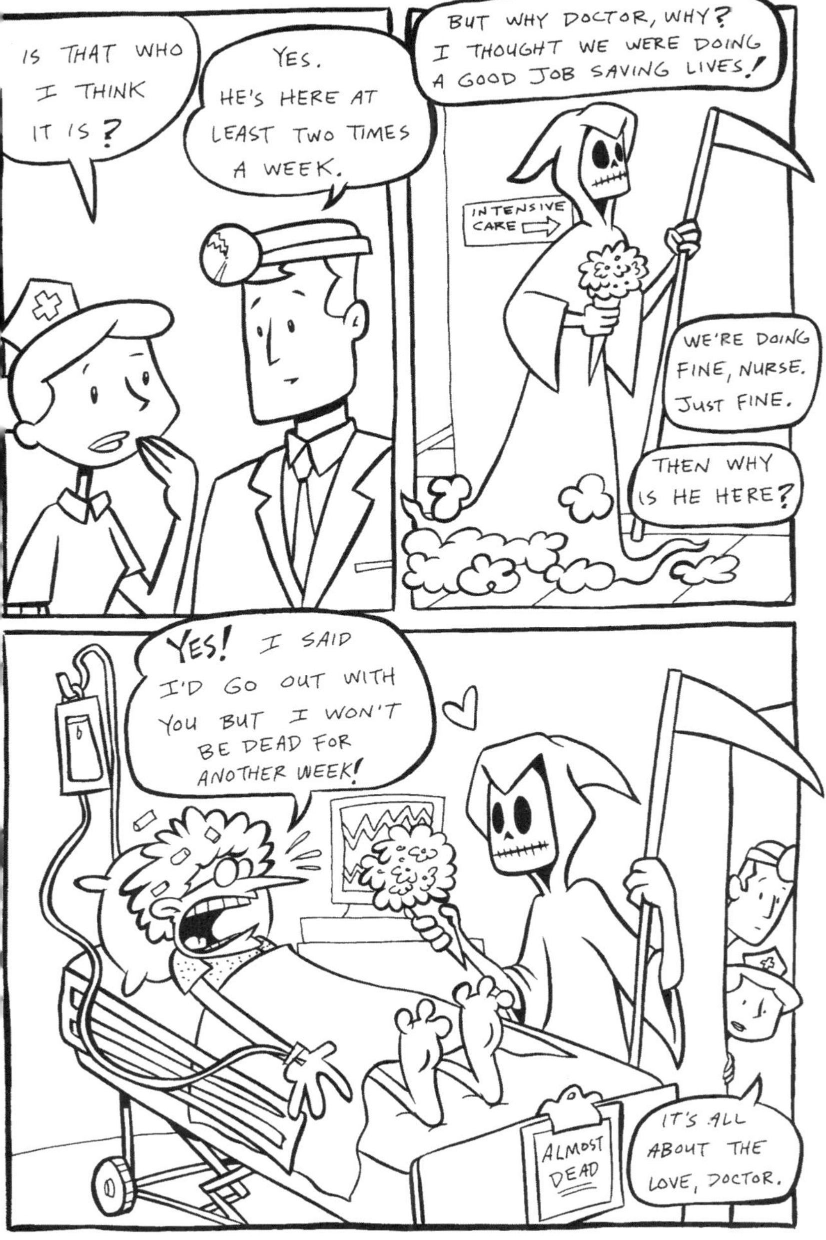
IS THAT WHO I THINK IT IS?
YES. HE'S HERE AT LEAST TWO TIMES A WEEK.
BUT WHY DOCTOR, WHY? I THOUGHT WE WERE DOING A GOOD JOB SAVING LIVES!
INTENSIVE CARE
WE'RE DOING FINE, NURSE. JUST FINE.
THEN WHY IS HE HERE?
YES! I SAID I'D GO OUT WITH YOU BUT I WON'T BE DEAD FOR ANOTHER WEEK!
ALMOST DEAD
IT'S ALL ABOUT THE LOVE, DOCTOR.

AND NOW...

BRAND NEW NEVER-BEFORE-SEEN

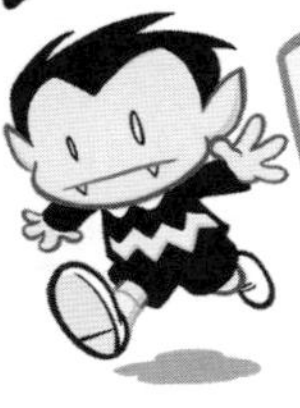

PATRICK THE WOLF BOY

COMICS!

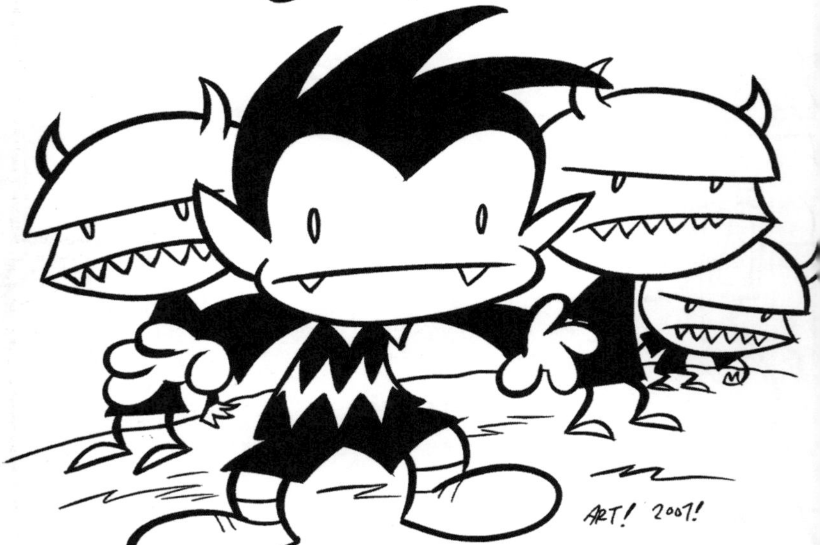
ART! 2007!

BY ART & FRANCO!

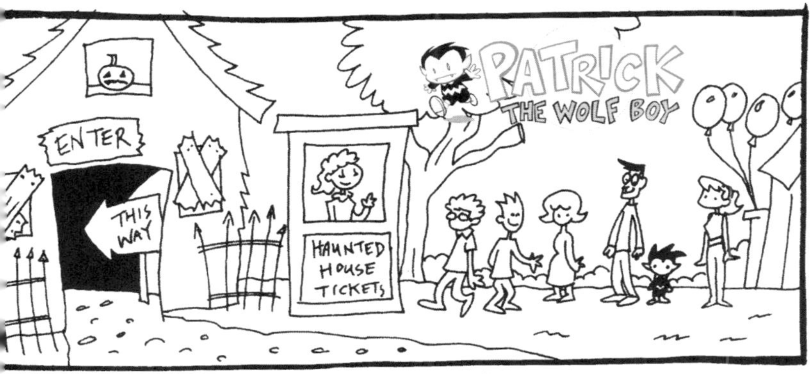
ENTER
THIS WAY
HAUNTED HOUSE TICKETS
PATRICK THE WOLF BOY

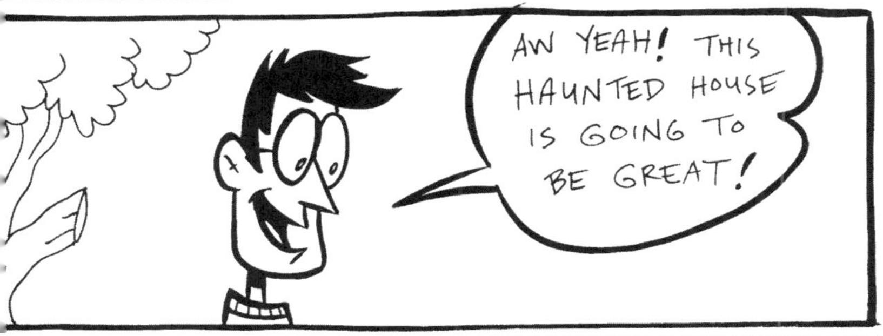
AW YEAH! THIS HAUNTED HOUSE IS GOING TO BE GREAT!

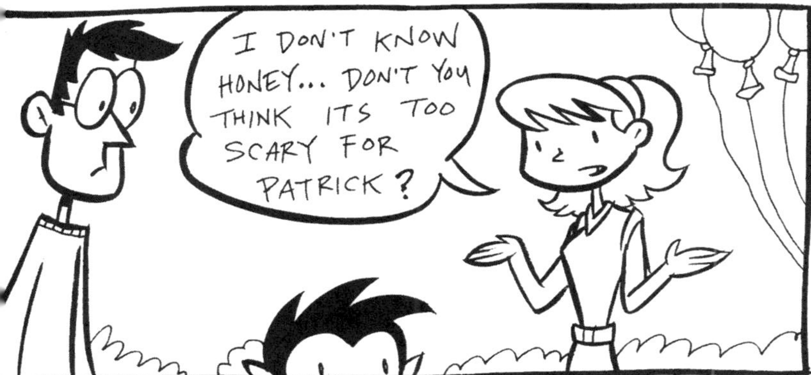
I DON'T KNOW HONEY... DON'T YOU THINK ITS TOO SCARY FOR PATRICK?

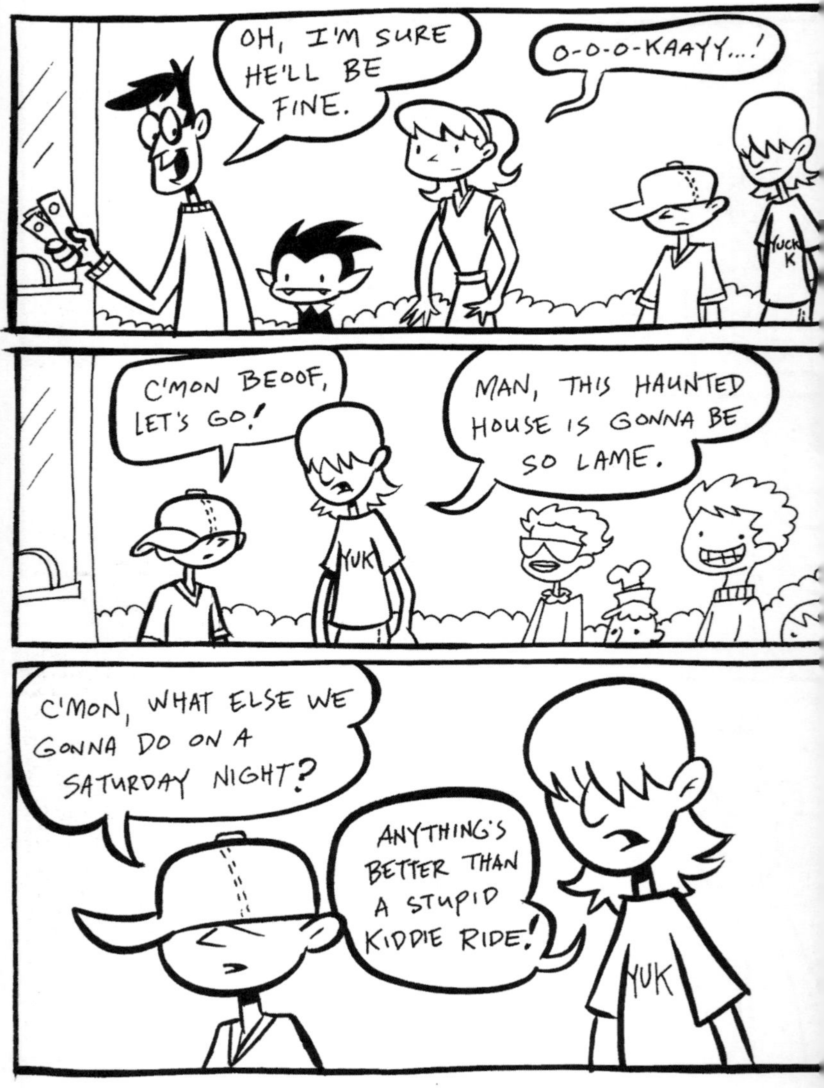

OH, I'M SURE HE'LL BE FINE.
O-O-O-KAAYY...!
YUCK
C'MON BEOOF, LET'S GO!
MAN, THIS HAUNTED HOUSE IS GONNA BE SO LAME.
YUK
C'MON, WHAT ELSE WE GONNA DO ON A SATURDAY NIGHT?
ANYTHING'S BETTER THAN A STUPID KIDDIE RIDE!
YUK

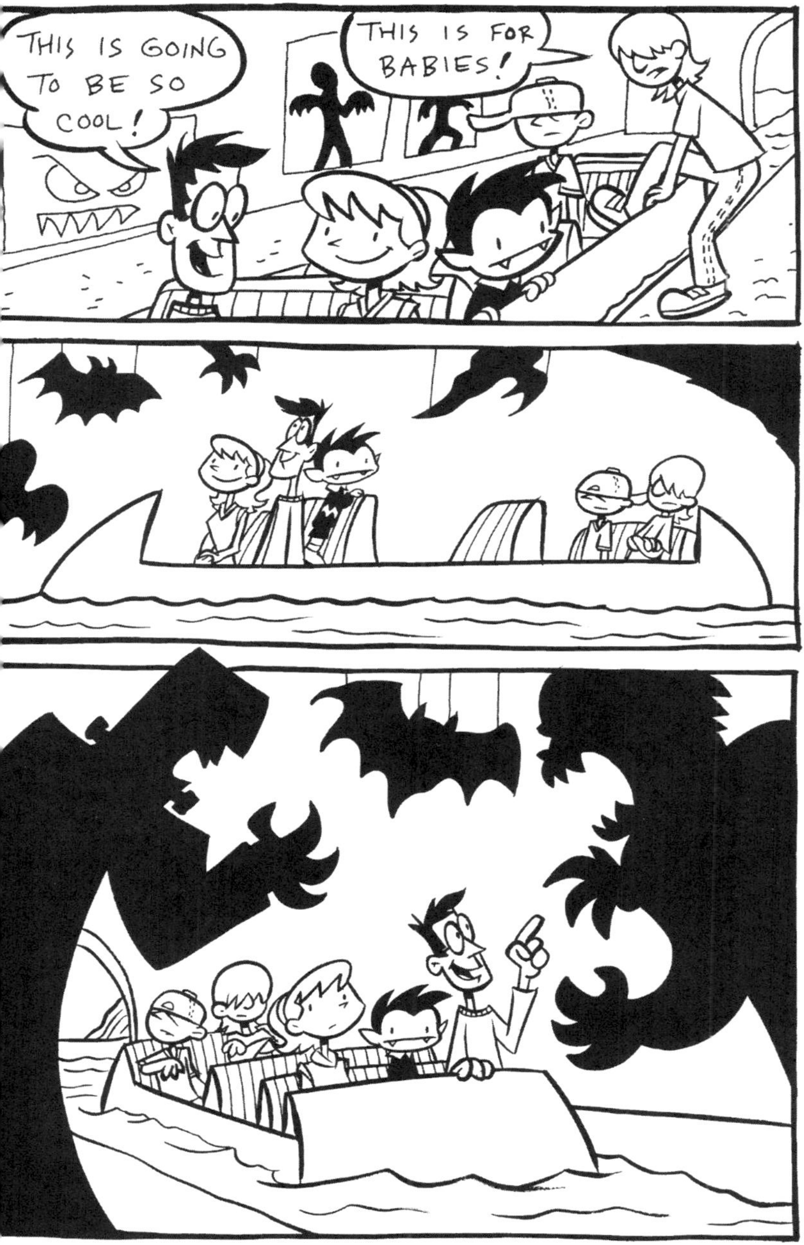
THIS IS GOING TO BE SO COOL!
THIS IS FOR BABIES!

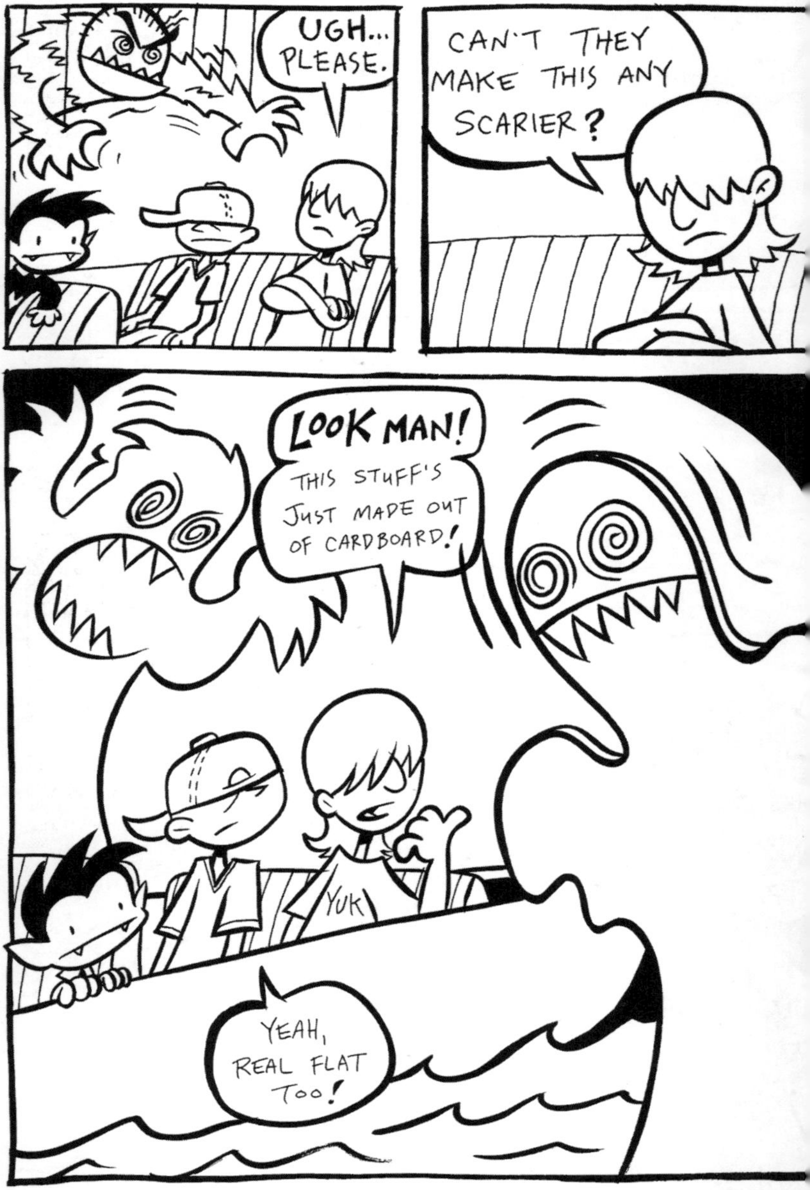
UGH... PLEASE.
CAN'T THEY MAKE THIS ANY SCARIER?
LOOK MAN! THIS STUFF'S JUST MADE OUT OF CARDBOARD!
YUK
YEAH, REAL FLAT TOO!

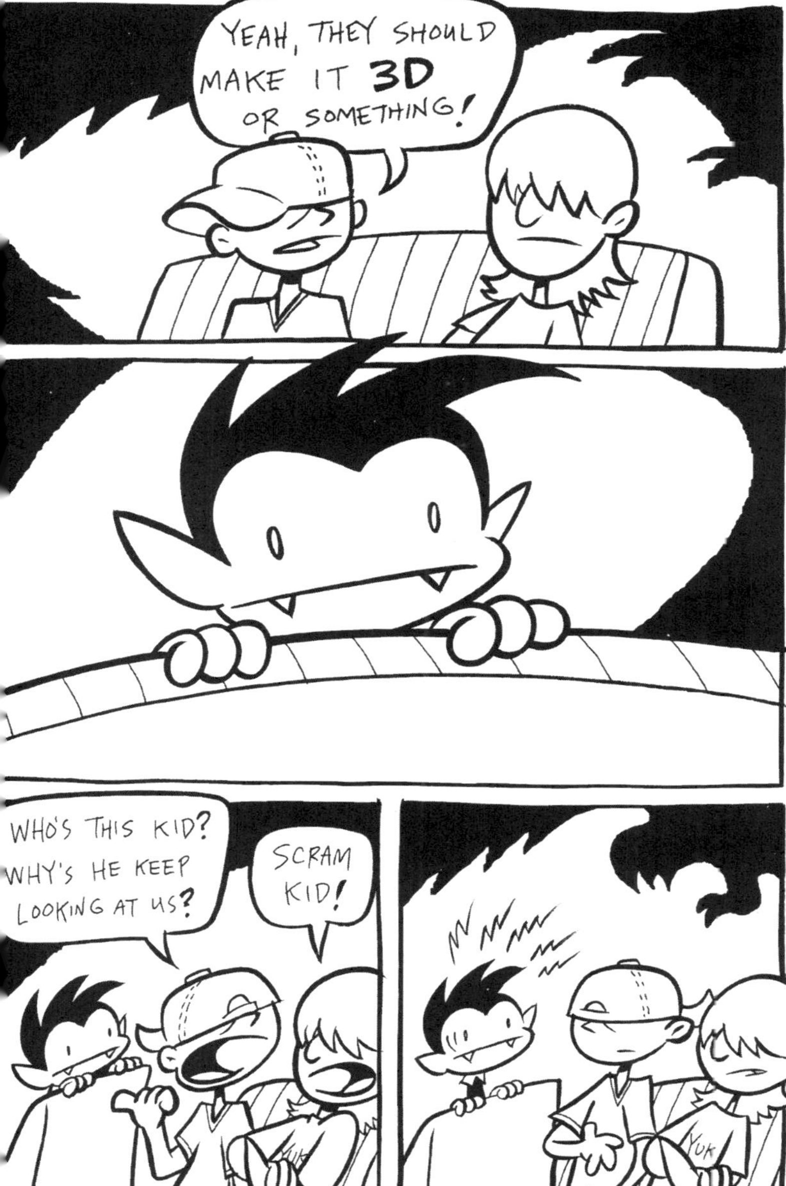
YEAH, THEY SHOULD MAKE IT 3D OR SOMETHING!
WHO'S THIS KID? WHY'S HE KEEP LOOKING AT US?
SCRAM KID!
YUK

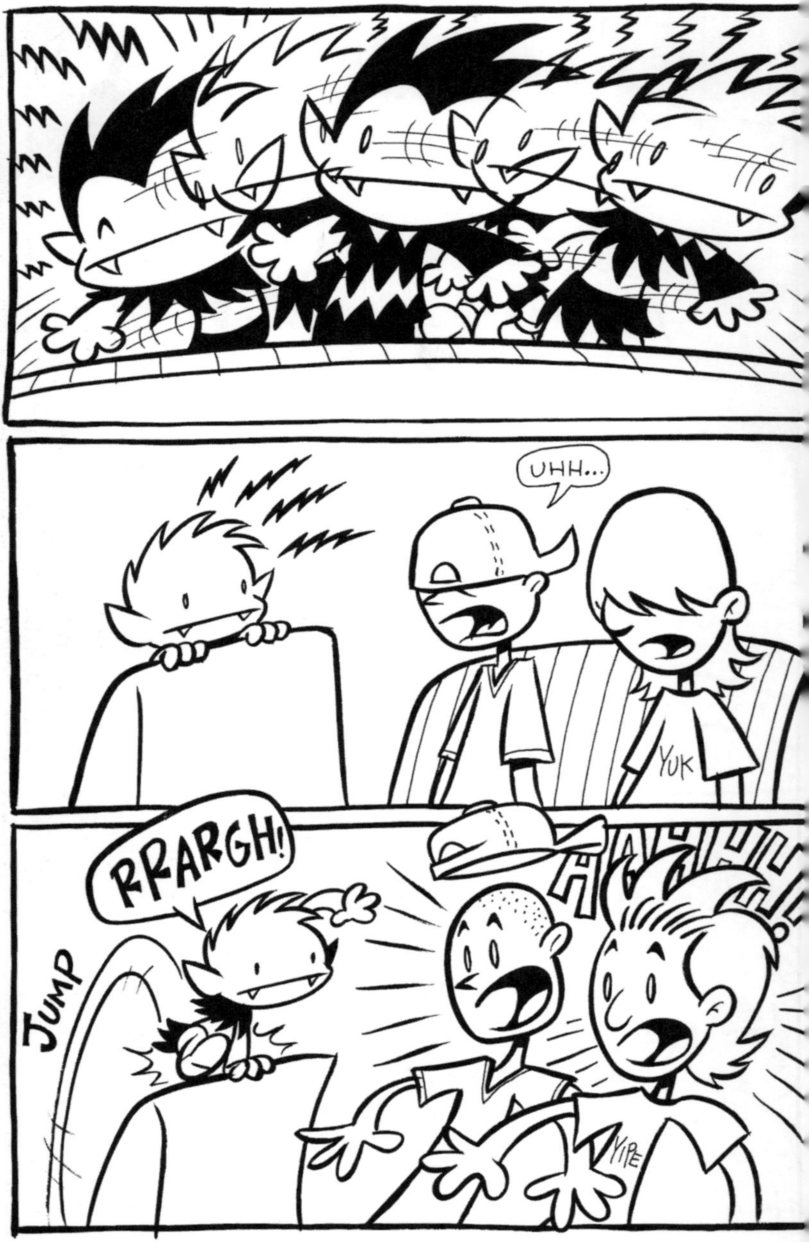
UHH...
YUK
RRARGH!
JUMP
YIPE

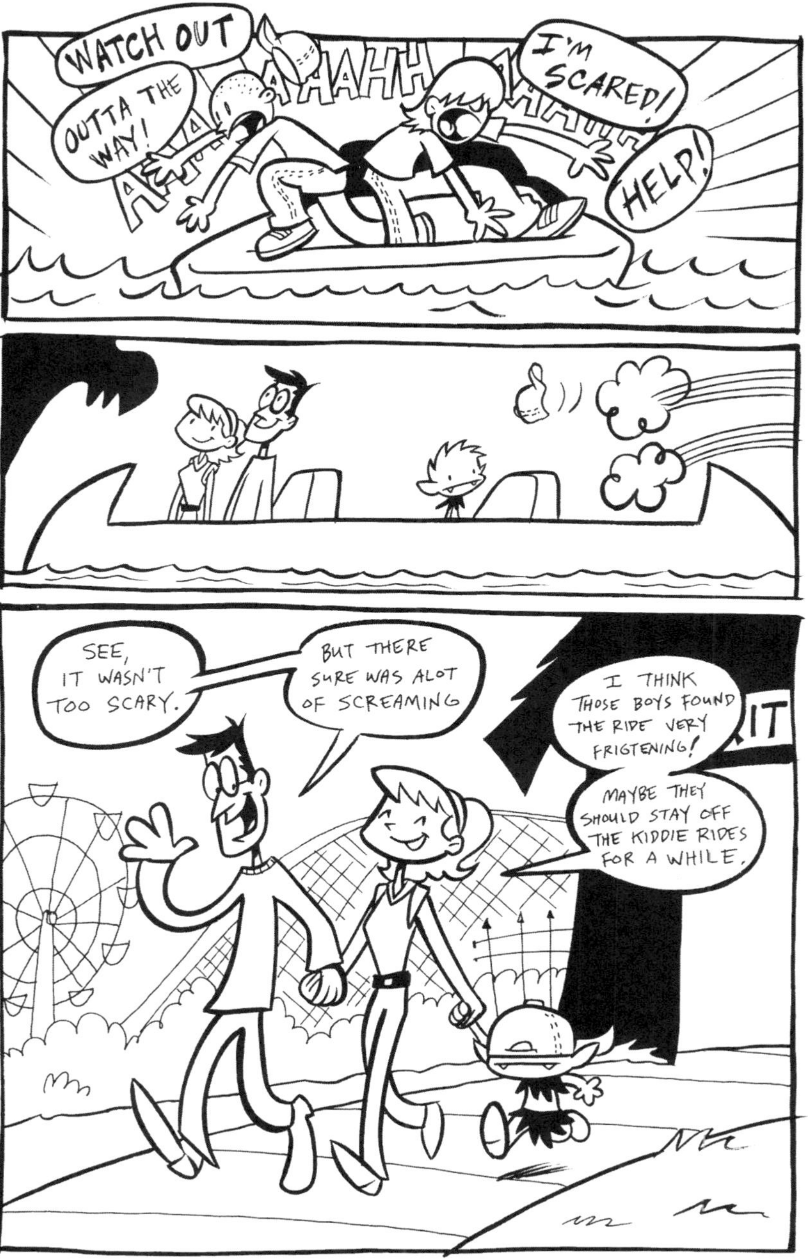
WATCH OUT
OUTTA THE WAY!
AAAHHH
I'M SCARED!
HELP!
SEE, IT WASN'T TOO SCARY.
BUT THERE SURE WAS ALOT OF SCREAMING
I THINK THOSE BOYS FOUND THE RIDE VERY FRIGTENING!
MAYBE THEY SHOULD STAY OFF THE KIDDIE RIDES FOR A WHILE.

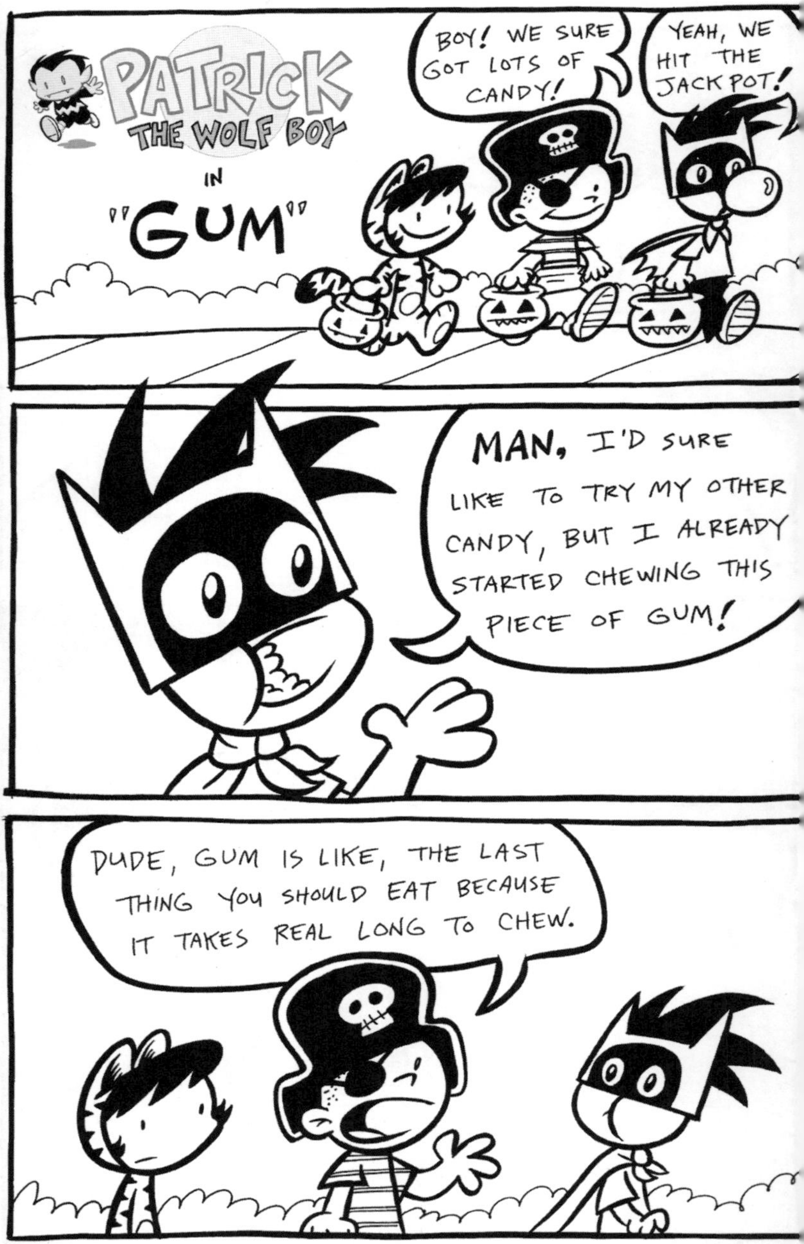
PATRICK THE WOLF BOY
IN
"GUM"
BOY! WE SURE GOT LOTS OF CANDY!
YEAH, WE HIT THE JACKPOT!
MAN, I'D SURE LIKE TO TRY MY OTHER CANDY, BUT I ALREADY STARTED CHEWING THIS PIECE OF GUM!
DUDE, GUM IS LIKE, THE LAST THING YOU SHOULD EAT BECAUSE IT TAKES REAL LONG TO CHEW.

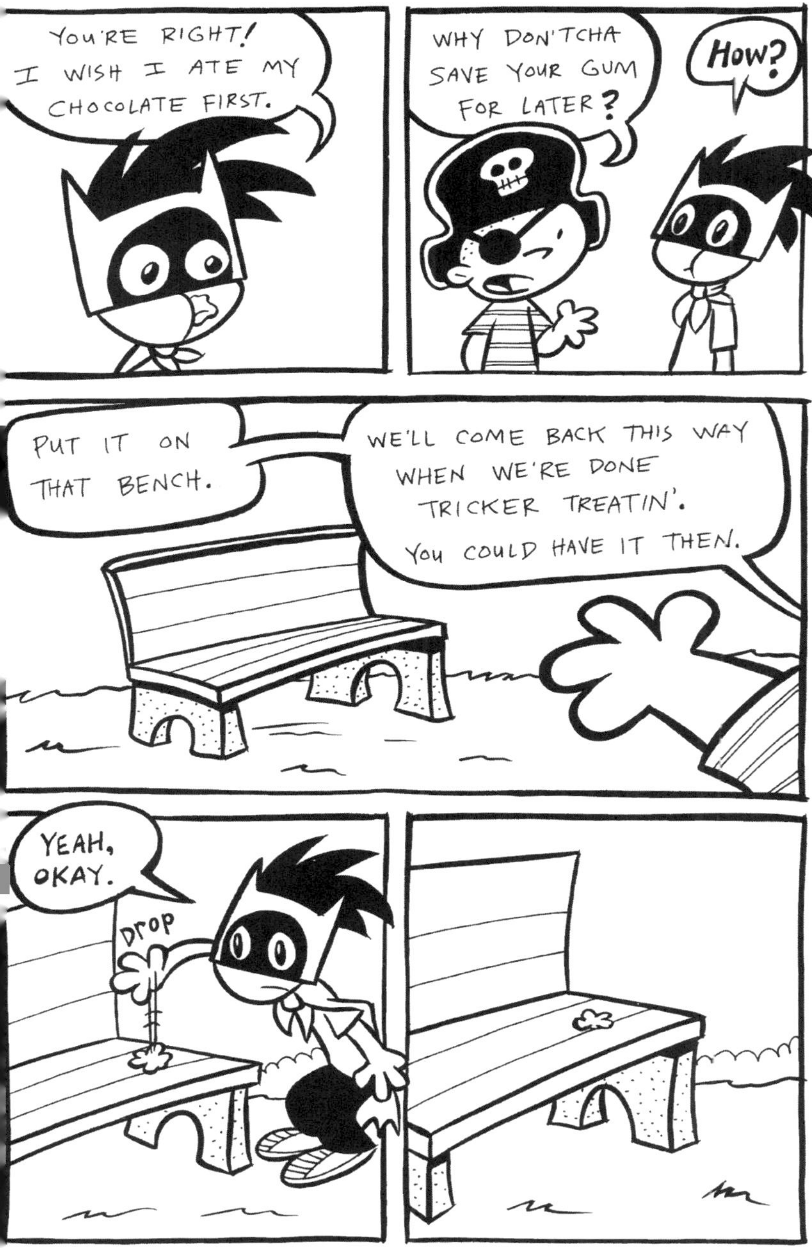
YOU'RE RIGHT! I WISH I ATE MY CHOCOLATE FIRST.
WHY DON'TCHA SAVE YOUR GUM FOR LATER?
How?
PUT IT ON THAT BENCH.
WE'LL COME BACK THIS WAY WHEN WE'RE DONE TRICKER TREATIN'. YOU COULD HAVE IT THEN.
YEAH, OKAY.
Drop

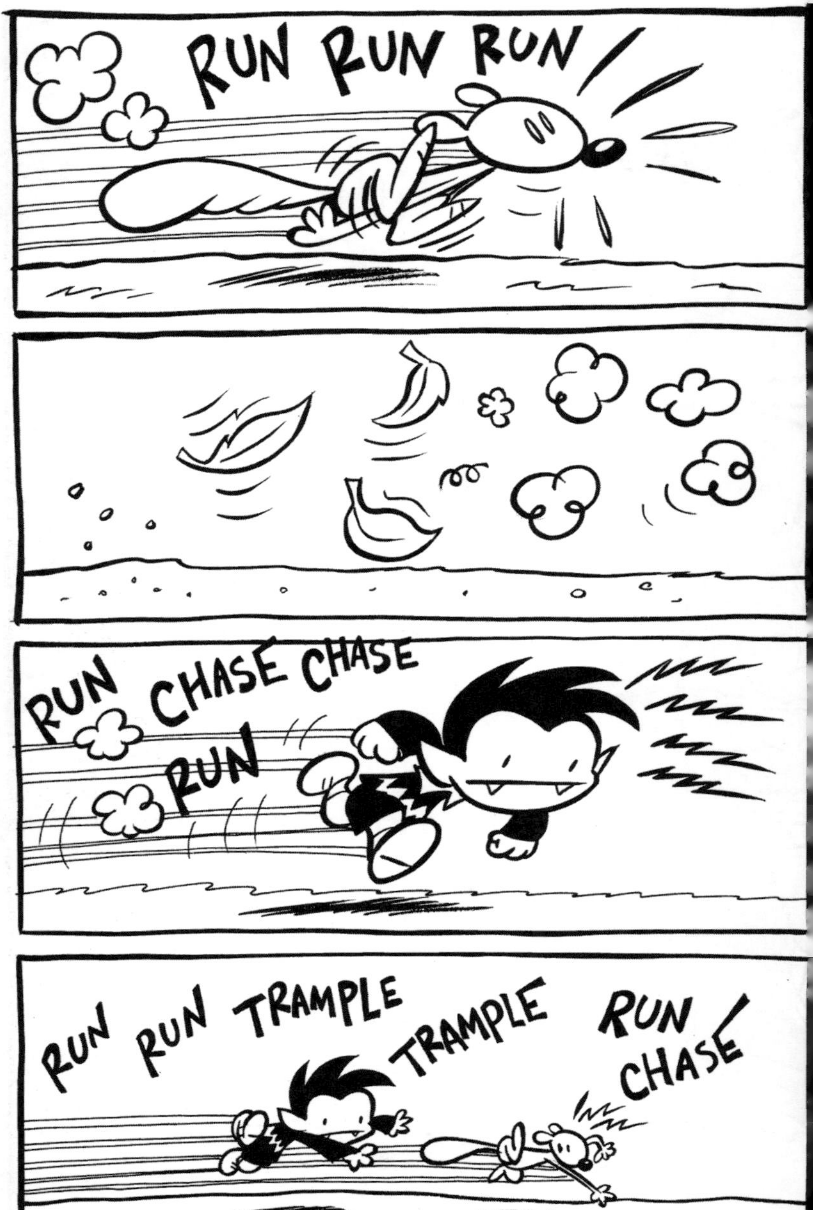
RUN RUN RUN
RUN CHASE CHASE
RUN
RUN RUN TRAMPLE
TRAMPLE RUN
CHASE

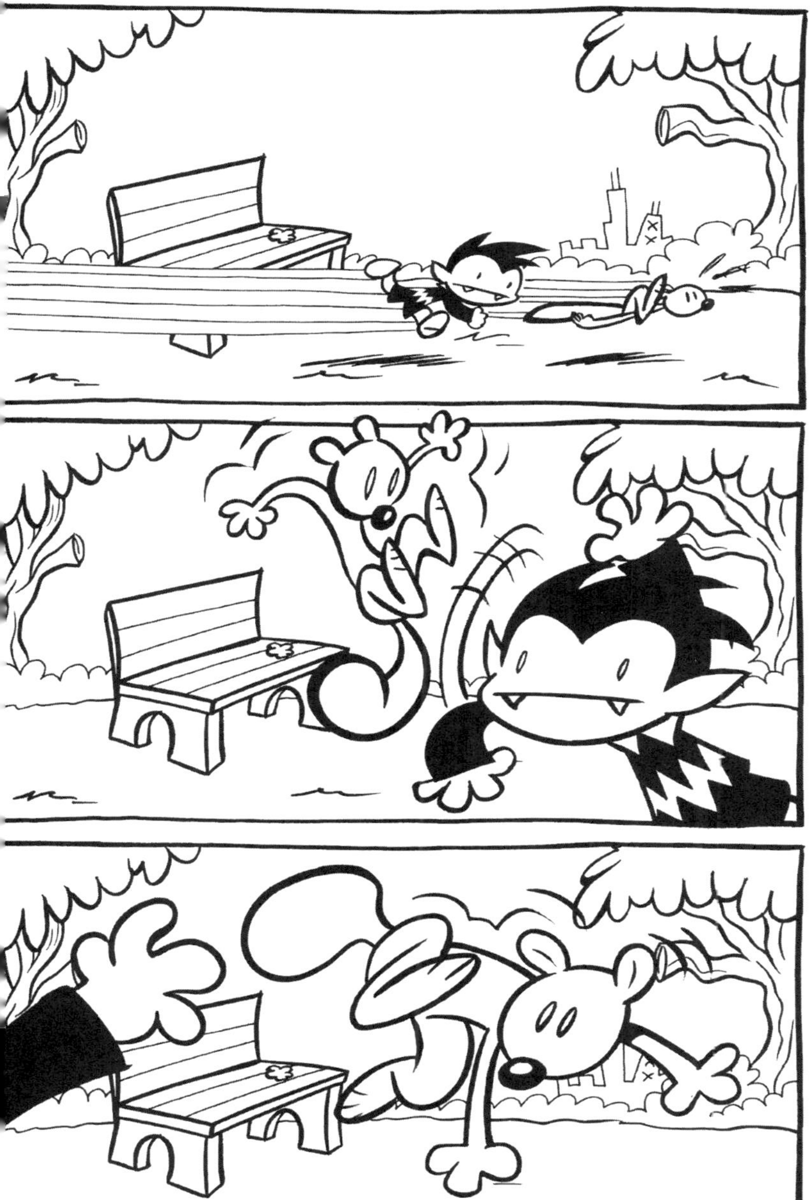

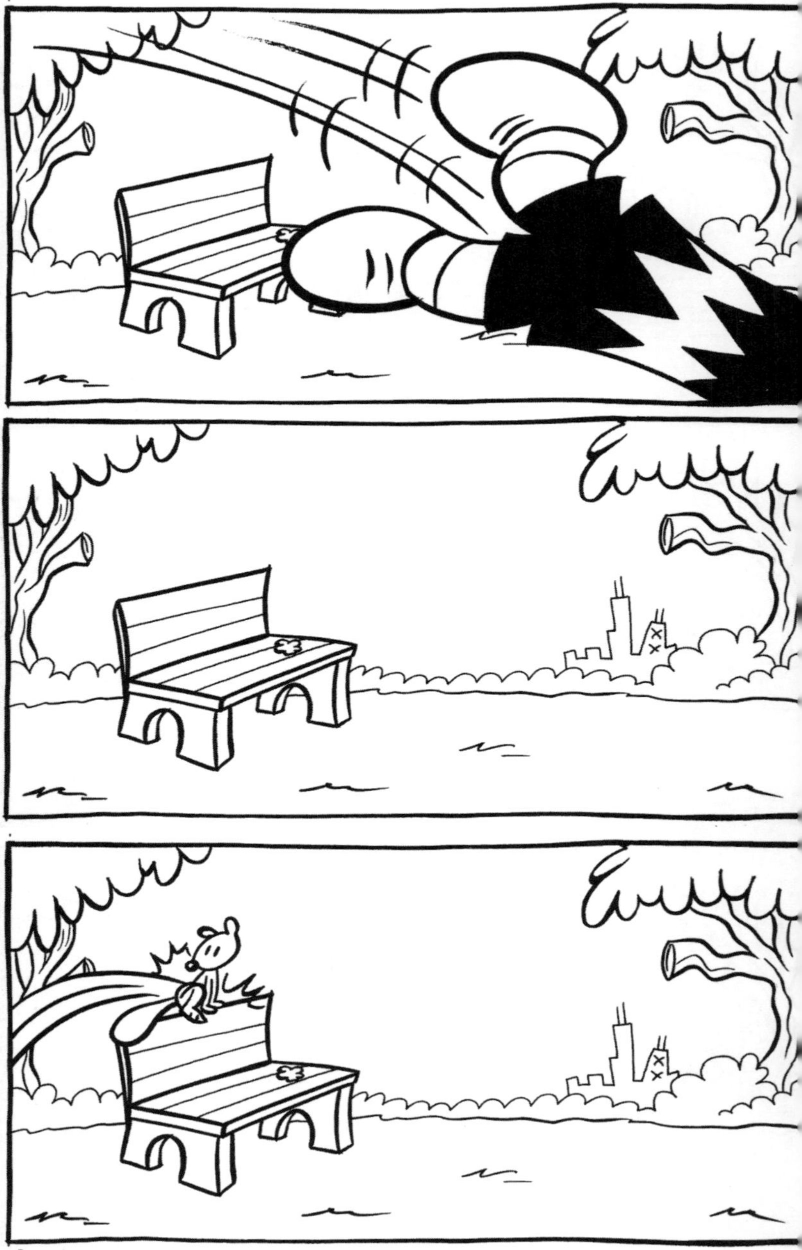

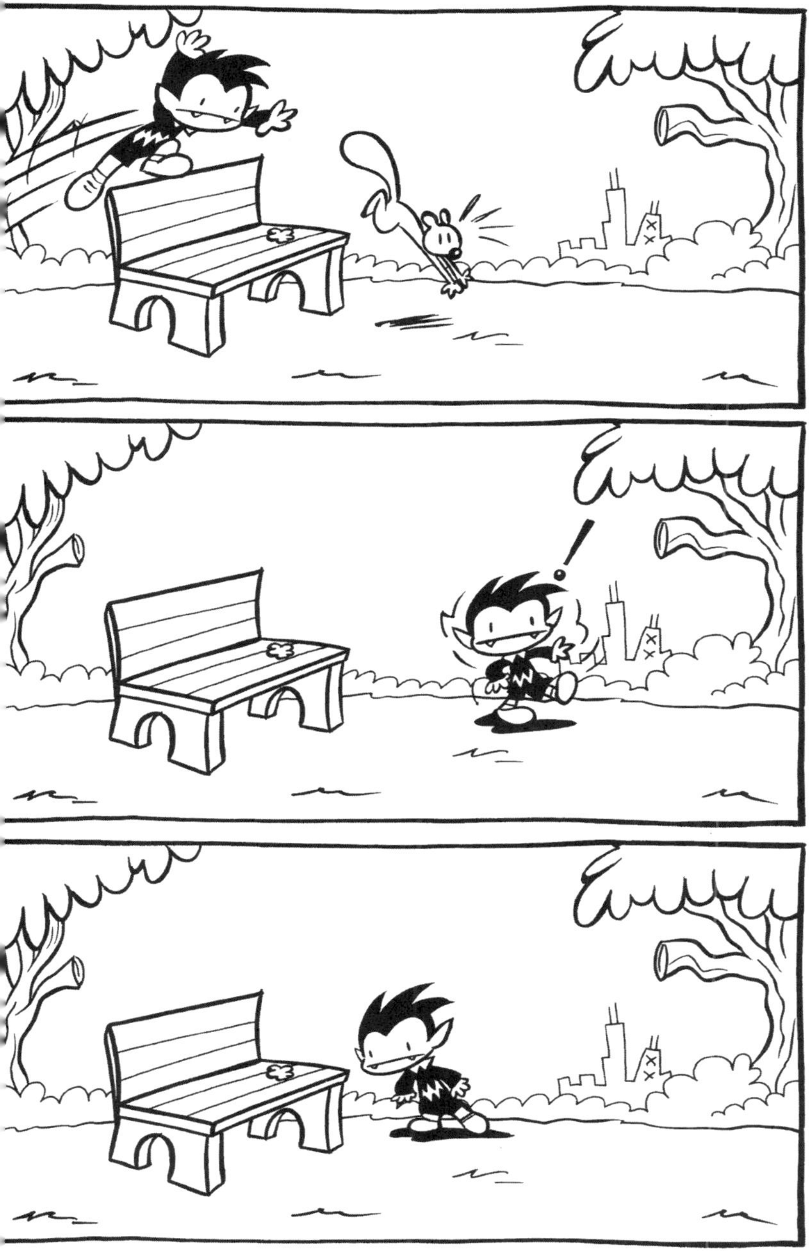

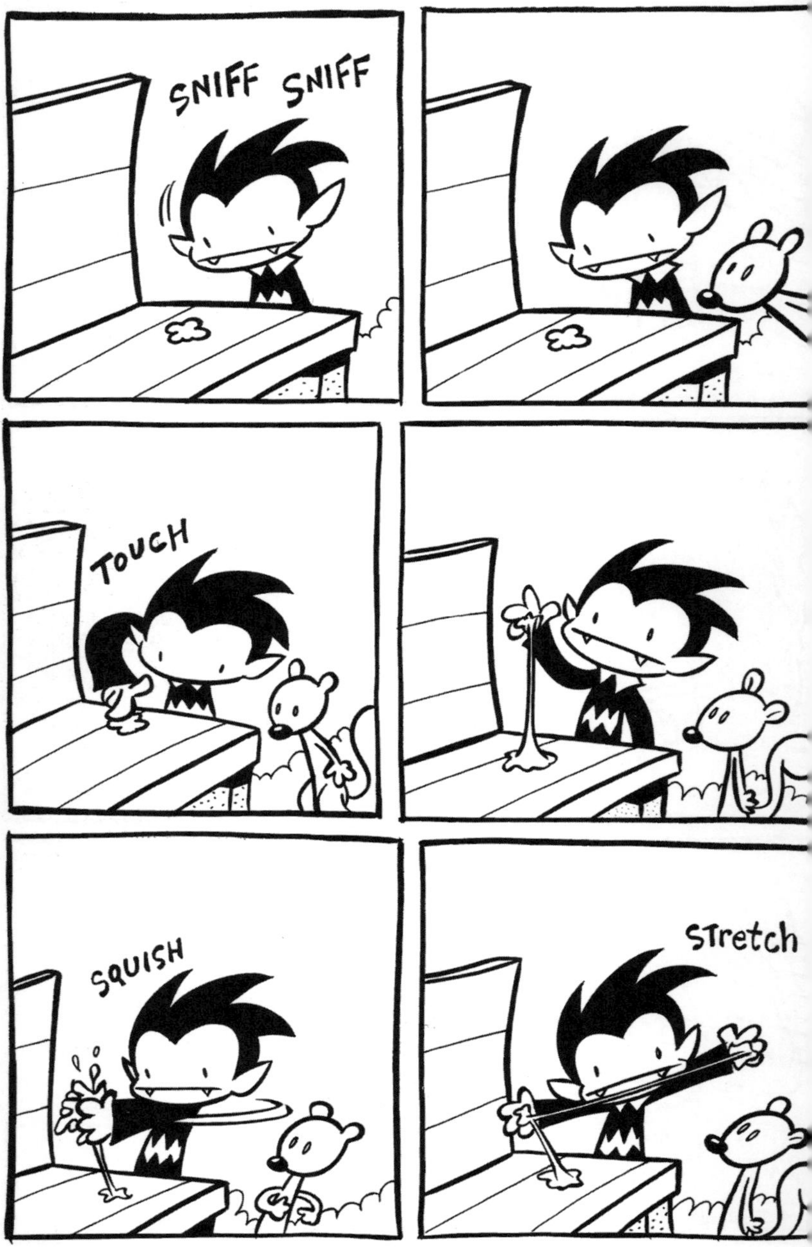
SNIFF SNIFF
TOUCH
SQUISH
STretch

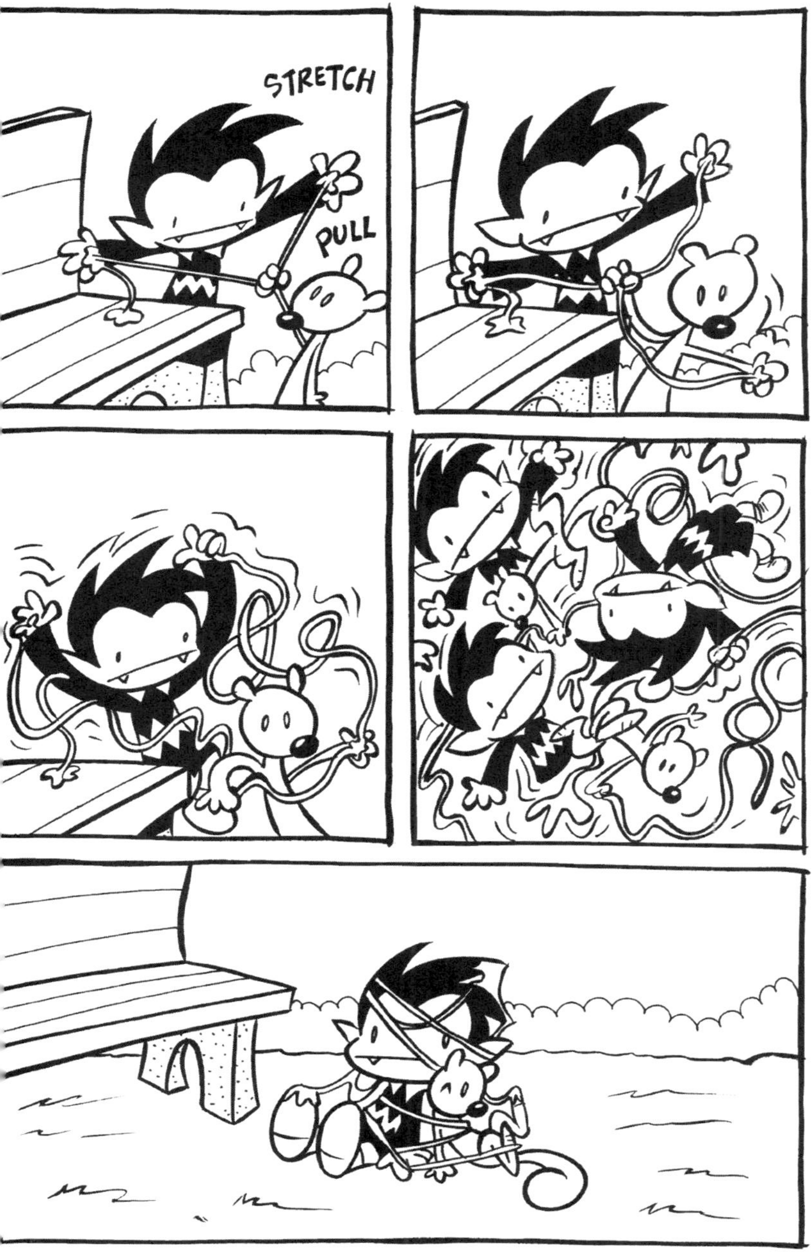
STRETCH
PULL

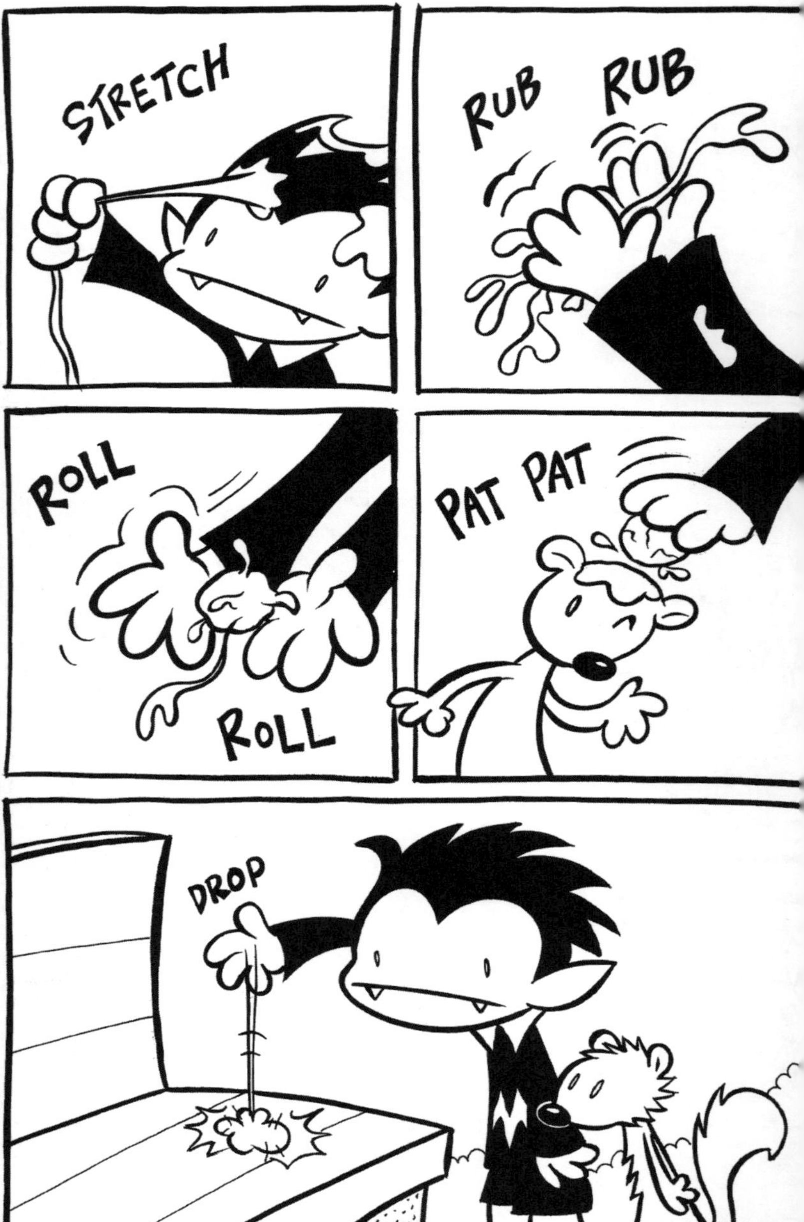
STRETCH
RUB RUB
ROLL
ROLL
PAT PAT
DROP

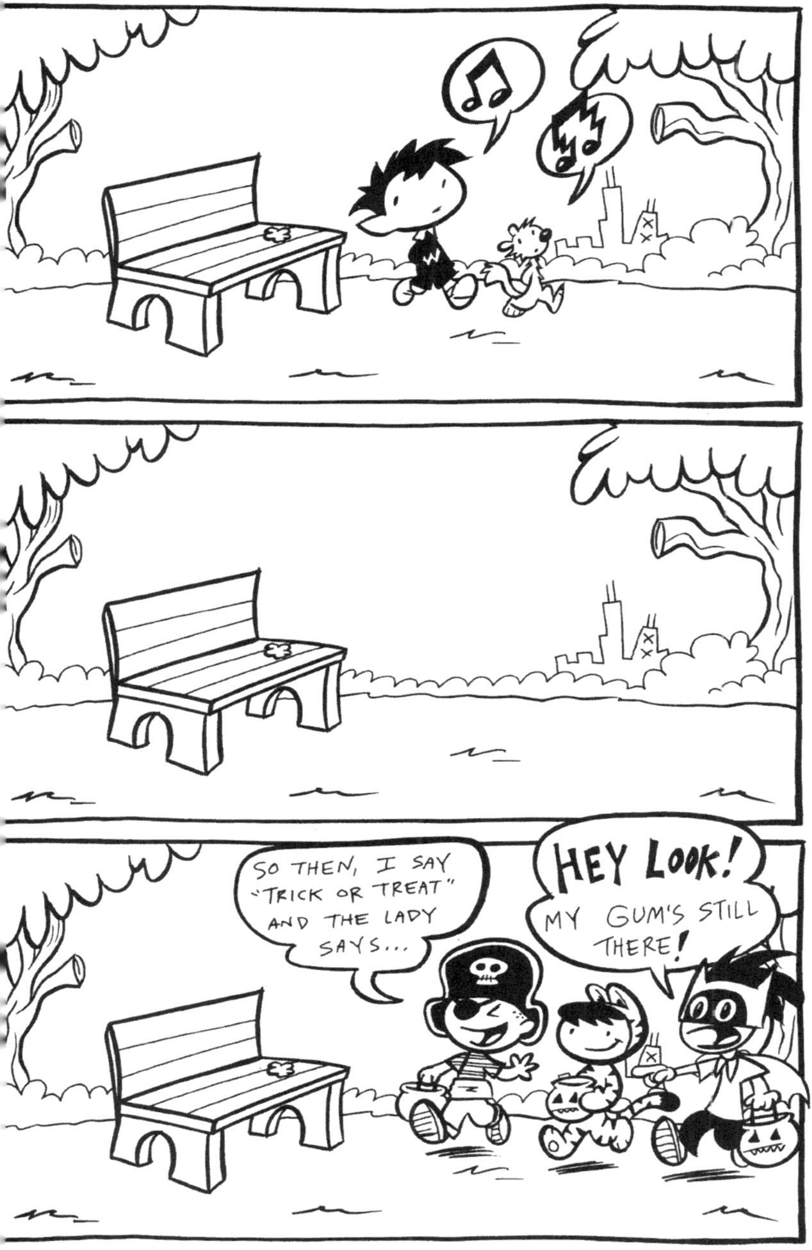
SO THEN, I SAY "TRICK OR TREAT" AND THE LADY SAYS...
HEY LOOK! MY GUM'S STILL THERE!

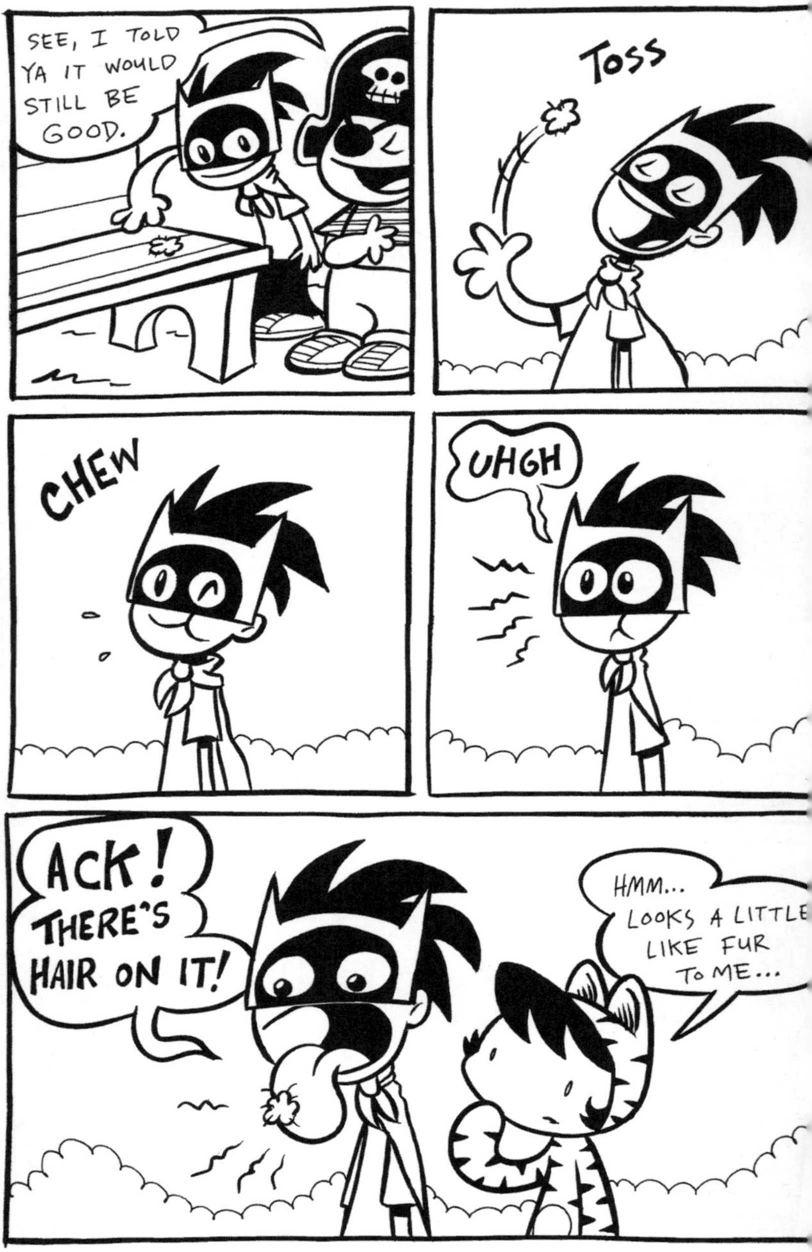
SEE, I TOLD YA IT WOULD STILL BE GOOD.
TOSS
CHEW
UHGH
ACK! THERE'S HAIR ON IT!
HMM... LOOKS A LITTLE LIKE FUR TO ME...

PATRICK THE WOLF BOY

BY ART BALTAZAR & FRANCO

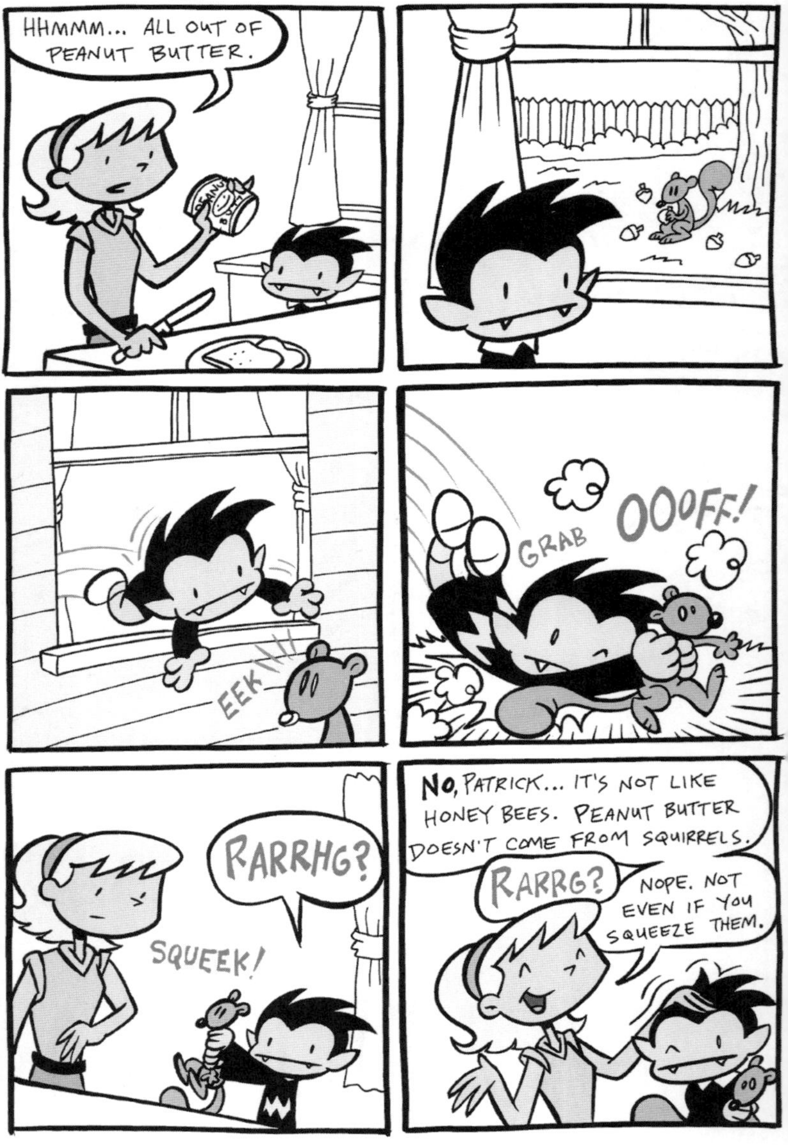
HHMMM... ALL OUT OF PEANUT BUTTER.
EEK
GRAB
OOOFF!
RARRHG?
SQUEEK!
NO, PATRICK... IT'S NOT LIKE HONEY BEES. PEANUT BUTTER DOESN'T COME FROM SQUIRRELS.
RARRG?
NOPE. NOT EVEN IF YOU SQUEEZE THEM.

PATRICK THE WOLF BOY

BY ART BALTAZAR & FRANCO

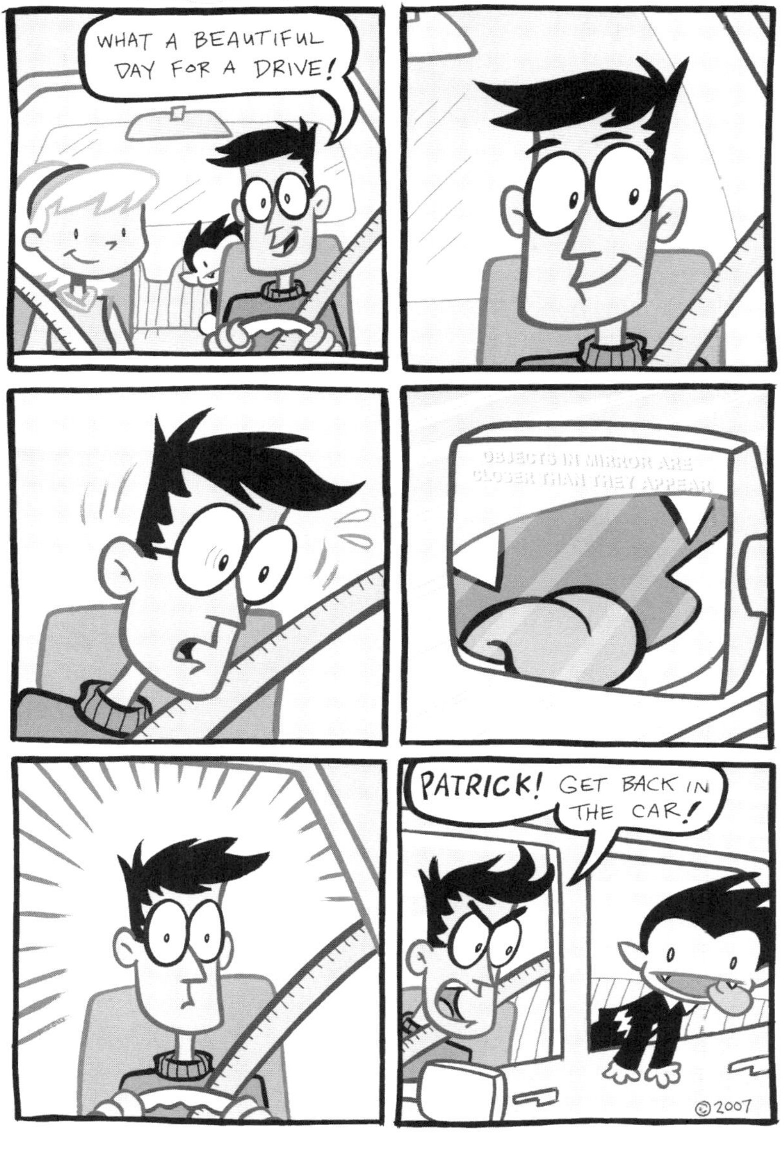
WHAT A BEAUTIFUL DAY FOR A DRIVE!
OBJECTS IN MIRROR ARE CLOSER THAN THEY APPEAR
PATRICK! GET BACK IN THE CAR!
©2007

PATRICK THE WOLF BOY

BY ART BALTAZAR & FRANCO

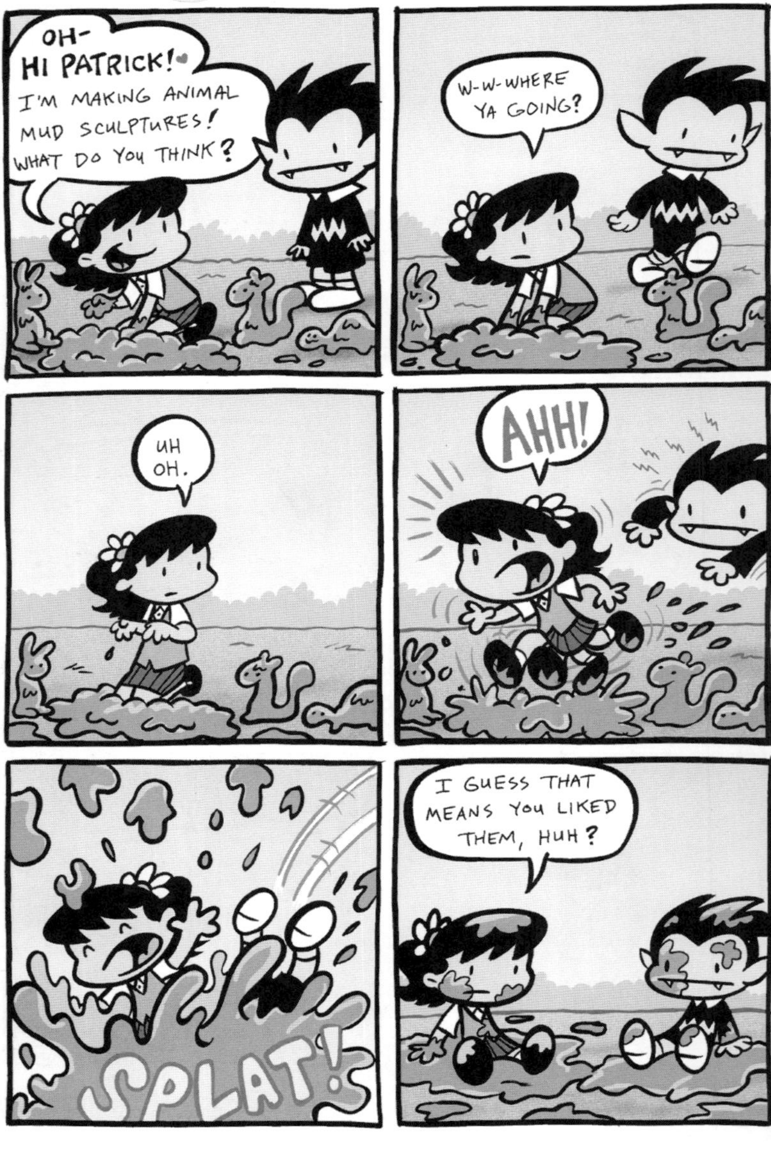
OH-
HI PATRICK!
I'M MAKING ANIMAL MUD SCULPTURES! WHAT DO YOU THINK?
W-W-WHERE YA GOING?
UH OH.
AHH!
SPLAT!
I GUESS THAT MEANS YOU LIKED THEM, HUH?

PATRICK THE WOLF BOY
BY ART BALTAZAR & FRANCO
YES, TEACHER I DID MY HOMEWORK!
I WROTE ABOUT THE BIG CAKE MY MOM MADE FOR MY BIRTHDAY!
I EVEN DREW A NICE COVER WITH CRAYONS AND EVERYTHING!
BUT... BUT... I DON'T HAVE IT ANYMORE... SORRY.
NEVE, ARE YOU TRYING TO TELL ME "YOUR DOG ATE YOUR HOMEWORK"?
NO!
PATRICK DID!
©2007

PATRICK THE WOLF BOY

BY ART BALTAZAR & FRANCO

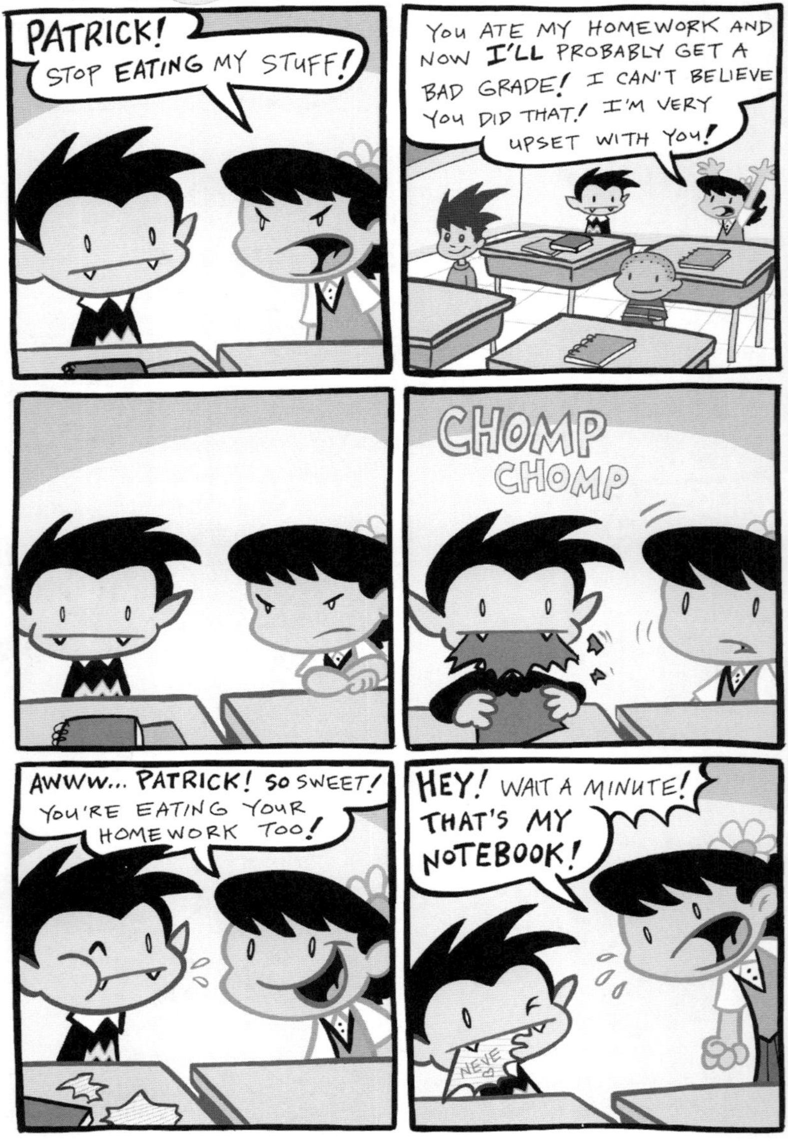
PATRICK!
STOP EATING MY STUFF!
YOU ATE MY HOMEWORK AND NOW I'LL PROBABLY GET A BAD GRADE! I CAN'T BELIEVE YOU DID THAT! I'M VERY UPSET WITH YOU!
CHOMP
CHOMP
AWWW... PATRICK! SO SWEET! YOU'RE EATING YOUR HOMEWORK TOO!
HEY! WAIT A MINUTE!
THAT'S MY NOTEBOOK!
NEVE

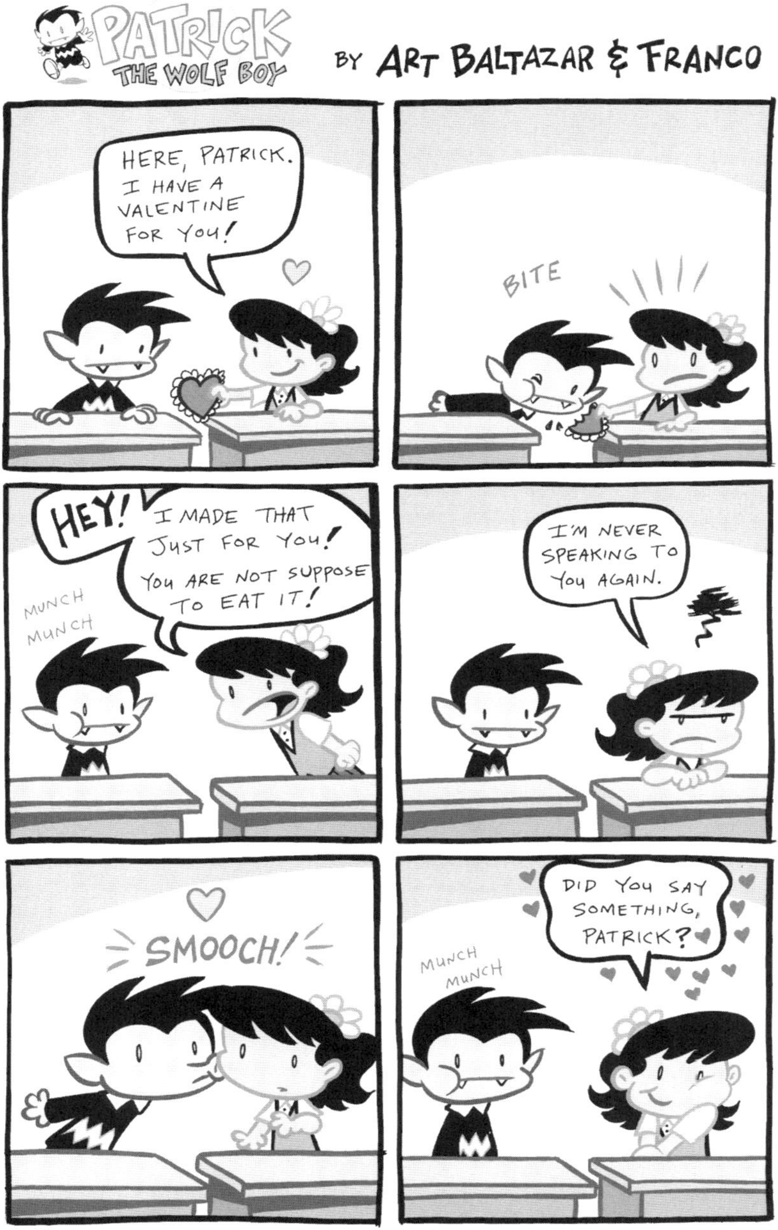
PATRICK THE WOLF BOY
BY ART BALTAZAR & FRANCO
HERE, PATRICK. I HAVE A VALENTINE FOR YOU!
BITE
HEY!
I MADE THAT JUST FOR YOU! YOU ARE NOT SUPPOSE TO EAT IT!
MUNCH MUNCH
I'M NEVER SPEAKING TO YOU AGAIN.
SMOOCH!
MUNCH MUNCH
DID YOU SAY SOMETHING, PATRICK?

Patrick the Wolf Boy

By Art Baltazar & Franco

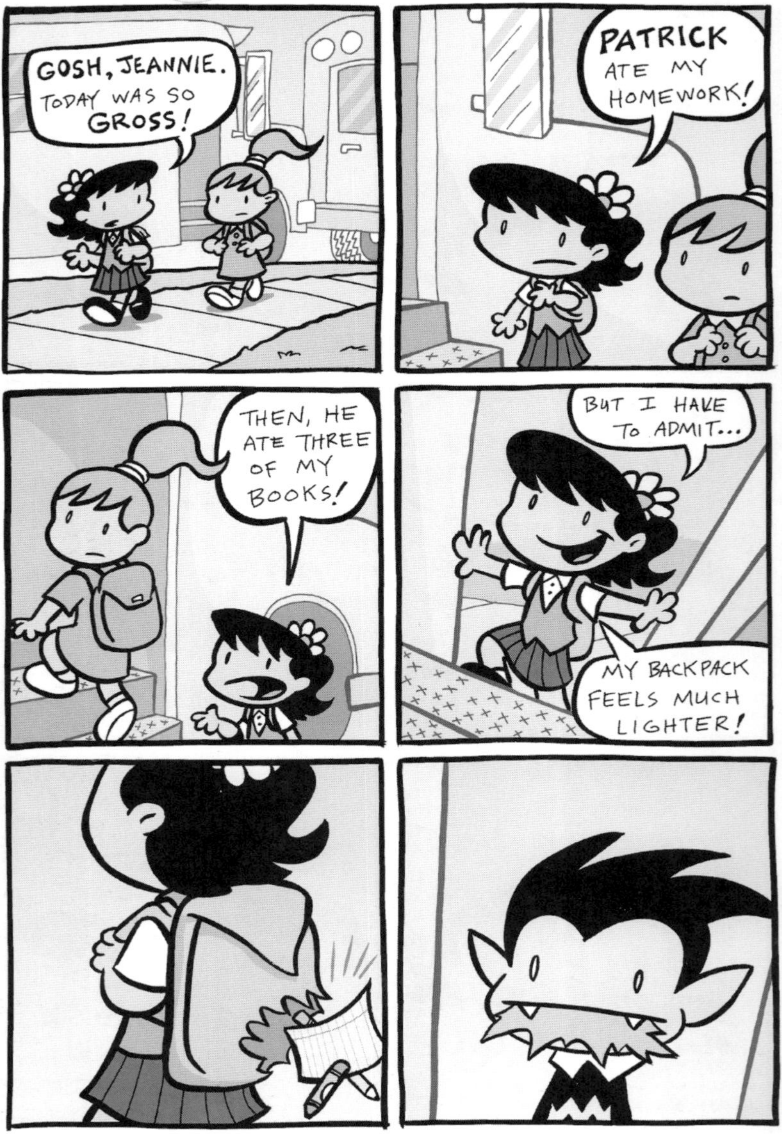
GOSH, JEANNIE. TODAY WAS SO GROSS!
PATRICK ATE MY HOMEWORK!
THEN, HE ATE THREE OF MY BOOKS!
BUT I HAVE TO ADMIT...
MY BACKPACK FEELS MUCH LIGHTER!

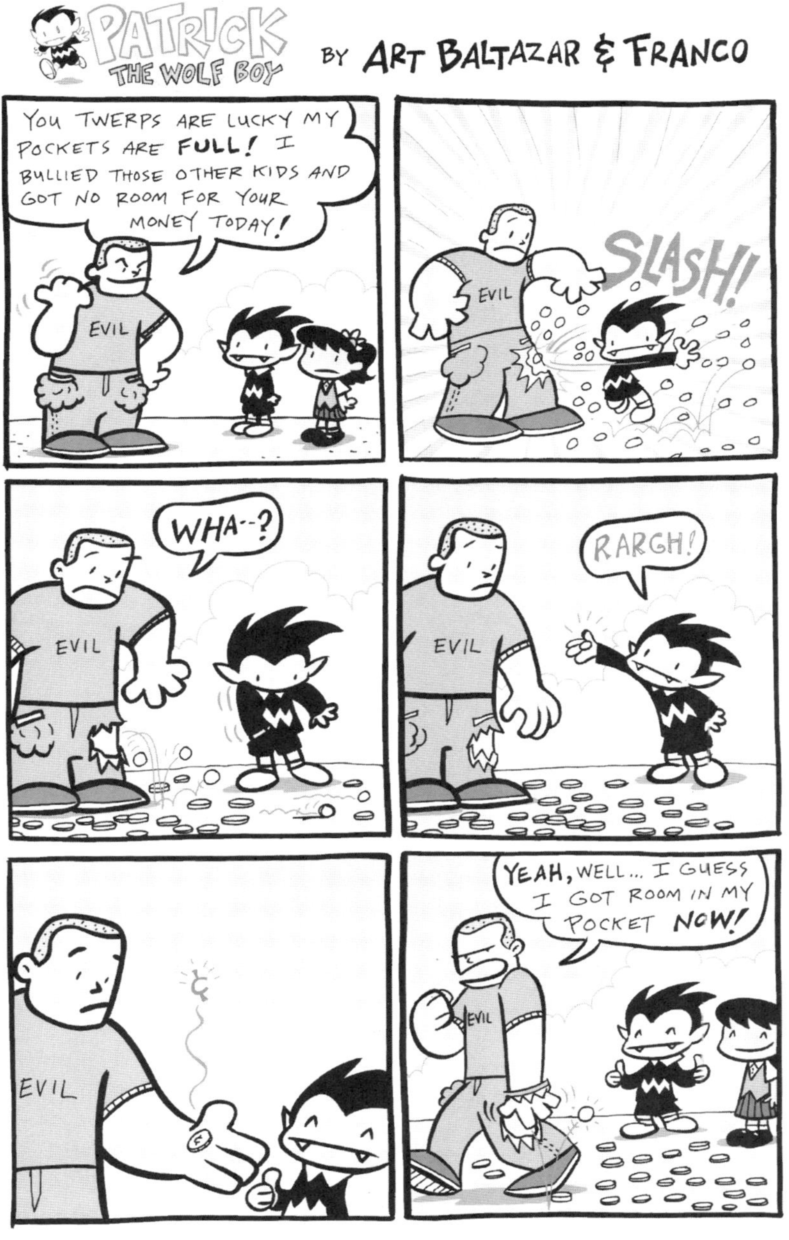
PATRICK THE WOLF BOY
BY ART BALTAZAR & FRANCO
YOU TWERPS ARE LUCKY MY POCKETS ARE FULL! I BULLIED THOSE OTHER KIDS AND GOT NO ROOM FOR YOUR MONEY TODAY!
EVIL
SLASH!
EVIL
WHA--?
EVIL
RARGH!
EVIL
EVIL
¢
YEAH, WELL... I GUESS I GOT ROOM IN MY POCKET NOW!
EVIL

PATRICK THE WOLF BOY

BY ART BALTAZAR & FRANCO

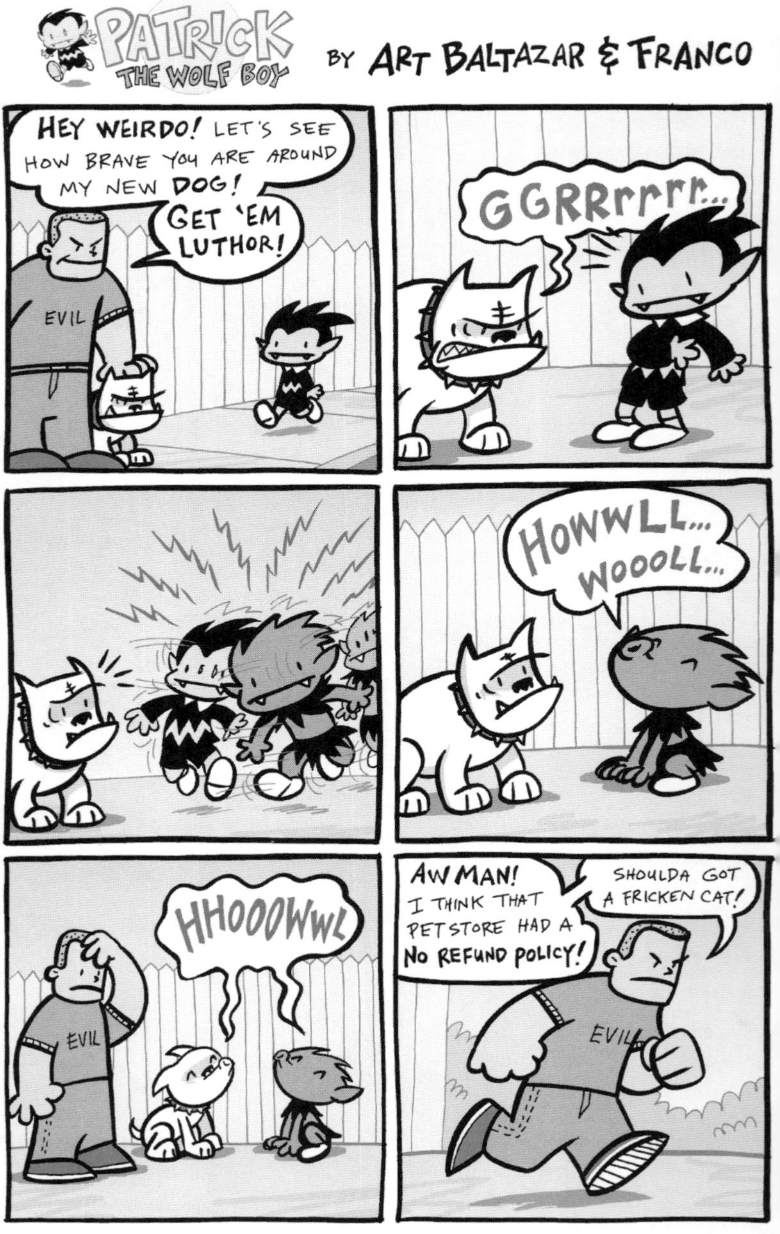
HEY WEIRDO! LET'S SEE HOW BRAVE YOU ARE AROUND MY NEW DOG!
GET 'EM LUTHOR!
EVIL
GGRRrrrrr...
HOWWLL... WOOOLL...
HHOOOWWL
EVIL
AW MAN! I THINK THAT PETSTORE HAD A NO REFUND POLICY!
SHOULDA GOT A FRICKEN CAT!
EVIL

PATRICK THE WOLF BOY BY ART BALTAZAR & FRANCO

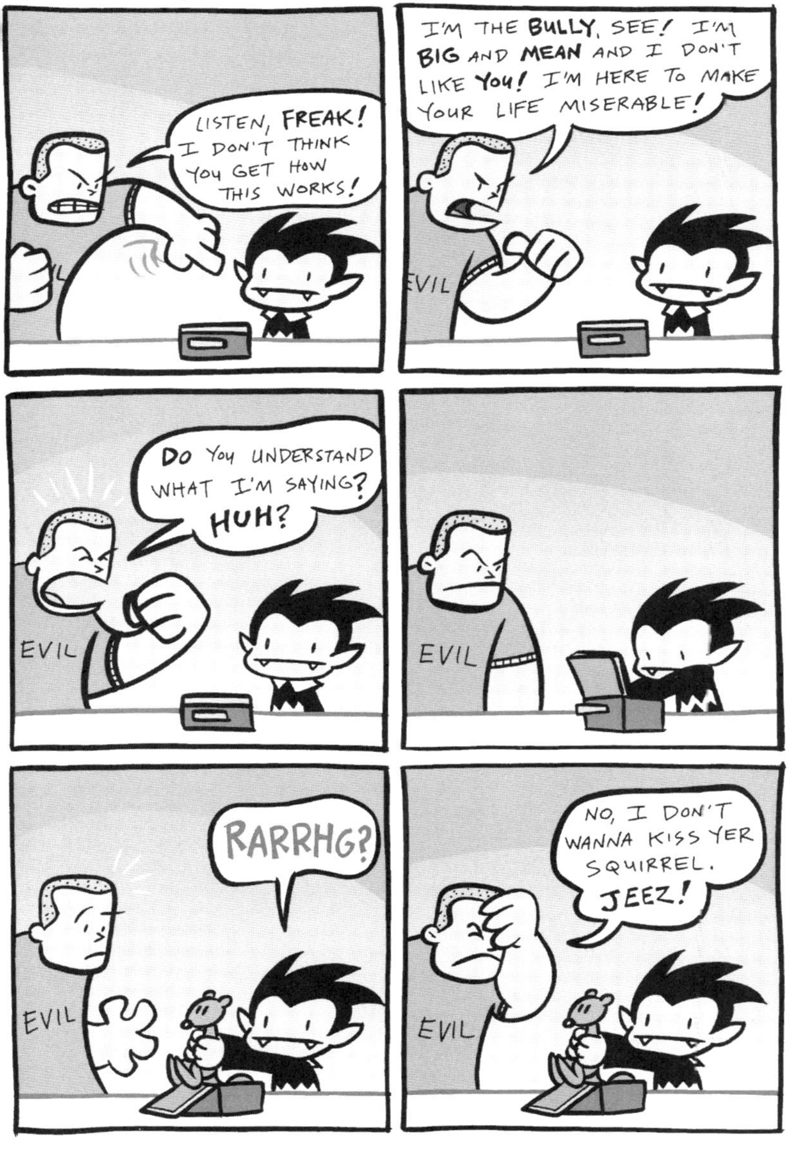
LISTEN, FREAK! I DON'T THINK YOU GET HOW THIS WORKS!
EVIL
I'M THE BULLY, SEE! I'M BIG AND MEAN AND I DON'T LIKE YOU! I'M HERE TO MAKE YOUR LIFE MISERABLE!
EVIL
DO YOU UNDERSTAND WHAT I'M SAYING? HUH?
EVIL
EVIL
RARRHG?
EVIL
NO, I DON'T WANNA KISS YER SQUIRREL. JEEZ!
EVIL

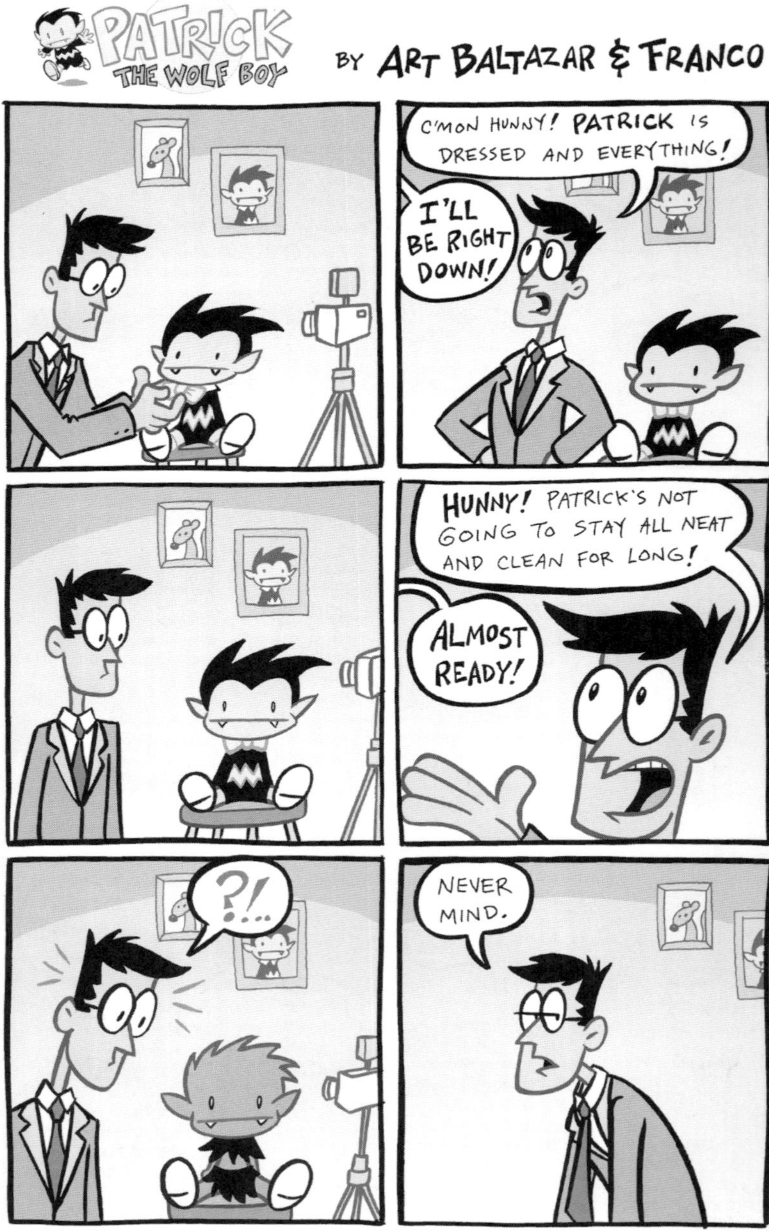
PATRICK THE WOLF BOY
BY ART BALTAZAR & FRANCO
C'MON HUNNY! PATRICK IS DRESSED AND EVERYTHING!
I'LL BE RIGHT DOWN!
HUNNY! PATRICK'S NOT GOING TO STAY ALL NEAT AND CLEAN FOR LONG!
ALMOST READY!
?!...
NEVER MIND.

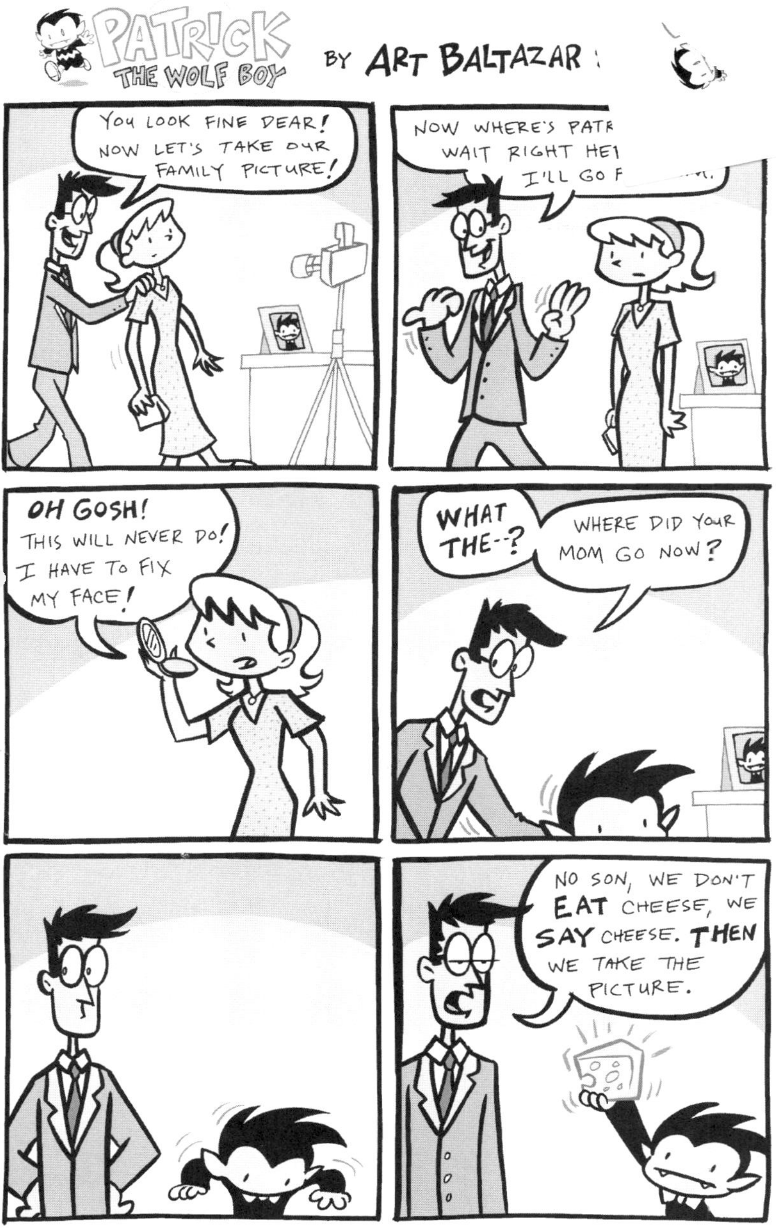
PATRICK THE WOLF BOY
BY ART BALTAZAR
YOU LOOK FINE DEAR! NOW LET'S TAKE OUR FAMILY PICTURE!
NOW WHERE'S PATR
WAIT RIGHT HE
I'LL GO F
OH GOSH! THIS WILL NEVER DO! I HAVE TO FIX MY FACE!
WHAT THE--?
WHERE DID YOUR MOM GO NOW?
NO SON, WE DON'T EAT CHEESE, WE SAY CHEESE. THEN WE TAKE THE PICTURE.

PATRICK THE WOLF BOY

BY ART BALTAZAR & FRANCO

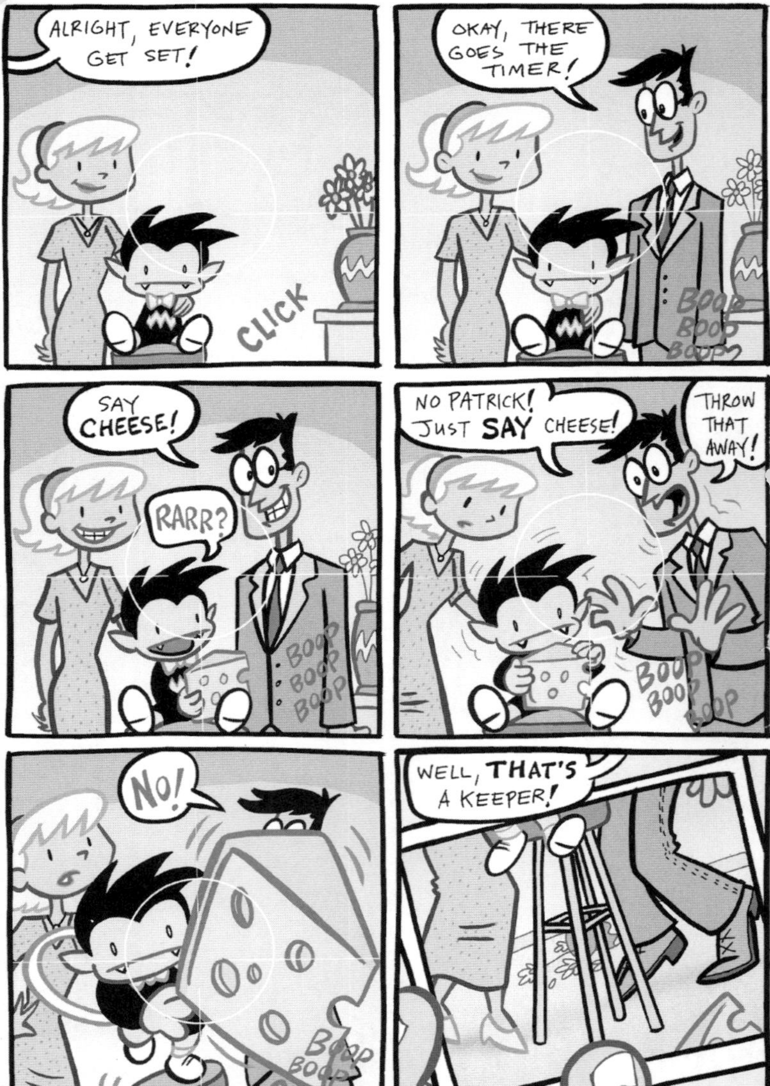
ALRIGHT, EVERYONE GET SET!
CLICK
OKAY, THERE GOES THE TIMER!
BOOP BOOP BOOP
SAY CHEESE!
RARR?
BOOP BOOP BOOP
NO PATRICK! JUST SAY CHEESE!
THROW THAT AWAY!
BOOP BOOP BOOP
NO!
BOOP BOOP
CLICK
WELL, THAT'S A KEEPER!

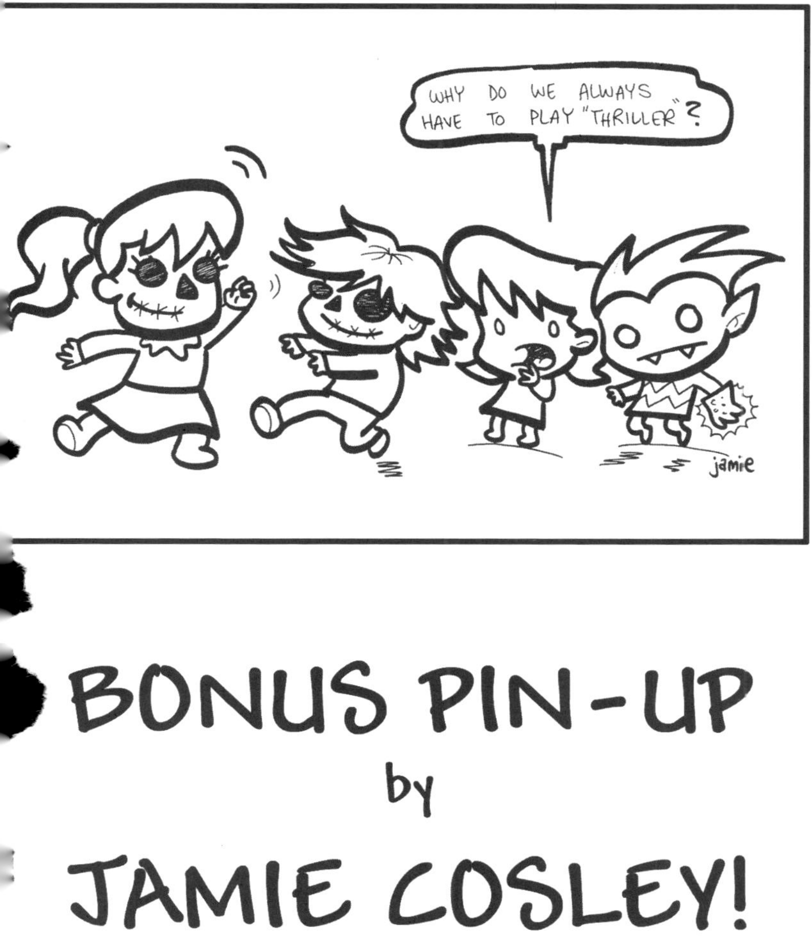
WHY DO WE ALWAYS HAVE TO PLAY "THRILLER"?
jamie

BONUS PIN-UP
by
JAMIE COSLEY!

Art Baltazar

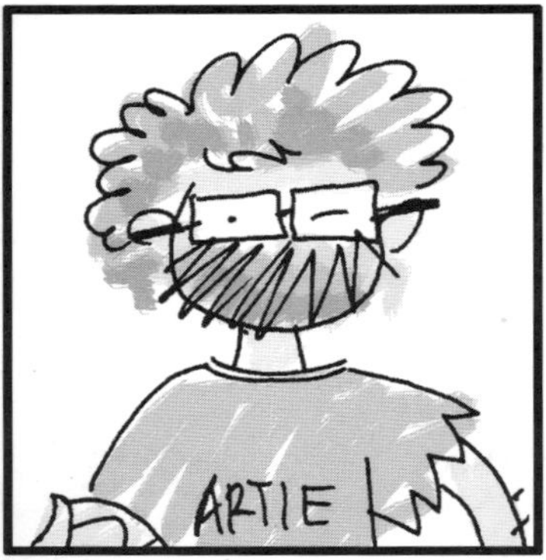
ARTIE

Art's a super cartoonist from Chicago! He's the artist, co-write and co-creator of Patrick. He works on Gorilla Gorilla comic strip for Disney Adventures and also likes to BBQ cheeseburgers Art is secretly working on a project with DC Comics. Its real secret. Can't tell no more. Art knows Josh Blaylock.

www.artbaltazar.com

Franco Aureliani

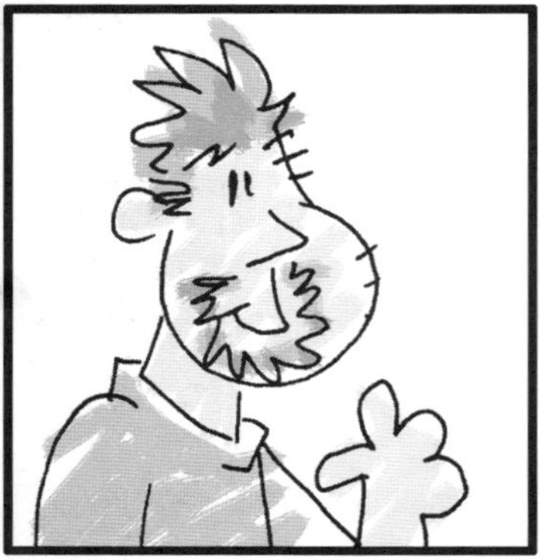

Franco is very tall. He likes to r comics and play and draw with little boy. He is a prolific (he had to look that word up) writer and artist. He has worke on many things but Patrick is the one that keeps him the sanest. He washes his hands after every visit to the restroom and his favorite color is blue! Franco knows Josh Blaylock.

www.blindwolfstudios.com